SUFI SAINTS

ENCYCLOPAEDIC SURVEY OF ISLAMIC CULTURE SERIES

SUFI SAINTS

Edited by
MOHAMED TAHER

ANMOL PUBLICATIONS PVT. LTD.
NEW DELHI-110 002 (INDIA)

ANMOL PUBLICATIONS PVT. LTD.
4374/4B, Ansari Road, Daryaganj
New Delhi-110 002

Sufi Saints

First Edition 1998
ISBN 81-7488-939-6

PRINTED IN INDIA

Published by J.L. Kumar for Anmol Publications Pvt. Ltd., New Delhi-110 002 and Printed at Mehra Offset Press, Delhi.

Contents

Preface

The *Encyclopaedic Survey of Islamic Culture* is a unique reference source. This series seeks to anthologise the most important primary and secondary materials on a wide variety of topics and writers of Islamic culture and civilisation. The scholar, the student and the layman will find in various volumes not only a generous selection of reprinted articles, but original essays, bibliographies, and other materials brought for the first time in a comprehensive and exhaustive fashion.

The need for this collation grew out of our awareness that there is no comprehensive source of information for the study and research of the field. Other published works are too specialised in the topics discussed or neglect the institutional as well the individual role which the Islamic system plays. Few encyclopaedic works do exist, and few anthologies also have appeared. Fewer books, again, have systematically covered such topics as Islam in Africa, Islamic sociology, Islamic polity, Islamic thought, etc. Although these topics have been addressed separately, no attempt has been made to discuss them as part of a united treatment of the literature of the field.

Islam brought a total change in all spheres of life. It revolutionised many societies, both in the east and the west. But this is not always accepted and acknowledged. To quote Major Arthur Leonard from his work: Islam; her moral and spiritual value:

"Never to this day has Europe acknowledged in an honest and whole hearted manner the great and everlasting debt she owes to Islamic culture and civilisation. Only in a lukewarm and perfunctory way has she recognised that when, during the dark ages, her people were sunk in feudalism and ignorance, Muslim civilisation under the Arabs reached a high standard of social and scientific splendour that kept the flickering members of European society from utter decadence.

"Do not we, who now consider ourselves on the top most pinnacle ever reached by culture and civilisation, recognise that, had it not been for the high culture, the civilisation and intellectual, as well as the social splendours of the Arabs and soundness of their school system, Europe would to this day have remained sunk in the darkness of ignorance. Have we forgotten that the Muslim maxim was that, the real learning of a man is of more public importance than any particular religious opinions he may entertain, that Muslim liberality was in striking contrast with the then intolerant state of Europe? Does the magnificent valour of the Arabs, inspired as it was by a theism as lofty as it was pure, not appeal to us? Does not the moderation and comparative toleration shown by them to the conquered, notwithstanding the fierce and burning ardour to regenerate mankind that impelled them onward to conquest, also appeal to us? Does it not all the more appeal to us when we contrast this with the bitterness of the attitude of the Christian sects towards one another? Especially when we consider that in Christendom, as it was then constituted, extortion, tyranny and imperial centralisation, combining with ecclesiastical despotism and persecution, had practically extinguished patriotism, by substitution in its place schismatic and degenerate Church?"

Further the same writer continues to say:

> "Is it possible that Europe is unmindful of, and has the ingratitude to ignore the splendid services of the scientists and philosophers of Arabic? Are the names of Assamh, Abu Othman, Alberuni, Albeithar, Abu Ali Ibn Sina (Avicenna) the great physician and philosopher, Ibn Rushd (Anempace) besides a host of others but dead letters? Is the great work that they have done and the fame they have left behind them in their books to be consigned to the limbo of oblivion, by an ungrateful but antipathetic Europe?

"It cannot be that already we have lost sight of the amazing intellectual activity of the Muslim world during the earlier part of the `Abbaside' period more especially. It cannot be that we have quite forgotten the irrecoverable loss that was inflicted on Arabian literature, and on the world at large, by the wanton destruction of thousands of books that was promoted by Christian bigotry and fanaticism? It cannot be surely said of Christian Europe that for centuries now she has done her best to hide obligations to the Arabs; yet most assuredly, obligations such as these, are far too sacred to lie much linger hidden."

This is one side of the story. The other side is that the West has definitely absorbed much of the Islamic contributions and is "unaware." To quote Marcus Marby and William Underhill "Bold new visions from ancient landscapes" (*Newsweek*, May 29, 1995): Christian and Islamic civilizations have been in conflict for most of their history. But as often as they have clashed, they have enriched each other. In this ninth century, Moors brought advanced architecture, astronomy and medicine to occupied Spain. While Europe lingered in the Dark Ages, courtly poetry from Persia inspired the troubadours, whose verse evolved into the literature of the early French Renaissance. Even whiling away hours over coffee and conversation—the basis for the cafe—came from Arab culture... France's most popular dish today is not escargots but couscous. French slang is peppered with Arab words like kif-kif (50-50) and Insha Allah (God willing). The hottest new music is Arab-inspired rai" (p. 28). The list of Arabic borrowed words in English and Western usages are many more, not mere algebra, alchemy, azimuth, albatross, timbal, zenith, etc.

There is, in short, a lot of misinformation and incorrect representation about Islam. And more so there is a need today to describe and interpret the issues and express in clear terms what this thought actually deals with. Due to social and cultural changes, the salient aspects of the field require examination. The post cold war era has left the world with a unipolar political system. Islam is a system which promises the world that if applied in toto it would solve the multi-dimensional problems of the modern era. But is there any one who wishes to test this module and try it in a space and time to see the truth of the statement?

The primary purpose of this encyclopaedic survey is to serve as a basic handbook on significant topics of Islamic culture. To facilitate an understanding of the field, the series presents a survey and an analysis of the various socio-cultural forces that shape both the structure and functions of the field as well as by the way this society has changed. We also analyse the larger forces outside the community, such as assimilation and acculturation, and forces inside the community, like, role of the leadership, role of the social and cultural groups and the so much alleged 'imbalance' in the theory and practice of the faith.

We are confident that this work will make a permanent and significant contribution to the study of Islam. Its style is simple, and it is presented in a style accessible to a wide audience. Its target audience is faculty, students, and all concerned with the understanding of the faith of the second largest following in the world. While it has scholarly materials, it is nevertheless also of use to those who have no knowledge of the field, as well as to those who are working in related and allied fields. Most important, we hope that this series will be useful in teaching and learning as an educational resource in the academic world.

The series is planned to be both, multi-volume and multi-faceted set, which will run into hundreds of numbers. The compilation of such a huge set is a gigantic task and requires the support and encouragement of all concerned. It requires feed-back and also support from the literary market place and literary circles all over.

A collection of articles, or an anthology, has many benefits, like, it renews our acquaintance with literature which we have neglected, it reveals to us material of which we were ignorant, and it exposes relationships where we did not suppose them to exist. This is the ultimate purpose of our efforts and we wish and pray that this is fulfilled.

A word of acknowledgement is due to the inspiration of the idea of a comprehensive, commulative and compact set of literary works on the Islamic culture. These inspirers are from all walks of life and their efforts must be acknowledged which includes contributors, authors and editors, as well as the publishers who have graciously contributed to this project and we duly acknowledge their cooperation. The well wishers are many more and listing all the concerned by names is impossible here. Each must be duly rewarded for this gesture, and this is our sincere prayer.

—Editor

1

Imam Musa Al-Kazim and Sufi Tradition

HAMID ALGAR

It is well-known that the Imams from the *Ahl al-Bayt* enjoyed, both during their lifetime and posthumously, the respect and veneration of many within the Islamic community who were not, in the strict sense, their followers. This was no doubt a principal reason for the persecution and confinement to which the Imams were repeatedly exposed. Prominent among those who did not belong to the Shi'ah faith but nonetheless held the Imams in high esteem were those ascetics and Sufis who came to believe, like the Shi'ah, in the initiatic transmission of a special body of knowledge and, seeing in the Imams exemplars of the spiritual virtues, included them among their spiritual teachers and forebears. Thus al-Kalabadhi (d. 385/995) begins his listing of "those who spoke concerning the sciences of the Sufis" with a mention of the first six Imams; Hujwiri (d.ca. 465/1071) lists them immediately after the *Rashidun* Caliphs as "the *imams* of the Sufis"; and Farid al-Din 'Attar opens his celebrated compendium, the *Tadhkirat al-Awliya'*, with a detailed mention of Ja'far al-Sadiq and closes it will a similar account of Muhammad al-Baqir, thus symbolically including the numerous Sufis whose lives he describes between these two Imams from the Household of the Prophet.

It is indisputable that the early Sufis drew inspiration, in a general sense, from certain dicta and teachings of the Imams. In addition, however, widespread traditions—repeated down to the present — associate each of the first eight of the Twelve Imams personally with one or more of the well-known Sufis. These traditions have not yet been evaluated in any systematic way, and it is possible that at least in some cases their foundation in historical fact may be weak. Nonetheless, the very existence of these traditions, together with their persistence, demonstrates how the Imams have served as poles of the spiritual world for many Muslims, even after the Sunni-Shi'i division crystallized in more or less sectarian form. We propose to examine here the accounts that link to Imam Musa al-Kazim the names of Shaqiq Balkhi (d. 194/810), Bishr al-Hafi (d. 227/841), and Ma'ruf Karkhi (d. 200/815) and to suggest in what additional ways the Imam played a role in the shaping of Sufi tradition.

All who have written of Imam Musa al-Kazim are unanimous in ascribing to him high spiritual virtues. In addition to *al-Kazim* ("the one who vanquishes anger"; cf. al-Qur'an, III:134), he was known to his contemporaries as *al-`abd al-salih* ("the righteous servant of God") and was celebrated for his asceticism, piety, mildness of demeanor, and trustworthiness in transmitting *Hadith*. He was much given to prolonged prostration and to supplicatory prayer, declaring of the latter that it was able to repel even that which had been predetermined. Some of the prayers he composed have been preserved in both Shi'i and Sufi manuals of devotion. Among his predecessors in the line of Imams, he has been well-compared with Imam 'Ali Zayn al-`Abidin for gentleness of character and asceticism of nature. All this suggests that in both Madinah and Baghdad he must have served as a pole of attraction for those who sought to cultivate the spiritual life and shun what was perceived as the corruption of the day. In a sense, he continued to fulfil this function after his death in 183/799, for his tomb in Baghdad became a favoured place of pilgrimage where prayers were thought likely to be accepted; among the people of the city, it was known as *bab al-Hawa'ij* ("the gate to the fulfilment of needs"). None other than Imam Shafi'i is reported to have said that his tomb was "a well-proven antidote" (*taryaq mujarrab*).

Shaqiq Balkhi is the Sufi whose name is most commonly linked to that of Imam Musa al-Kazim. According to the conventional accounts, Shaqiq was deflected from a life of worldly neglect by a series of encounters and incidents experienced during his travels as a merchant, becoming thereafter a pupil of the well-known ascetic, Ibrahim b. Ad'ham (d.c. 165/782). He is said to have been martyred at Khuttalan in Transoxiana in 194/810. The dicta attributed to him relate mostly to *tawakkul*, and his principal disciple was Hatam al-Asamm.

There is, however, a lengthy story, not found in the earliest Sufi compendia, that associates Shaqiq with Imam Musa al-Kazim. It is said that while on his way to the Hajj in the year 149/766, Shaqiq noticed among his fellow travellers, during a pause at Qadisiyah, a young man of striking appearance—handsome, slender and dark brown in complexion. Telling himself that the young man must be a mendicant Sufi, intent on exploiting the charity of the pilgrims, Shaqiq went up to him with the intention of reproaching him. But before he had a chance to utter a word, the young man said, "O Shaqiq, 'avoid excessive suspicion, for some suspicion is sinful'". Overcome with remorse, Shaqiq tried to follow him in order to ask him to pray for the forgiveness of his sins, but he lost sight of him in the crowd. Somewhat later, he glimpsed him again, now standing in prayer, "with his limbs trembling and his tears flowing down." When he had completed his prayers, he turned to Shaqiq and said, "O Shaqiq, recite this saying of the Almighty: Certainly I am oft-forgiving to those who repent, believe and do right, and who are ready to accept true guidance'". Thus the young man had again divined what Shaqiq had intended to say, leaving him with the conviction that he must be one of the *abdal*. After a further interval, Shaqiq noticed him preparing to fill his water-skin. Hiding in a nearby well, Shaqiq saw the water rise up miraculously to fill the waterskin. The young man then made his ablutions with the water and filled the skin with sand. He shook the skin, turning the sand into water, which he then drank. Shaqiq now made his presence known, and begged to be allowed to drink of the water that had been miraculously transmuted from sand. The young man consented, saying, "O Shaqiq, the bounties of God reach us unceasingly, both apparent and hidden, so view your Lord with favour." Shaqiq drank from the waterskin and, according to some venisons of the story, found it to contain a substance akin to *sawiq*, a kind of mash made from corn and dates. Thereafter he felt neither hunger nor thirst for several days. It was not until reaching Makkah that Shaqiq finally discovered the identity of the mysterious young man. Seeing him surrounded by hundreds of devotees as he circumambulated the Ka'bah, Shaqiq asked a bystander who it was that had aroused such fervour, and he was told that it was Imam Musa al-Kazim.

Absent not only from the standard sufi biographical dictionaries but also from early authoritative accounts of the lives of the Imams, such as the *Kitab al-Irshad* of Shaykh al-Mufid (d. 413/1022), this narrative is to be found in a wide variety of later works, of both Sunni and Shi'i authorship. It is worth stressing, however, that the story makes its first appearance in Sunni sources. The earliest author to record it seems to have been Abu Muhammad al-Hasan b. 'Abd al-Rahman b. Khallad Ramhurmuzi (d.ca. 360/970), a *qadi* of Khuzistan better known to posterity as a *Hadith* scholar than as a biographer of Sufis. Ramhurmuzi's *Karamat al-Awliya'*, a work now apparently lost, is cited by many later authors as one of their principal sources for the story of Shaqiq's encounter with Imam Musa al-Kazim. Next come two words of the celebrated Hanbali *faqih, muhaddith* and historian, Ibn al-Jawzi (d. 597/1200), *Sifat al-Safwah,* a critical digest of Abu Nu'aym Isfahani's *Hilyat al-Awliya'*; and a still unpublished work referred to by various titles of which the most correct appears to be *Muthir al-Gharam al-Sakin fi Fada'il al-Biqa' wa'l-Amakin.* The Istanbul manuscript of *Sifat al-Safwah* cites as authority for the story Khushnam b. Hatam al-Asamm, who heard it from his father, who heard it from Shaqiq himself. The next author to write of the encounter between Shaqiq and the Imam was al-Hafiz Abu Muhammad 'Abd al-'Aziz b. al-Akhdar al-Junabadhi (d. 611/1214-15), a Hanbali *faqih* of Baghdad originally from Nishapur. His still unpublished *Ma'alim al-'Itrat al-Nabawiyah* is cited as authority for the story by a number of later writers.

A full *sanad* is given by the historian al-Sibt ibn al-Jawzi (d. 654/1256) for his telling of the story in *Tadhkirat al-Khawass;* it contains eight names, the last of which is again Khushnam, the son of Hatam al-Asamm. Contemporary with al-Sibt ibn al-Jawzi was a certain Kamal al-Din Muhammad b. Talhah al-Halabi (d. 652/1254), a Shafi'i *muhaddith* who taught in Aleppo and Damascus. He tells the story of Shaqiq's encounter with Imam Musa al-Kazim in his *Matalib al-Su'ul fi Manaqib Al al-Rasul,* giving precisely the same *sanad* as al-Sibt ibn al-Jawzi.

Two further Sunni compendia on the lives of the Imams content themselves with a retelling of the story as found in earlier sources (notably Ramhurmuzi, ibn al-Jawzi and al-Junabadhi) without supplying any *sanad.* These are the *Kashf al-Ghummah fi Ma'rifat al-A'immah* by Abu'l-Hasan 'Ali b. 'Isa al-Irbili (d. 692/1293) and *al-Fusul al-Muhimmah fi Ma'rifat al-A'immah* by Nur al-Din 'Ali b. Muhammad (d. 885/1451), known as Ibn al-Sabbagh, a Maliki *faqih* resident in Makkah. Finally, we may cite the well-known anti-Shi'i polemic, *al-Sawa'iq al-Muhriqah,* of the Shafi'i *muhaddith* and *faqih*, Ibn Hajar al-Haythami (d. 973/1565); he quotes as his sources for the encounter of Shaqiq with Imam Musa al-Kazim Ibn al-Jawzi and Ramhurmuzi.

It is to be noted that in none of these sources is there any indication of further contact having taken place between Shaqiq Balkhi and Imam Musa al-Kazim, or of the threefold encounter on the road to Makkah having served as an initiatic experience for Shaqiq. The same is true of the first two Shi'i sources to speak of an encounter between Shaqiq and Imam Musa al-Kazim: the *Manaqib Al Abi Talib* of Ibn Shahrashub (d. 588/1192) and the *Minhaj al-Karamah* of 'Allamah Hilli (d. 726/1325). The account given by Ibn Shahrashub is the second (or possibly the third) oldest of all tellings of the story, whether in Sunni or Shi'i sources, but it seems hardly ever to have been quoted, even in later Shi'i works. For his part, Ibn Shahrashub cites as his source a work unmentioned else where, the *Amthal al-Salihin* of an unnamed author. 'Allamah Hilli recounts the story as told by Ibn al-Jawzi in *Sifat al-Safwah,* without adding any comment of his own.

By contrast, a near-contemporary of 'Allamah Hilli asserts flatly that Shaqiq Balkhi was the *murid* of Imam Musa al-Kazim, while dispensing with all anecdotal evidence. This is Sayyid Haydar Amuli, the Shi'i gnostic of the eighth/fourteenth century who maintained true Sufism to be identical with true Shi'ism. Describing in the *Jami' al-Asrar wa Manba' al-Anwar* the alleged transmission of esoteric knowledge by the Imams to certain among the Sufis and ascetics, he asserts that one line of transmission went from Imam Musa al-Kazim to Shaqiq Balkhi and "from him to his students and disciples." Amuli was followed some hundred years later by Ibn Abi Jumhur al-Ahsa'i (d. post 901/1496) who similarly stated in his *Kitab al-Mujli* that Shaqiq was the disciple of (*akhadha an*) Imam Musa al-Kazim. A further element was added to Shaqiq's association with the Imam by Qadi Nur-Allah Shushtari (d. 1019/1610), who claimed in his *Majalis al-Mu'minin* that Shaqiq was in fact a Shi'i and was even martyred for his beliefs in Transoxiana (*ba tuhmat-i rafd shahid shud*). This identification of Shaqiq as a Shi'i was not widely followed by later Shi'i authorities. Muhammad Baqir Majlisi (d. 1111/1700), for example, contents himself with a retelling of the story as found in the works of Ibn al-Jawzi, al-Irbili and Ibn al-Sabbagh, not even making of Shaqiq a disciple of Imam Musa al-Kazim. Muhammad Baqir Khwansari (d. 1313/1895), author of a well-known biographical dictionary of Shi'i notables, *Rawdat al-Jannat fi Ahwal al-'Ulama' wa 'l-Sadat*, records non-committally of Imam Musa al-Kazim that he has been related to be the master (*ustadh*) of Shaqiq Balkhi, without classing Shaqiq as a Shi'i. Finally, Muhammad Ma'sum Shirazi, known as Ma'sum 'Ali Shah (d. 1344/1926), draws together in the encyclopaedic work on Sufism the evidence of both Sunni and Shi'i sources, and concludes that Shaqiq Balkhi was invested with a cloak (*khirqah*) by Imam Musa al-Kazim, making him a *murid* of the Imam but not an adherent of the Shi'ah.

The second Sufi whose name has been linked to that a Imam Musa al-Kazim is Abu Nasr Bishr b. al-Harith al-Hafi, usually referred to as Bishr al-Hafi. According to the standard Sufi biographies, he was redeemed from a life of dissipation and drunkenness by the simple act of cleansing and perfuming a scrap of paper bearing the divine name that he found on the road.

Other sources, however, attribute his salvation to Imam Musa al-Kazim and relate the following story. One day the Imam was passing in front of Bishr's house in Baghdad and was distressed to hear echoing from it the sound of music and frivolous rejoicing. A maidservant emerged from the house, and the Imam asked her whether the owner of the house was a freeman or a slave. She replied that he was a freeman, where upon the Imam observed that must indeed be the case, for it he were a slave, he would engage in acts of servitude (i.e., worship of God). When the maid-servant returned inside, Bishr asked her what had delayed her. She recounted what Imam Musa al-Kazim had said, and Bishr was overwhelmed with remorse. Barefooted, he rushed out of the house and catching up with the Imam fell penitently at his feet.

It appears again to have been Ibn al-Jawzi who first related this story. Muhammad Baqir Khwansari writes in his *Rawdat al-Jannat* that he had seen the autograph copy of a work by Zayn al-Din al-'Amili al-Shahid al-Thani (d. 966/1588) citing the *Kitab al-Mud'hish* of Ibn al-Jawzi as authority for this narrative of Bishr's repentance. In the telling of the story, however, the Imam in question is 'Ali Zayn al-'Abidin, not Musa al-Kazim, a gross chronological error that it is difficult to attribute either to Ibn al-Jawzi or to al-Shahid al-Thani. It is also worth noting that Ibn al-Jawzi makes no mention of encounter between Bishr and Imam Musa al-Kazim in the section he devotes to the former in the *Sifat al-Safwah.* It nonetheless seems probable that the story entered circulation sometime before the seventh/thirteenth century, for it is taken up by 'Allamah Hilli in *Minhaj al-Karamah.* Hilli is cited in turn by Qadi Nur-Allah Shushtari in *Majalis al-Mu'minin* and by Ma'sum 'Ali Shah in *Tara'iq al-Haqa'iq*. However, the story never came to enjoy the same widespread circulation as that relating to Shaqiq Balkhi, and it is completely absent from the well-known Sunni works on the lives of the Imams.

The third and last Sufi said to be connected with Imam Musa al-Kazim— if we ignore the manifestly a historical claim made by the *Khaksar derwishes* of Iran that the Imam nominated Hallaj as the *qutb* of the age—was Ma'ruf Karkhi. For more commonly, Karkhi is held to have been an associate of the eighth Imam, 'Ali b. Musa al-Rida, who is said to have presided over his conversion to Islam. However, Shah Ni'mat-Allah Wali (d. 834/1437), founder of the Ni'matullahi order of *derwishes* and one of the principal figures in the history of Shi'i Sufism, attributes the conversion of Karkhi to Imam Musa al-Kazim and states that he acted as the Imam's gatekeeper for ten years. The same view was expressed by the author of *Usul al-Fusul*, who added that Karkhi kept his position as gatekeeper during the Imamate of 'Ali b. Musa al-Rida. Ma'sum 'Ali Shah—himself, of course, an affiliate of the Ni'matullahi order—regards this as possible, and suggests even that Karkhi may have enjoyed the company of Imam Ja'far al-Sadiq. By contrast, another relatively modern Shi'i-Sufi author, Ihsan-Allah Istakhri of the Dhahabi order, rejects any association of Ma'ruf Karkhi with the Shi'i Imams before the time of 'Ali b. Musa al-Rida.

The accuracy of these various accounts linking Sufis with Imam Musa al-Kazim must now be assessed. The fact that they are not included in the earliest Sufi and Shi'i sources counts, no doubt, as an argument against their authenticity. In his attempted refutation of Hilli's *Minhaj al-Karamah*, Ibn Taymiyah (d. 728/1328) dismisses, with his customary acerbity, the Shi'i scholar's telling of the stories concerning Shaqiq Balkhi and Bishr al-Hafi as mere "lies." The modern Iraqi scholar, Mustafa al-Shibi, was has written a detailed and fully documented study of the historical relations between Sufism and Shi'ism, casts doubt on the historicity of the traditions in question, suggesting that they are a by-product of the Sufi claim to initiatic descent from 'Ali b. Abi Talib. From a somewhat different perspective, the Lebanese writer Hashim Ma'ruf al-Hasani, determined to prove what he calls "the great gap" between Sufism and Shi'ism, denies even the possibility of sympathetic contact having taken place between any of the Imams and any of the Sufis.

It may be argued, on the other hand, that although we are in the habit of calling Sufi *tadhkirahs* biographical dictionaries, works such as 'Attar's *Tadhkirat al-Awliya'* are in fact remarkably sparse in strictly biographical information; far more attention is given in them to the dicta of the Sufis in question than to the details of their travels and encounters. It is therefore conceivable, in principle, that Shaqiq Balkhi and Bishr al-hafi should have and initiatic encounters with Imam Musa al-Kazim that went unnoticed by the earliest Sufi writers. That Musa al-Kazim had contacts beyond the immediate circle of his followers is suggested by the occurrence of *hadith* narrated by him in such Sunni books of tradition as the *Musnad* of Ibn Hanbal, the *Sunan* of al-Tirmidhi, and the *Sunan* of Ibn Majah.

In the case of Shaqiq Balkhi, it is true, as Ibn Taymiyah points out, that in 149/766—the year of the alleged encounter with Imam

Musa al-Kazim while *en route* to the Hajj—the Imam was still resident in Madinah; his father, Imam Ja'far al-Sadiq, had died the previous year, and it was not until the caliphate of al-Mahdi began, some ten years later, that Imam Musa al-Kazim was taken to Baghdad. The does not exclude, however, the possibility of the Imam having undertaken himself an earlier journey to Baghdad, and in any event not every telling of the story supplies a year for the encounter. Most sources place it, in fact, after the release of Imam Musa al-Kazim from confinement in Baghdad by the Caliph al-Mahdi. The *sanad* given by al-Sibt ibn al-Jawzi and Muhammad b. Talhah al-Halabi must count as an argument in favour of the authenticity of the story, and it seems unwise to dismiss it out of hand. The most judicious conclusion in that of Ma'sum 'Ali Shah, who suggests that while Shaqiq Balkhi counts primarily as a disciple of Ibrahim b. Ad'ham, he also received the spiritual grace (*fayd*) of Imam Musa al-Kazim. The Indian hagiographer Ghulam Sarwar Lahuri enchoes this conclusion with the statement that Shaqiq Balkhi kept the company of both Imam Musa al-Kazim and Ibrahim b. Ad'ham.

As for Bishr al-Hafi, the story of his repentance at the hands of Imam Musa al-Kazim occurs in relatively few sources, and in none of them is a *sanad* cited. The argument of Ibn Taymiyah that Imam Musa al-Kazim was unlikely to be walking through the popular quarters of Baghdad and thus chance on the house of Bishr clearly deserves attention. The story may nonetheless be taken as indicating a certain attachment to the Imam on the part of Bishr, for Qushayri reports a dream in which Bishr saw the Prophet and was told by him that his spiritual attainments were due, in part, to his love of the *Ahl al-Bayt*.

By contrast, the tradition linking Ma'ruf Karkhi to Imam Musa al-Kazim lacks all plausibility, given the greater weight of those traditions that associate him with Imam 'Ali b. Musa al-Rida. If Ma'ruf was indeed converted to Islam by the eighth Imam, it is hard to see on what basis he could have been associated with his predecessor.

In short, the historicity of the narratives linking these three Sufis to Imam Musa al-Kazim is unproven; only the story of Shaqiq Balkhi's encounter with him can be regarded as fully plausible. The traditions in question nonetheless have their historical and even spiritual significance. First occurring in almost exclusively Sunni sources of the fourth/tenth to seventh/thirteenth centuries, they demonstrate how pro-'Alid segments of Sunni opinion gave shape and substance to the veneration of the Imams as part of the spiritual patrimony of all Muslims. That Sufis were chosen to figure as associates of Imam Musa al-Kazim (as well as of other Imams) suggests, too, that a particular affinity was seen to exist between the Sufi and Imamite traditions.

The place of Imam Musa al-Kazim in Sufi tradition is not limited to the stories—apocryphal or otherwise—that link him to individual Sufis. Insofaras he is the predecessor of Imam 'Ali al-Rida, who is regarded in turn as the preceptor of Ma'ruf Karkhi he belongs to the ancestry of all those numerous Sufi lineages that claim descent from Ma'ruf Karkhi. In other words, he forms the penultimate link in what is known as the Golden Chain (*silsilat al-dhahab*), i.e., the initiatic line connecting the Sufis through the first eight of the Twelve Imams with the Messenger and with the Source of Revelation.

Remarkable, too, is the number of Sufis who claim physical descent from Imam Musa al-Kazim (or on whose behalf such descent is claimed). Earliest among them is Junayd Badhdadi (d. 298/910), separated—according to the *Tiryaq al-Muhibbin* of Taqi al-Din al-Wasiti (d. 774/1373)—from the Imam by five generations of descent. This genealogy appears difficult to reconcile with the predominant view that Junayd was of Iranian ancestry. By contrast, the Musawi genealogy of Sayyid Ahmad al-Rifa'i (d. 578/1183), eponym of the Rifa'i order, seems to be universally agreed on; fourteen generations of descent connect Ahmad al-Rifa'i with Imam Musa al-Kazim.

Real or pretended descendants of Imam Musa al-Kazim came to play an important role in the eastern Islamic lands in general and Iran in particular during the eighth/fourteenth and ninth/fifteenth centuries, a period of intense interaction between Sufism and Shi'ism. Many Sufis gave new prominence to their traditional devotion to the Family of the Prophet, re-emphasizing the role of the Imams as a fountainhead of spiritual tradition; while at the same time some Shi'is experimented with the organizational forms of Sufism. It is thus not surprising that a number of Sufi movements with Shi'i or proto-Shi'i colouring came into being, at least four of which were founded by persons regarded as the descendants of Imam Musa al-Kazim. First among them was Hajji Bektash (Haci Baktas), said to have been born in Nishapur sometime during the seventh/thirteenth century and to have migrated by way of Makkah and Najaf to Anatolia, where he established the beginnings of the order that came to bear his name. The Bektashi order certainly cannot be designated as Shi'i in any real sense of the term, given its general disregard for the *Shari'ah;* nonetheless it professed loyalty to the Twelve Imams. Hence, it was claimed on behalf of Hajji Bektash that he was the son of Muhammad b. Musa, a great-grandson of Imam Musa al-Kazim. This is clearly impossible for chronological reasons, but the possible remains that Hajji Bektash was indeed born to a family of Musawi *Sayyids* in Nishapur and that the full genealogical record was lost somewhere between Khurasan and Anatolia. By contrast, the Musawi lineage with which the Safavid family sought to adorn itself in the course of its transformation from Sufi order to ruling dynasty is now generally recognized as spurious, the outcome of an attempt made not later than the reign of Shah Tahmasp (930/1524—984/1576) to efface the humble Kurdish origins of the Safavids. Nonetheless, the choice of Imam Musa al-Kazim as the ancestor is a further illustration of the prestige that attached to Musawi descent. Another claimant to Musawi lineage active in the ninth/fifteenth century was Sayyid Muhammad Nurbakhsh (d. 869/1464), founder of the Nurbakhshi order that branched off from the Kubrawiyah and survived in various regions of Iran until the mind-Safavid period. Finally, mention may be made of Sayyid Haydar Tuni (d. 830/1426), sometimes regarded as the ultimate ancestor of the infamous Haydari gangs that plagued numerous Iranian cities in the Safavid the Qajar periods. This Sufi claimed both physical and spiritual descent from Imam Musa al-Kazim, his initiatic chain going back through five generations to a certain Sayyid Ibrahim Khwarazmi, described as a "devoted follower" of the Imam.

It might be thought that this prominence of claimants to descent from Imam Musa al-Kazim in various Shi'i-Sufi movements simply reflected the numerical predominance of Musawi *Sayyids* in Iran. After all, Imam Musa al-Kazim fathered no fewer than thirty-seven children, more than any other of the Imams, an many of them had lived and died in Iran. The shrines built over their tombs came indeed to function as some of the principal sites of pilgrimage in Iran, even in pre-Safavid times. Notable examples are the shrine of Husayn b. Musa in Qazvin (known popularly as Shahzadah Husayn), that of Ahmad b. Musa in Shiraz (designated locally as Shah Chiragh), that of Hadrat Fatimah bint Musa in Qum, and above all, of course, that of the eighth Imam, 'Ali b. Musa al-Rida in Mashhad. These shrines certainly helped to anchor the lineage of Imam Musa al-Kazim in the pious awareness and the religious consciousness of Iran, and to establish real or alleged descent from him as a title to honour and pious repute. It seems unwise, therefore, to attribute the popularity of a Musawi lineage among the founders of Sufi-Shi'i movements to mere statistical chance.

In short, Imam Musa al-Kazim won in his own lifetime a reputation for piety, asceticism and spiritual virtue that transcended the boundaries of the Shi'ah. The accounts linking various Sufis to him, even if not of proven historical authenticity, serve to illustrate the posthumous echo of the appeal he exerted. It is noteworthy that these accounts first occur almost exclusively in Sunni sources and were taken up by Shi'i authorities only after a considerable interval.

It was also in Sunni Sufism that descent from Imam Musa al-Kazim first came to be regarded as spiritually prestigious before emerging as a prominent factor in the crystallization of Shi'i forms of Sufism in the eighth/fourteenth and ninth/fifteenth centuries.

The memory of Imam Musa al-Kazim thus played a role in the evolution of Sufism. This can be taken as a minor illustration of the way in which the Twelve Imams of the *Ahl al-Bayt* have formed part of the spiritual patrimony of the Muslim community as a whole.

Aspects of Al-Mubarrads Linguistic Thought of the Glorious Qur'an

The birth and scholastic work of al-Mubarrad in the city of Basra shows the rise of an Arab grammarian and philologist who left his mark on the whole Arab and Islamic thought in general and in the field of Qur'anic linguistics in particular. In Basra, al-Mubarrad was taught by well-known scholars of his time such as Abu 'Umar al-Jarmi, Abu 'Uthman al-Mazini and Abu Hatim al-Sijistani, the pupil of Asma'i.

When al-Mubarrad went to Baghdad, he became "a very busy teacher," and the "Imam of the Arabic language." Moreover, he led seminars devoted to the study of Sibawayh's *al-Kitab* after he "had mastered it at the hands of his Basrite masters who, in turn, allowed him to teach *al-Kitab* at a young age."

Al-Mubarrad's works are numerous and are mentioned in many sources. However, one of them, namely, *Kitab Ma'ttafaqa Lafzuhu wa Khtalafa Ma'nahu* (On Words Which Have the Same Utterance but Different Meanings) seems not to have received enough attention.

A careful examination of the long list of al-Mubarrad's works reveals that he probed many fields: linguistics, prose, poetry, rhetoric, prosody, grammar and Qur'anic semantics and sciences. In order to thoroughly understand and appreciate his book, *Kitab Ma'ttafaqa Lafzuhu wa' Khtalafa Ma'nahu*, it is important to examine similar works by other authors.

We first examine Sulayman al-Balkhi's book entitled *al-Ashbah wa'l Naza'ir fi'l-Qur'an al-Karim*. This book is considered the first of its kind to appear in that very field of study. It would seem that because of al-Balkhi's pioneering effort, some writers later on benefitted from it. In fact, after a careful examination of al-Bakhi's *al-Ashbah wa'l-Naza'ir fi'l-Qur'an al-Karim* and Yahya b. Sallam's *al-Tasarif*, we find that both books share essentially the same approach as well as the same issues.

In addition to the book of *al-Tasarif* by Yahya b. Sallam (A.H. 200) there are other works which fit the topic under discussion, such as *Tahsil Naza'ir al-Qur'an* by al-hakim al-Tirmidhi (A.H. 320), *al-Wujuh wa'l-Nasa'ir* by al-Damighani (A.H. 478), and *Nuzhat al-A'yun al-Nawazir fi 'Ilm al-Wujuh wa'l-Naza'ir* by Ibn al-Jawzi (A.H. 597).

With the exception of al-Hakim al-Tirmidhi's book, which has its own approach, all the aforementioned works are concerned with *al-ashbah wa'l-naza'ir* and all reflect the following observations:

1. They tend to interpret the Qur'an through the meaning and the sense of the word as well as its place in the verse. Therefore, words such as *al-iman* (faith), *al-tayyibat* (peasant things), *al-fasad* (corruption), *al-islah* (reform), or *al-khalq* (creation), as well as other words which could bear several aspects and meanings are dealt within the context of the verses in which each word occurs. Moreover, these books are also concerned with the clarification as well as the interpretation of all the probable meanings of all such words in their positions in the verse.
2. Al-Balkhi's book *al-Ashbah wa'l-Naza'ir fi'l-Qur'an al-Karim* is considered the first of its kind in this field although it includes the same information as the other books.
3. The meanings of one word vary, ranging from two to sixteen aspects such as the word *al-huda*, and sometimes seventeen aspects. However, a careful examination of both al-Damighani (*al-Wujuh wa'l-Naza'ir*) and Ibn al-Jawzi (*Nuzhat al-A'yun*), shows that both works share the following features:

   (a) Both follow the old tradition in the discussion of *al-wujuh wa'l-naza'ir* in terms of the linguistic meaning and the science of interpretation.
   (b) Both are concerned with the causes of *nuzul* (the revelation of certain verses and why they were revealed) and linguistic issues as well, i.e. the circumstances in which a certain verse in the Qur'an may be interpreted.
   (c) Both follow the same system of arrangement, i.e., alphabetical.
   (d) In their interpretation of unusual words (*gharib*) in the Qur'an, they rely on the word's form and case in the verse regardless of its origin (*asl*) and the extra letters added to such origin or not.

However, the two writers differ in certain aspects.

(a) While Ibn al-Jawzi elaborates in his detailed discussion and explanation, al-Damighani tends to be brief and general. This is why Ibn al-Jawzi's book is considered the most comprehensive in the field of *al-wujuh wa'l-naza'ir*.

(b) In addition to the lexical arrangement of Ibn al-Jawzi's book, he also observes the internal arrangement of the single word as well as arranging its consonants according to the numerous derivations from the word. Al-Damighani's book lacks such a system.

4. Al-Tirmidhi's work in this field differs from the rest of the books. For example, he denies the several aspects of a single word as well as the commonness of the utterance (*al-mushtarak al-lafzi*). Consequently, he followed a unique linguistic approach, namely, that a word has only one meaning.
5. Compared with the aforementioned books, al-Mubarrad's work is relatively small and brief, or, in terms of the field of *wujuh* and *naza'ir*, a short study. In his introduction, he presents the synonyms and "the common utterance." Then, he moves to the words which agree in their utterance but differ in meaning in the Qur'an, providing the reader with a simple example and supporting his argument by citing the Qur'an, the Arabic language, and sometimes the *Hadith*.

Moreover, al-Mubarrad discusses the *majaz* (metaphor) in the Glorious Qur'an and its use in a relationship or evidence. His approach may be summarized as follows:

(a) The difference in utterances and meanings, as in verbs: *dhahaba*, "to go"; *ja'a,* "to come", *qama,* "to rise"; and *qa'ad,* "to sit";
nouns: *yadd*, "hand", *rijl*, "leg", *rajul*, "man"; *faras* "horse"

(b) Two different utterances and one meaning, as in verbs: *zanantu* and *hasibtu* = to think (that)
qa'adtu and *jalastu* = to sit
nouns: *dhira'* and *sa'id* = arm
anf and *mirsan* = nose

(c) The same utterances but different meaning:
wajada, "to find"; *wajada* derived from *mawjida* (feeling, passion, anger, grudge); and *wajada* meaning "to know."
Daraba has three different meanings: *Darabtu Zaydan,* "I hit Zayd;"
Darabtu mathalan, "I gave an example"; and *Darabtu' - arda,* "I roamed the earth."

He also cites another example of names such as the word *'ayn* with its different meanings: *al-'ayn,* "truth", "the present wealth," "the visual organ," "the scale," "the clouds coming from the *qibla* direction," and "the water spring."

Then al-Mubarrad discusses the words which have the same utterances but convey opposite meanings, e.g. *jalal*, which provides two opposite meanings: "inferior" (*haqir*) and "great" (*`azim*). For the first meaning, "inferior," he cites the following verses:

Kullu shay' in ma khala-llahu jalal
(All things are inferior except God)

wa'ara Arbada qad faraqani
(And I find out that Arbad had left me)

wa mina'rruz'i kabirun wa-jalal
(For calamity can be great or small)

In both verses the word *jalal* means small or inferior.

For the second meaning, "great", al-Mubarrad cites the following verse:

rasmi darin waqaftu fi talalihi
(In a mansion's ruins I stood)
kidttu aqdi'l-hayata min jalalihi
(Almost spent my life viewing its greatness)

However, he also cites the word *jawn* as having opposite meanings: "black" and "white" However, al-Mubarrad's use of these words was derived from classical Arabic poetry as well as Arab rhetoric, such as that of al-Hajjaj b. Yusuf al-Thaqafi.

Thus far, al-Mubarrad seems to have presented the above terms as an introduction to the words actually occurring in the Glorious Qur'an from which he cites the following examples:

1. *al-muqwi,* to mean both "the weak" and "the strong". For the first meaning, "the weak", the following verse is cited: *wa-mata'an li'l-muqwin*

For the second meaning, "the strong," he cites a general Arabic expression:

aktharu min fulan fa' innahu muqwin.
(Know well so and so because he is powerful).

2. The word *zann* means both "doubt" (*shakk*) and "certainty" (*yaqin*). To express doubt, al-Mubarrad cites the following verse:
"...who know not the Book, but (see there in their own) desires and they do nothing but conjecture."

For "certainty," he cites this verse:

"I did really understand that my account would (one day) reach me."

In this book al-Mubarrad is careful to mention certain words in the Glorious Qur'an which are repeated twice in the verse where the meaning of the first differs from the second. Some of the examples he cites are:

1. "The recompense for an injury is an injury equal thereto (in degree)."

The second word of *sayyi'ah* (injury) is not an "offense" or "misdeed" against the person, but similar in reprehension because he is judged by the second.

2. They say, "We are really with you; we (were) only jesting. God will throw back the mockery on them."

The word *mustahzi'un* (jesting) is a kind of disobedience, but God's *istihza'* (throw back their mockery) in His "punishment" of them.

3. 'They plot and plan, and God also plans.'

Again, *yamkurun* is a sin as far as man is concerned but for God it means "torture" and "to punish severely".

In many places in his book al-Mubarrad deals with linguistic and grammatical, as well as rhetorical issues in order to convey the intended meanings of the Qur'anic terms to the reader. In this respect, he exploits certain linguistic features of the Qur'anic verses, e.g. omission (*hadhf*) and summarization (*ikhtisar*), as well as Arabic speech, to explain certain words in the Glorious Qur'an. For example, when al-Mubarrad discusses the Qur'anic style of the verse, "and what will make thee realize what the sure reality is," he says, "(There is) no explanation of this, but for those who have insight, the predicate (the answer to the question), was omitted since the addressed person is known." This is done for a certain purpose, namely, to magnify or glorify the matter, as when one says, "If one sees someone holding a sword in his hand," which would have a certain impression on the person who hears such a statement and which would normally be labelled as "exaggeration" (*tahwil*).

However, al-Mubarrad goes further and discusses not only words of different utterances with the same meanings, but also the styles which have the same utterances and various rhetoric aspects contextually.

He cites the interrogative style as an example.

> *Ma'adraka?* and *ma yudrika?*
>
> The Almighty said, "And what will explain to thee what this is?"
>
> Then the Almighty continues: *narun hamiyah*
>
> (It is) a fire blazing fiercely.
>
> In another place

> "And what will explain to thee what the Day of Judgement is?... (It will be) the Day when no soul shall have power (to do) aught for another."

Moreover, *wa ma adraka ma'l-qari'ah. . . .*

> "And what will explain to thee what the (Day) of Noise and Clamor is? (It is) a day where on men will be like moths.."
>
> Also, He said, *wa ma adraka ma'l-hutamah. . . .*
>
> "And what will explain to thee that which breaks to pieces? (It is) the fire of (the wrath of) God kindled (to a blaze)."

A careful examination of these verses reveals that after each verse a "clarification" (*bayan*) is given. The interrogative style therefore refers to glorification (*ta'zim*) and determination (*taqrir*).

At the same time, al-Mubarrad cites other examples from the Qur'an of the same style but with no "clarification," as in the following example:

> "And what will explains to thee what Hell-fire is? Naught doth it permit to endure and naught doth it leave alone."

Al-Mubarrad explains the omission of "clarification" as an indication of glorification and determination. This justification is based on other *surahs*, such as:

> "If there were a Qur'an with which mountains were moved, or

> the earth were cloven asunder, or the dead were made to speak, butt truly, the Command is with God in all things".

The response is not given because the addressed person, a persons, knows it through the expected response of the conditional "if' (*laww*), i.e. "this Qur'an would have been it."

Finally, al-Mubarrad writes about *al-majaz* in the Qur'an through certain statements or words which are used differently from what they mean linguistically to indicate a relationship or factual evidence. This occurs as a result of contraction or abbreviation, one of the common styles used by Arabs. It the respect, al-Mubarrad cites an example from the Glorious Qur'an:

"Ask at the town where we have been and the caravan in which we returned."

Obviously, the "town" (*al-qaryah*) is an inanimate object and so is the "caravan" (*al-'ir*). Consequently, they cannot be "asked" nor can they "respond" to any question. Therefore, the actual meaning is omitted al-though it is understood to mean "the town people" and the "caravan owners."

Al-Mubarrad continues his discussion of abbreviations in the Qur'anic *majaz* (metaphor), buttressing his arguments with Arab verses or statements as well as the *Hadith*.

Last, but not least, al-Mubarrad discussed another linguistic phenomenon, namely, *al-tahwil*. In this respect, al-Mubarrad's use of a modern linguistic idiom deserves serious attention. He cites the verse

> "Such were the treasures we had bestowed on him, that their very keys would have been a burden."

In the verse, the *'usbah* (bundle of keys) have been burdened by the keys, instead of "their very keys have been a burden." Here, al-Mubarrad indicates the linguistic phenomenon of diversion in Qur'anic verses as well as in the speech of the Arabs when they say, "The posterior (or buttocks) would have been a burden on the woman," actually meaning that the woman has been burdened by her posteriors.

This linguistic style becomes clearer in certain Arabic expressions cited by al-Mubarrad such as:

"I put the hood in my head".

The real meaning is obvious, namely, "I put the hood on my hand." The same occurs with another expression:

"I put the slipper in my foot".

The actual meaning is, "I put my foot in the slipper," i.e. "I put on my slipper."

2

Abu'l Hasan Al-Shadhili's *Ahzab*

AWAD M. AL-JEMAEY

Abu'l-Hasan al-Shadhili was born in Ghumara, a village near Sabta in Morocco, in 593/1196. His full name was Abu'l-Hasan 'Ali Ibn 'Abd al-Jabbar, known as al-Shadhili. His descent goes back to al-Hasan ibn 'Ali ibn Abi Talib. Abu'l-Hasan memorized the Qur'an while he was young. Since his youth, he had shown a desire to lead the life of a Sufi. He received his *khirqah* from Abu 'Abd-Allah H. b. Harazim (d. 633/1236), a pupil of Abu Madyan. He also received from him knowledge of the principles of the *tariqah* (path).

It may be noted that Abu'l-Hasan had travelled to Tunis where he studied Arabic grammar and morphology as well as jurisprudence and *Tafsir, Hadith* and theology. He became a follower of Maliki school of law.

He travelled without delay to Egypt, Iraq, Palestine, Syria, and performed his pilgrimage to Makkah several times. During his travels in Iraq looking for a *qutb* (pole) he was told that he had left the *qutb* in his homeland. After that, he went back and then he met 'Abd al-Salam ibn Mashish who was identified as a *Qutb*. Later on, he was advised to travel to Africa and to live in Shadhila, hence his surname al-Shadhili.

In A.H. 642 he went to Egypt with a large number of his disciples where he used to preach here and there for a number of years before he lost his sight in A.H. 645. Finally, he died in Humaythira, a village near the Red Sea, in 656/1258.

It may be noted that among the teachers of Shadhili the most eminent were Ibn Harazim (d. 633/1236) and 'Abd al-Salam ibn Mashish (d. 625/1228). His teaching was mentioned by his disciples. Among them was Abu'l-'Abbas Ahmad al-Mursi (d. 686/1287), who was considered as his successor, and Taj al-Din ibn 'Ata'-Allah 'Abbas (d. 709/1309) who wrote an account of the life and sayings of both Abu'l-Hasan and Abu'l-'Abbas.

However, Shadhili left us with no written books other than his *Ahzab* and *Awrad* which are discussed in this study.

These *Ahzab* and *Awrad* are scattered in various books such as in *al-Mafakhir al-'Aliyah fi al-Ma'athir al-Shadhiliyah, Lata'if al-Minan,* and in *Durrat al-Asrar*.

The term *Hizb* (plural *Ahzab*) has the real meaning of *'wird'* (litany), a collection of *adhkar* (remembrance) and supplication. In his book, *al-Mafakhir al-'Aliyah fi al-Ma'athir al-Shadhiliyah,* Ibn 'Ayyad al-Shafi'i summarizes, the function of the *Ahzab*, and explains as to how they should be used for both worldly affairs and those of hereafter. First of all, he begins with analyzing the meaning, the real concept of *Ḥizb*. He says, "*al-Hizb* is *al-wird* (litany) that is used for the sake of worshipping God... etc." Technically, *Ahzab* are a collection of *du'a'* (supplication). They are purposely composed for contemplation, remembrance, seeking refuge from evil, and for seeking knowledge, goodness, and uniting hearts in God, as well.

The difference between *wird* and *hizb*, says Padwick, is that a *wird* is a litany of approach developed not only for recitation in a *dervish* order, but also used by the general public. The term may be derived from the words for reaching a watering-place, or may have originated as divisions of the Qur'an or office of an order, or the order itself. A *wird* is generally taught orally. It may be called *hizb*; but the term *hizb* has more of a connotation of semi-magical protection. They imply guardianship and many are used to subdue hostile forces of men or nature. "Some would be considered real devotions by Christians; others are apparently constructed as magical formulae."

In her book *Mystical Dimensions of Islam*, Schimmel shows no such difference to exist between both *wird* and *hizb*. Both are "formulae given by the master to his disciples to be recited after the ritual prayer or in case of special need. Many of these prayers are credited with supernatural powers, and the most famous famous one is probably the *Hizb al-Bahr*, attributed to Shadhili and used mainly during travel as a protective charm." However, in his book, *Bayn al-Tasawwuf wa al-Adab*, al-Juyushi tried to differentiate between *wird* and *hizb: wird* is to be recited in a specific period of time whereas *hizb* is to be recited frequently and whenever the reciter wills. But this seems to be not correctly stated because if we, for instance, examine Shadhili's *Hizb al-Barr*, known as *al-Hizb al-Kabir*, (the Great *Hizb*), we find that this *Hizb* is to be recited after the *Fajr* prayer.

According to Ibn 'Ayyad al-Shafi'i these *Ahzab* did not exist in the first century of Islam, but were collected by some pious and saintly people who were interested in bringing themselves and others closer to God.

In fact, Shadhili left us some sixteen *Ahzab* among them are the following:

1. *Hizb al-Bahr* (Ocean): This *Hizb* is to be recited while crossing an ocean or sea in other to protect oneself from harm and damage from the ocean. Its function also is to prevent man from evil, enemies, and to brighten hearts.
2. *Hizb al-Ayat* (Signs): This *Hizb* is to be read for devotion and brightening hearts. Shadhili used to read it sometimes with *Hizb al-Barr*, and sometimes without it.
3. *Hizb al-Fath* (Victory) known as *Hizb al-Anwar* (lights) is to be read at dawn. Its function is to strengthen *Imam* (faith) of believing that there is no God save Allah, Muhammad is His messenger, Adam is His viceregent, *Nuh* (Noah) is His messenger, Abraham is His *Khalil* (friend). Moses is His spokesman, Jesus in His spirit and Muhammad is His beloved.
4. *Hizb al-Nur* (Light): This *Hizb* is almost the same as *Hizb al-Fath* (victory) with a slight difference of not having the

same verses when they both start and end. It contains two Qur'anic verses. Devotion seems to be its main purpose.

5. *Hizb al-Latif* (Protector): It is to be recited when there are difficulties and hardships. It begins with *Surat* "al-Fatihah" (the Opening). Its function is to protect from evil.
6. *Hizb al-Ikhfa* (Hiding): This *Hizb* is to be read during night and day in order to help prevent evil and harm from enemies and from illness.

The above-mentioned are some of the Shadhili's *Ahzab* and their functions. As far as *Hizb al-Barr* (land) is concerned, it begins with the following Qur'anic verse, "When those come to you who believe in Our Signs, say peace be on you: your Lord has inscribed for Himself (the rule of) Mercy: verily, if one did evil in ignorance, and thereafter repented, and amended (his conduct): He is Oft-forgiving, Most Merciful." This *Ayah* (verse) is call *Ayat al-Istiftah* (opening). Shadhili begins his *Hizb* with it because it gives hope to those who had committed sins and wanted to repent. It also indicates the authority given to the Prophet for asking forgiveness for those who repent after they wronged themselves and ask for forgiveness. The Qur'an says, "And if, when they had wronged themselves, they had but come unto thee and asked forgiveness of Allah, and the Apostle had asked Forgiveness for them, they would have found Allah instead Forgiving, Merciful."

His saying "O God, you know that I am known is ignorance while you are described by knowledge," gives the following inspirations:

1. Man's acknowledgement of his being ignorant.
2. God has knowledge of everything.
3. God's Mercy can cover everything.
4. God has power above everything.
5. Man should seek help from God.

As far as *Alif-Lam-Ra, Kaf-Ha-ya-'Ayn-Sad, Ha-Mim-Sin-Qaf,* are concerned, they might be considered here *Fawatih al-Suwar* (openings of *surahs*). However, numerous interpretations have been undertaken about these particles that occur in the beginning of some Qur'anic *surahs*. Ibn 'Abbas says about *Kaf-Ha Ya-'Ayn-Sad* that *Kaf* is from *Kafi* (protector), *Ha* is from *Hadi* (guide), *Ya* is from *Hakim* (wise), *'Ayn* is from *'Alim* (knowing), and *Sad* is from *Sadiq* (Truthful). Thus, Shadhili is using them here for protection and guidance.

By his saying "Make us slaves of you at all times in all situations, and teach us wisdom with which we become perfect in both life and death," Shadhili wants to be slave to God at all times in all situations. As a result, he asks of *`ilm* (wisdom, knowledge) with which someone can be pure and perfect. As a matter of fact, he does not ask for any knowledge, but for the useful one which leads to perfection and happiness. Shadhili refers to these Qur'anic verses: "Observe your duty to God. For it is God that teaches you." "For any to whom God giveth not light, there is no light," says Khamis. In tradition, the Prophet himself used to ask for useful knowledge, and to take refuge from harmful knowledge, because knowledge can be helpful while, at the same time, it can destroy. Says Shadhili that knowledge to hearts is like money in hands. They can be used in both ways, useful and harmful.

Finally, *Hizb al-Barr* is a famous *hizb* and an influential one among Shadhili's *Ahzab*. Containing in very deep meanings, spiritually and intellectually, it is written in a very concrete and graphic style. According to Zaki Mubarak, *Hizb al-Barr* points to profound and secret meanings that can only be understood by the greatest ones among wise people.

THE QADIRIYAH (KUNTA HAJJI) *TARIQAH* IN NORTH-EAST CAUCASUS: 1850-1987

The Origins

The North-Eastern part of the Caucasus, that is, the present-day Checheno-Ingush and Daghestan republics, is probably one of the last areas of the Muslim world to be penetrated by the Sufi brotherhoods. Today two *tariqahs* are represented there, the Naqshbandiyah, which predominates in Daghestan and Eastern Chechnia, and the Qadiriyah, centred in the Chechen and Ingush territories.

The history of the Naqshbandiyah in the Caucasus is fairly well-known. It penetrated in Northern Daghestan for the first time in late 18th century from Turkestan and for the second time in early 19th century to the Southern Daghestan from the Shirwan and India. The Naqshbandi *murids* led the two major holy wars against the Russian invaders—in 1785-1791 under the conduct of Imam Mansur and in 1824-1859 under the three Daghestani *mams*, Ghazi Muhammad, Hamzat Beg and Shamil.

By contrast, the shorter but curious history of the Caucasian Qadiris is very little known. The *tariqah* appeared in North Caucasus only around 1850, at a time when the great resistance movement led by Shamil was already doomed, and when the Russians—who at that time had in North Caucasus a half-a-million strong army—appeared as unavoidable victors.

In 1848 or 1849, a Daghestani shepherd, Kunta Kishiev, left the Caucasus for a pilgrimage to mecca. He was a Turk (Kumyk) native from the village of Inkho in Northern Daghestan, but lived in the Chechen village of Eliskhan-Yurt in the district of Gudermes, and spoke Chechen. On his way back home, he stopped in Baghdad and visited the tomb of Shaykh 'Abd al-Qadir Gilani, the founder of the Qadiriyah brotherhood. According to a Chechen legend, while at the tomb Kunta Hajji was initiated into the order by the founder himself. Back to his country he started his missionary activity, but in 1858 he had to leave Caucasus for a second *Hajj* to Mecca because of the hostility of Imam Shamil (who then was fighting his last battles against the Russians) towards his pacifist sermons. Kanta Hajji Kishiev returned to the Caucasus only after Shamil's final defeat. All the North Caucasus and particularly the mountainous areas of Chechnia and of Upper Daghestan lay in ruins. After a fierce thirty-five years long war, the human losses were appalling, especially among Chechens who have been the staunchest fighters of the Naqshbandi *Jihad*. Kunta Hajji preached non-resistance and acceptance of Infidel domination—slogans which became quite popular among the war-weary mountaineers.

The new brotherhood was known in the Caucasus under the name of "Kunta Hajji *tariqah*". In the beginning, until 1863 at least, says one Russian observer, its preachings had an ascetic and mystical character quite detached from worldly problems. It fitted well in the atmosphere of profound pessimism and of "end of the world" which prevailed in North Caucasus following the Russian victory. The new *tariqah* practised the loud *dhikr* (*dhikr al-jahriyah*) as opposed to the silent *dhikr* of the Naqshbandis, with ecstatic dances, songs and later, the use of musical instruments, drums and violins. In enjoyed an immediate and spectacular success especially in Chechnia and in the high mountains of Avaristan—areas where the Russian pressure had been particularly hard. From western Chechnia, the Qadiri adepts penetrated into Ingushetia, which had remained until then a nearly entire animist territory, and converted the Ingush to Islam. The last Ingush animist village became Muslim in 1870.

However, very rapidly, by 1863, the adepts of the Kunta Hajji *tariqah* were faced with the same political-religious dilemma which had confronted the leaders of the Naqshbandiyah in the early 1820s. Is it possible for a mystical to travel along the path leading to God without joining the *jihad* against Infidels when these dominate a Muslim land? In the Northern Caucasus the Russian presence was oppressive though they never attempted to mix up with the religious life of the mountaineers, and all Christian missionary activity was forbidden in Chechnia and Daghestan.

The majority of Kunta Hajji's adepts were Naqshbandi *murids* former warriors of Shamil. Their spirit has not been broken by the defeat. They were still conscious of their fighting qualities. The new *tariqah* was a tightly know organization by an iron discipline and an absolute devotion to their *murshid* (preceptor). Disappointed by the remorseless harshness of the Russian administration, the Qadiris began to switch from the "non-resistance to evil" to the idea of resistance to the rule of the Infidels.

In January 1864, Russian authorities alarmed by the fast-growing number of Qadiri *murids* (disciples), and convinced that the *tariqah* was preparing a new uprising, arrested Kunta Hajji and several dozens of his *murids*. The *murshid* was not tried but simply declared insane and jailed in a prison-hospital in Central Russia where he died in May

1867. His companions were accused of planning a "rebellion" against the Russian rule and deported to hard-labour camps in Siberia.

On 18th January, 1864, some four thousand *murids* who gathered in the Chechen village of Shah were attacked by Russian troops and dispersed by gunfire. More than 200 of them were killed, a thousand were wounded and hundreds were arrested and deported to Siberia. The Kunta Hajji brotherhood was not officially outlawed, but the loud *dhikr* was strictly prohibited and those who were convinced of practising it were arrested and deported to Siberia.

In 1865 took place a massive migration of Chechens and Ingushes to the Ottoman territory. Some five thousand families (a minimum of 30,000 persons, mostly Qadiri adepts, left North Caucasus. But in spite of all that the expansion of the *tariqah* was not slowed down. It continued to expand westward into Ossetia and even the Kabarda, and eastward in the direction of Daghestan. Kunta Hajji did not leave and direct lineage. After his deportation the spiritual unity of the brotherhood was maintained for a short while by his mother. After his death the order split into four groups (called *wirds* in Russian literature) with his former *vekils* at their head who became their hereditary *murshids*. They were:

(a) Bammat Giray Hajji Mitaev from the village of Avtura in the Chechen territory. At the beginning the *wird* was limited to one Chechen clan (the "Gunoy" clan), but later on it extended to the entire Chechen nation. The leadership is hereditary in the Mitaev family.

(b) Batar Hajji Belhoroev, from the village of Surhohi in the district of Nazran in Ingush territory. At first limited to some Ingush clans, the brotherhood gained adepts in the Chechen territory and in Northern Daghestan. From the start, the first *murshid* inculcated in his followers a spirit of radical puritanism. Members of the Batal Hajji brotherhood were not supposed to marry outside their *wird* and were even forbidden to share a meal with the non-initiated. The principles of *Jihad* were strictly observed. During the century-long life of this order, nearly all its *murshids* and a large number of its adepts met violent death at the hands of Russian (Tsarist or Soviet) authorities.

The leadership of the Batal Hajji is still in the Belhoroy(ev) family.

(c) Chim Mirza, from the village of Mayrtup in the district of Shali in Chechen territory. The adepts of Chim Mirza use drums during their *dhikr*, and are sometimes called "Drummers" (*Barabanshchiki*) in Russian and Soviet literature.

(d) The "regular" brotherhood of Kunta Hajji known in Russian and Soviet literature as "Kunta Haji," was directed after the death of its founder by six of his former *vekils*—two were Daghestanis `Umar Hajji (a Kumyk) and Rajab Dibir Aliev of Tsumada (an Avar); two were Chechens: Qahraman Hajji of Shali and Yusuf Hajji of Mahkema in the district of Vedeno; and two Ingushes: Husayn Hajji of Plievo and Gharabig Hajji of Nazyr-Korta in the district of Nazran. The *tariqah* covered the territory of the present-day Checheno-Ingush republic and of North Eastern Daghestan.

The Struggle for Survival

In 1877/78 during the Russian-Ottoman war a great uprising against Russian domination took place in Daghestan-Chechnia. It was led by the feudal nobility but both Caucasian *tariqahs*—the Naqshbandiyah and the Qadiriyah—joined the revolt and played a significant role in it. In the Chechen country most of the insurgents were Qadiri adepts.

The uprising was crushed down in 1878 and the repression that followed was extremely harsh. Those of the leaders who had not been killed in the battle were hanged and thousands of *murids* were deported to Siberia, others emigrated to the Ottoman Empire.

Nevertheless, the defeat of 1878, far from marking the decline of Sufism in North Caucasus, served as a starting-point for its new and spectacular expansion. But after 1878 the nature of North Caucasian Sufism changed. The "Infidel" ruler being too powerful, the idea of an open *Jihad* was momentarily discarded and both the *tariqahs*, particularly the Qadiriyah, acquired the character of underground secret organizations which provided them considerable prestige. "Between 1878 and the 1917 Revolution," writes a Soviet historian, A. Salamov, "almost all of the adult population of Chechnia-Ingushetia belonged to a Sufi brotherhood."

By a curious historical paradox, the Sufi brotherhoods had practically absorbed the official Islamic establishment in Daghestan and Chechnia (nearly all Chechen *'Ulama'* were members of a *tariqah*) and identified themselves with the national resistance to the Russian rule.

Such was the situation in North Caucasus when the October Revolution and the Civil War took place. It took there a specific character different from all other Muslim areas of the former Russian Empire: Middle Volga, Transcaucasia, Turkestan, or the Kazakh Steppes where the leadership of the national movement was assumed by the liberal or moderate left-wing political parties. The moderate leaders caught in the maelstrom of the REvolution, for which they were badly prepared, tried in vain to manouevre between the Bolsheviks and the White counterrevolutionaries. And the end they failed and collapsed, the majority were forced to emigrate or to join (in 1920) the winning side, the Bolsheviks.

Contrarily the North Caucasian conservatives, led by Sufi *tariqah*, never hesitated, they fought back first the White Armies (1918 to 1920), then after their victory, the Bolsheviks (1920-1921). It were the Naqshbandis who led the last desperate revolt against the Bolsheviks. The nominal head of the 1920-21 revolt was Sa'id Beg, Shamil's grandson, but the effective leader was the Naqshbandi's *murshid*, Imam Najm al-Din Gotsinski. The revolt was finally quelled only in 1925 when the Bolsheviks captured and executed Najm al-Din Gotsinski and the few surviving Naqshbandi leaders. It was followed by a ferocious repression, but, as after Shamil's defeat, the military defeat did not lead to the decline of the Sufi orders. In particular, the Qadiriyah's influence was growing last.

According to Soviet official sources, in the mid-1920s there were in Daghestan alone some 61,200 adepts (*murids*), 19 *murshids* and 60 *vekils*, mostly Naqshbandis. In Chechnia, there were, in 1926, some 60,000 adepts, mostly Qadiris, out of a total population of 400,000.

The Qadiris did not participate massively in 1920/21 rebellion. During the first years of the Soviet regime some of their leaders played even a political role. Shaykh 'Ali Mitaev, son and successor of the founder of the Bammat Giray Hajji *wird* which numbered some ten thousand adepts in 1920, was even for a short while (1920-1923) one of the leading members of the Chechen Revolutionary Committee set up by the Bolsheviks. Several Chechen Communist leaders were secret Qadiri adepts. Elderkhanov, president of the Chechen Central Executive Committee, did not hide his sympathy for the brotherhood.

The curious, unnatural cooperation between the Sufis and the new godless regime did not last. In late 1923 a violent anti-religious campaign was launched in North Caucasus. All the *Shari'at* courts were abolished, many mosques closed and *waqf* properties taken over by the Soviet State. At the same time the Red Army began to disarm the Chechen population. In April 1924, Shaykh 'Ali Mitaev was arrested as 'counter-revolutionary"; he was tried in 1927 and executed. In 1925, Elderkhanov and many leading Chechen communists suspected of sympathy toward the underground and now-outlawed Qadiri brotherhood were arrested and liquidated.

The year 1928 marked the beginning of the massive frontal offensive against Islam in North Caucasus (and elsewhere in the Muslim territories of the USSR as well). It was accompanied by an attempt to liquidate what Soviet authorities called the "clerical leadership and their followers," in other terms the two Sufi brotherhoods still active in Chechnia and Daghestan. It provoked a new wave of rebellions with Naqshbandiyah and different branches of the Kunta Hajji fighting side by side. It started in autumn 1929 and the guerrilla fighting went on until 1936 when it was quelled momentarily. At this time the Qadiris played leading role, especially the Batal Hajji group. Nine sons and seven grandsons of Batal Hajji Belhoroev, the founder of the order, were killed inn battle or executed by the Soviets.

One may ask what were the political and military goals of the rebels who have fought for nearly fifteen years without any external help. Soviet sources call the Sufi adepts "reactionaries," "counter-revolutionaries" and even "agents" of various imperialisms—Turkish,

British, and after 1933, Japanese and German. In reality, the rebels fought without any precise political goal in mind, simply because they could not submit to the new Soviet regime with its old Russian imperialism aggravated by its new militant Marxist atheism.

Deghestan and Chechnia-Ingushetia remained until the outbreak of war in 1941 an area of insecurity. Six month before the beginning of the German attack, in winter 1940, a major revolt took place again in Chechnia. Soviet historians maintain that it was manipulated by German agents, which is certainly contrary to historical reality. In February 1942, when German vanguards were still a thousand miles away from Chechnia, another major revolt broke out which was a large popular movement led by former members of the Communist Party. The Germans never reached Chechnia and the rebellion was crushed by the Red Army. The entire Chechen and Ingush population was rounded up in February 1944 and deported to Siberia and Kazakhstan. It is estimated that out of a total of some half a million deported mountaineers (including all Chechen and Ingush officers and soldiers serving in the Red Army) a quarter perished during the transportation to the camps.

The Sufi brotherhoods took an active part in the revolt and, because of their better organization, succeeded to hold on longer than other rebels. Their guerrillas led by Quraysh Belhoroy, the last surviving son of the founder of Batal Hajji, lasted in the higher mountains of Ingushetia and Eastern Ossetia until 1947 when the Shaykh was finally captured by the Soviet troop and deported.

Altogether over one million of North Caucasian Muslims were deported. But the deportation had an unexpected and paradoxical result: far from destroying the Sufi brotherhoods, it actually promoted their expansion. For the deported mountaineers deprived of everything, Sufi order, particularly the Qadiriyah, became not only the very symbol of their nationhood but also very efficient organizers ensuring their survival. The vitality of the Qadiris during the long years of deportation (1943-1955) in Siberia and Kazakhstan is revealed by the birth, around 1950, somewhere in Kazakhstan of the most radical and puritan Qadiri branch, the Vis (for Uwais) Hajj *tariqah* founded by a

Chechen Vis Hajji Zagev, which soon became the most popular of all the Qadiri branches and gained adepts outside the Caucasian community among the Turkestanis: Kazakhs, Uzbeks and Karakalpaks.

After Stalin's death, the deported Caucasians were absolved of the crime of "collective treason" and allowed to return to their mountainous homeland, but their social structure has been deeply modified. The clan system in particular, which has been before 1943 the verb basis of Chechen and Ingush communities, has been, if not completely destroyed, at least seriously disturbed. Moreover, during the deportation all the mosques of Chechen-Ingush republic had been destroyed. More than ever before the *tariqah*, especially the Qadiriyah, appeared as the only centre around which the surviving mountaineers could organize their national and spiritual life.

The Situation after Deportation

After their return to the Caucasus, Sufi brotherhood, particularly the Qadiris, were once again subjected to a systematic relentless pressure about which the Soviet press provides abundant information. Today the *tariqahs* have no legal existence; they are underground, unlawful organizations and their adepts are hunted down as "reactionaries," "anti-socialist elements" and even as "criminals." They are accused of immutable hostility towards Soviet regime, of economic sabotage, banditism, terrorism and even "armed rebellion," especially in the case of the Ingush *Batal Hajji* often called in Soviet press "Gangster brotherhood." Several important trials of Sufi adepts took place in Groznyi, the capital of Chechen-Ingush republic, and in Nazran, in Ingush territory, in 1958, 1963 and 1964. The accused were tried for "banditism." The penalty was death.

All Sufi brotherhoods being outlawed and because of their strict clandestinity, our knowledge of the inner life of the Caucasian Qadiris is necessarily incomplete, based mainly on Soviet sources which are biased by their extreme hostility.

The first and most paradoxical fact is the new geographical expansion of the Qadiriyah after World War II. Its centre is still today in the Checheno-Ingush republic, but it is fast spreading eastward to

Northern Daghestan and westward to the Muslim part of Ossetia and Kabarda. Farther west it had planted its roots among the two Turkic small nationalities which have been deported in 1943 together with Chechens and Ingushes: the Balkars, living in the high mountainous area of Kabarda, and the Karachais, who live in the piedmont territory of the Karachais-Cherkess Autonomous Region. The Qadiris have also strong groups in southern Kazakhstan and in northern Kirghizia. In these two areas the adepts are either native Kazakhs, Uzbeks and Kirghiz or North Caucasians who stayed in Central Asia after 1958.

The present-day number of adepts is impossible to estimate, but we can make some approximate estimates. In the beginning of 1926, in spite of the human losses of the Civil War, there are were 70,000 Sufi adepts in the Checheno-Ingush republic, 60,000 of them were Chechens (19% of the population) and 10,000 were Ingushes (13% of the population).

In 1930 after the heavy purges of "clerical elements," there were in the Checheno-Ingush republic, according to Oshaev, a Chechen historian, 10,000 adepts of the Bammat Giray Hajji, and 800 of the Batal Hajji brotherhoods alone completely clandestine at that time. According to another Soviet expert, in 1974 "more than half of the believers of the Checheno-Ingush republic were adepts of a Sufi brotherhood" which corresponds to a minimum of 62,000 adepts, mostly Qadiris in the Checheno-Ingush republic alone, to which may be added at least 10,000 Qadiris in Daghestan, Kabarda, Ossetia and in various republics of Central Asia. A total of 70,000 Qadiris in the whole USSR may be considered as a reasonable figure. Thus the *tariqah* has succeeded to survive seventy years of hard anti-religious pressure, several uprisings followed by severe repression, and, between 1943 and 1958, an authentic attempted genocide.

Today all the four traditional Qadiri groups, formed after the deportation and the death of Kunta Hajji Kishiev ("Bammat Giray," "Batal Hajji," "Chim Mirza" and the original Kunta Hajji) are active, and to them was added a new group formed during the deportation in the 1950s, the "Vis Hajji," today probably the most numerous, the leadership of the groups is hereditary; it is still in the families of the founders, Mitaev (for the Bammat Giray), Belhoroy (for the Batal Hajji), Chim Mirza and Zagiev (for Vis Hajji). The leaders of the groups do not claim to be *murshids*, head of a new *tariqah* but simply *vekils* of Kunta Hajji. The four "*wirds*", as they are called in Soviet literature, are distinguished by their organization, ritual differences and their political attitudes towards the Soviet regime. All the Qadiris practise the loud *dhikr* with songs and dances. Chim Mirza use drums and Vis Hajji violins. All *wirds* are well-structured hierarchies. The head of the brotherhood has *vekils* or delegates of his own who control and direct the "elders" (in Chechen *tkhamada*) who are the brotherhood's representatives at the district level. Under the *tkhamada* the brotherhood is represented at the village level by a special category of executives (*turkhi* in chechen). According to Soviet sources, Batal Hajji are distinguished by their puritanism, their secrecy (they intermarry only with in their group) and their strong anti-communism attitude. In spite of their differences, all Qadiri groups are closely tied by a strong common sense of purpose. Moreover, a new trend has appeared among them during the recent years: the attempt to "federate" different *wirds* under a collective leadership, each group maintaining its characteristics while accepting collegial decisions of important political concern. The leading role is played today by the most dynamic and the most anti-Soviet of the *wirds*, the Vis Hajji.

The Qadiri groups are active in several spiritual and educational fields:

(i) They control numerous "holy places," generally *mazars* (tombs) of Sufi saints (most of them having fought Russian invaders) which are still visited by a number of pilgrims. In all North Caucasus and especially in the Checheno-Ingush country, where most of the mosques have been destroyed in 1942-44, the holy places represent real centres of religious life.

(ii) Sufi adepts run numerous clandestine religious schools where Arabic and elementary knowledge of Islamic theology are taught to children and adults.

(iii) Above all, they conduct a vigorous and constant missionary work among the population.

(iv) They publish underground works of purely religious character.

Soviet sources accuse all Sufi brotherhoods, in particular the Qadiris, of "conspiratorial political activity." Can we accept these malevolent assertions? It is true that from the standpoint of the Soviet legislation on the separation of the Church from the State, Sufi orders are illegal bodies. It is also true that to such dedicated believers as the adepts of a *tariqah*, the entire Soviet system with its huge (but not very efficient) anti-religious propaganda machinery appears as godless and therefore evil. But it is difficult to accept at their face value various Soviet accusations launched from time to time against the Sufis, especially against the Qadiris, like criminal activity, banditry, armed resistance to Soviet justice, manslaughter, etc.

I believe that for Soviet authorities the real social and political "danger" of Sufism lies elsewhere:

(1) Militant religious radicalism represented by the Sufi orders, sanctifying the traditional Muslim way of life, presents the greatest obstacle to the assimilation (the so-called "sovietization") of the Muslims by the Russians;

(2) The Sufi brotherhoods are the breeding ground of the most radical form of nationalism and of the anti-Russian and anti-communist feelings of the Muslim population. Sufis are denounced for encouraging believers and unbelievers alike to isolate themselves from the "Infidels," to refuse to learn Russian and to avoid any contact with the Soviet public organizations dominated by Russian, such as the Communist Party or the Komsomol;

(3) Less frequently, Sufi brotherhoods are accused of being channels through which "subversive" foreign propaganda (radio broadcasts, literature) reaches the Muslim territories of the Soviet Union;

(4) Sufi (especially the Qadiri) communities are closed societies which live outside the Soviet establishment. In the North Caucasus, Sufi rural communities are generally more prosperous than the official kolkhoz. I believe that the Sufi

> brothers are the main target of Soviet propaganda because they provide eloquent testimony that large, well-organized communities with their own rules and discipline and their own institutions can survive and expand entirely outside Soviet political control. By their very survival Sufi brotherhoods demonstrate that even the most rigorous religious group can resist, indeed prosper, in spite of Soviet pressure, without losing a single element of its creed, ritual or way of life. Sufism is an implied promise to Soviet Muslims that the final historical competition between Islam and Marxism will be decided in favour of Islam.

What could be the future of Sufism and especially of its most puritan form, the Qadiri, in Soviet Union? It depends mainly on Moscow's religious policy. The vitality of the *tariqah* depends to an important extent on the lack of vitality of the official Muslim Establishment. Sufism thrives on adversity. As long as official Islam remains a mere facade Sufism will continue to play an important role in the life of the believers. To weaken militant Sufism, Soviet authorities must give a new life to the official Islamic Establishment, which means to open more mosques and more religious schools and lessen anti-Islamic propaganda. For the time being, however, there is absolutely no evidence that Moscow is considering any change in its anti-religious strategy.

3

Shaikh Nizam-ud-din Auliya

R.N. DAS

Shaikh Nizam-ud-din Auliya holds a unique position among the Sufi saints of medieval India. In an age full of internecine wars, intrigues and assassinations he held fast to the duty which he chose to impose upon himself and carried on his mission quietly, undisturbed alike by the hostility of the Sultans and the glamour of the royal court. Whereas the contemporary Sultans of Delhi came and went, dynasties rose and sank into oblivion after a brief spell, this celebrated saint may be said to have passed into immortality—his memory being adored by the succeeding generations. The tombs of the majority of the Sultans have mostly disappeared or are only a debris of bricks and plaster while that of the saint at the ancient village of Ghiyathpur, a suburb of Delhi, which is now called Nizam-ud-din Auliya Ki Basti, continues to be a place of pilgrimage for the high and the low, the rich and the poor alike. Not a day passes without fresh flowers being strewn on the saint's grave which is visited by pilgrims all the year round. The anniversary ('urs) of the saint is celebrated at his shrine with as much solemnity, pomp and grandeur to-day as it was several centuries ago. People have conferred various titles of their own on Nizam-ud-din Auliya , e.g., 'Sultan-ul-Auliya' (the king of the saints) and Mahbub-e Ilahi (the beloved of God). In his *Siyar-ul-Auliya* (Lives of the saints) Amir Khurd has given him the title of 'Sultan-ul-Mashaikh' (the king of the saints). While paying eloquent tribute to Nizam-ud-din Auliya, Prince Dara Shikoh in his *Safinat-ul-Auliya'* uses the same title. To the people of Delhi he came to be better known as 'Nizam-ud-din Auliya.' Md. Habib has pointed out the incongruity of the appellation, for 'Auliya' means 'Saints.'

Some western scholars have done Nizam-ud-din Auliya less than justice by casting aspersions on his character. But they have not cared to prove their contention with reference to the original sources. Wolseley Haig' observes, "relations between Ghiyas-ud-din Tughluq and the Shaikh remained strained until his death, in which it is not improbable that the Shaikh was implicated." Similar is the case with Sleeman and Cooper, who have also denounced Nizam-ud-din Auliya. Their contention is that Nizam-ud-din Auliya had an understanding with Ulug Khan (later known a Muhammad bin Tughluq) to murder Ghiyath-ud-din Tughluq and brought it about through some of his devoted disciples.

In order to find out the justification or otherwise of such a grave accusation against the saint for taking an active part in some of the political events that occurred in his life-time, it will be convenient for us to attempt a brief review of his career with special reference to his relationship with the various Sultans of Delhi.

Of the sources of our information relating to Nizam-ud-din Auliya, the *Fawaid-u'l-Fuwad*, compiled by Amir Hasan Dihlavi, deserves special mention. As a trust worthy reproduction of the sayings of the saint, it provides us with plenty of material for the study of the character of the saint. The fact that the contents of this book were revised by the saint himself definitely enhances its historical value. Born at Badaun in 1238 A.D. Muhammad Nizam-ud-din lost his father at the age of five. His father's qualities of head and heart—more particularly his saintly habits—won recognition at the court of Qutbuddin Aibak. He grew up under the fostering care of his mother, a lady noted for her learning and piety. It is said that he imbibed his great love for things spiritual from his mother. Form his childhood he displayed wonderful development of mental powers and evinced also an intense fondness for sainthood. He was sent to Delhi to take lessons in the science of Tradition from the renowned teacher, Shamsu'l-Mulk. Soon he acquired great proficiency in Hadith (Tradition), Tafsir (commentary on the Qur'an) and literature. The brilliant academic career was sure to win for him a secure and comfortable position in life. But the expected did not happen. Before he was twenty the urge for spiritual enlightenment led him to cast all worldly temptations aside and he proceeded to Ajodhan with a view to making Shaikh

Farid-ud-din Mas'ud Ganj-i Shakar his spiritual preceptor. Nizam-ud-din Auliya' erudition, his spiritual bent of mind and the depth of his inner vision made such a profound impression upon Shaikh Farid-ud-din that he was nominated by the latter as his Khalifa or spiritual successor. The preceptor's words deserve to be quoted in this connection, "Outwardly it would seem that I have made Nizam-ud-din my disciple, but in reality he is the chief disciple of God and the Khalifa of the Prophet.' It was in 1265 A.D. that Nizam-ud-din moved to Ghiyaspur, adjacent to Delhi, yet away from the din of the capital. He was to spend the rest of his life there in the Khanqah constructed by one of his disciple, Maulana Ziauddin, and frequented by men from all walks of life irrespective of caste and creed. A man of vast erudition and singular piety, he used to spend his days in fasting, prayers and teaching. His way of life and magnetic personality drew around him a host of disciples whom he guided in their quest for spiritual salvation. It is said that the doors of his monastery were open to all and no one had to come back disappointed. Amir Hasan refers to wandering darweshes (jawaliq) who made it a point to include the sanctuary of Nizam-ud-din Auliya in their itinerary. He makes special mention of one occasion when one of the darweshes used very improper words before the saint whose equanimity was not in the least disturbed by so grave a provocation. Nizam-ud-din Auliya continued to listen patiently and was very kind to the said darwesh. He always laid great stress upon the virtues of "endurance, forbearance and contentment." One of his happy sayings runs thus: "Do as you would like to be done by and do not do as you would not like to be done by." In fact the wished 'to become a man of perfect virtue and to teach others without weariness.'

His whole career was one continuous struggle 'against sin, against poverty and against self.' He is reputed to have insisted upon his disciples complete severance of all worldly ties. He was not ready to permit them even to earn their livelihood. To him it appeared that the feeling of security about one's means of livelihood would imply dependence not upon God but upon somebody else. It may be mentioned here that the earlier mystics of the Chishti order sanctioned only two forms of livelihood, viz., Zamin-i-Ahya (the cultivation of barren land by the mystic's own hand) and Futuh ('unasked charity of the neighbours'). Nizam-ud-din Auliya was reluctant to approve of the former method and sanctioned charity which came unasked for.

Visitor to the Khanqah used to bring gifts to Nizam-ud-din Auliya. He would receive these private gifts only to give them away to others. Many stories of these presents that came to him became current. One of these relates to a traveller who, being robbed of all his possessions during the journey, approached the saint for help. The Sultan-ul-Auliya promised to give him whatever he would receive during the early hours of the next day. The traveller was beside himself with joy when he was given the entire amount of 12000 tankas collected during the stipulated period. If this is to be believed it will give us an idea of the richness of the presents offered to the saint as tokens of the high esteem in which he was held. The *Khair-ul-Majalis*, compiled by Hamid, is highly illustrative on this point. "Gifts flowed into the Jama'at Khana of Shaikh Nizam-ud-din Auliya like the waters of the Labia (a branch of the Jumna) that flowed before it. People came from morning to sunset and even at the time of the nigh prayer. But those who came with requests always exceeded those who came with gifts, and everyone who brought something also got something."

Obviously the growing popularity of the saint did not fail to attract the notice of the contemporary Sultans of Delhi. Nizam-ud-din Auliya lived through the reign periods of more than half a dozen rulers. But there is nothing on record to suggest that he ever cared for their favour or frown. Absolutely free from the lure of material gain, he never condescended to beg any favour from the temporal authority but relied solely on the will of the Almighty. The Sultanate of Delhi under Balban first sought his co-operation by offering him the exalted office of the Imamate. The Shaikh is said to have politely declined the offer with the words, "Namaz is the only valuable asset I possess, and the King wants to take even that away by making me his Imam." Balban's high regard for the integrity of the saint is revealed by the fact of his making yet another offer of the post of Qadi-ul-Quddat. The Sultan's offer met with the same fate as that of the first. In this connection it is pertinent to quote the words which Barani in his *Tarikh-i-Firuz Shahi* has put in the mouth of Shaikh Farid-ud-din

Ganj-i-Shakar: "Do not make friends with kings and nobles. Consider their visits to your home at fatal (for your spirit). Every Darwesh who makes friends with the kings and nobles, will end badly." It appears that Nizam-ud-din Auliya scrupulously followed his preceptor's advice.

The short period of Mu'izuddin's Kaiqubad's reign (1287-1290) was marked by a general outburst of licentiousness. The saints must have found the atmosphere in the realm not congenial to the pursuit of their mission. Only six months had elapsed after the accession of Kaiqubad to the throne of Delhi when he shifted from the Red Palace of Balban to the new one he had built at Kilughari on the banks of the Jumna. In his *Akhbar u'l Akhyar* Shaikh 'Abdul Haqq Dihlawi states that the shifting of the residential quarters to Kilughari resulted in making the locality congested. So many people started paying visits to Ghiyathpur that the saint began to contemplate leaving the place. At this juncture a young man approached him and humbly submitted that there could not be any special virtue in remembering God after one's withdrawal from the world. To succeed in an attempt to remember the Almighty in the midst of people would be all the more creditable. Further he pointed out that since Nizam-ud-din Auliya became "the full moon" it was only natural that the people should raise their fingers towards him. The words had their desired effect upon the saint who decided to stay on at Ghiyathpur.

The first Khalji Sultan was a pious, God-fearing Muslim who assumed the reins of administration at the ripe old age of seventy. Moved by the privation of the saint, Jalaluddin Firuz Shah Khalji requested him to accept the gift of a village. Despite the fact that Nizam-ud-din Auliya had to face hard times very often he stuck to his preceptor's advice by refusing to accept any favour from the kings and nobles of the court. Jalaluddin cherished an ardent desire to see the saint and he is said to have requested Amir Khusrau, a very favourite disciple of Nizam-ud-din Auliya, to use his influence for its fulfilment. But the persuasions of the poet-laureate were of no avail. It so happened that on hearing of the Sultan's intention to pay a surprise visit the saint went on a pilgrimage to Shaikh Farid-ud-din's tomb at Ajodhan. Thus it appears that this Sufi darwesh, who was absolutely free from the craving for earthly possessions, also highly detested the company of the kings. This may also be confirmed by a reference to Nizam-ud-din Auliya's relations with the next Khalji ruler.

'Alauddin Khalji, a great admirer of Nizam-ud-din Auliya, invited him to the royal court. But the Sultan-ul-Auliya firmly asserted that he was serving mankind in his own way. As he preferred a life of devotion and retirement he expressed his inability to accept the invitation. Even the Sultan's proposal to build a mausoleum for the saint did not meet with the latter's approval. Again, 'Alauddin's admiration for the saint led him to offer some costly presents for the maintenance of the Khanqah, which attracted a host of admirers. Convinced of the baneful influence of the worldly riches, Nizam-ud-din Auliya rejected the offer with the words, "A filled stomach keeps the soul subdued; where as when the stomach is empty the soul has free play." In spite of the saint's refusal to accept any favour from the Sultan, Barani assures us that no words ever passed the Sultan's lips to which the Shaikh could possibly object. Indeed it is highly interesting to note that 'Alauddin Khalji, who was opposed to ecclesiastical interference in matters of state, had the greatest veneration for Nizam-ud-din Auliya and sought his moral aid in times of political and military stress. For instance, 'Abdul Haqq Dihlawi refers to an occasion when 'Alauddin sent Prince Khidr Khan to Nizam-ud-din Auliya with some administrative proposals for his opinion. The latter he addressed to the saint ran thus: "The service of the Shaikh is for the (welfare of) mankind. The worldly and spiritual wants of a person are removed through you. God has bestowed on us the reins of the kingdom of the world. It is, therefore, necessary that every problem that faces the kingdom should be placed before you so that you may pronounce your opinion relating to the welfare of the state and the prudence of our measure. Accordingly, some problems relating to certain affairs have been submitted to you (for your opinion). Please signify your approval of those measures which you consider to be in the best interest (of the state), so that we may put them into execution." The saint did not care even to go through the contents of the letter. After the offering of a Fatiha (benedictory prayer) in company of those present he said, "Darweshes have nothing to do with the affairs of kings. I am a Darwesh and I have retired myself from the city. My business is to pray for the welfare of the kings and the Muslims. If after this the king speaks anything to me with regard to this matter, I shall leave this place." The saint's determination to keep aloof from the political controversies of the realm increased the Sultan's admiration for him. But 'Alauddin's proposal to visit the Shaikh at his Khanqah did not meet with his approval. What is more, when the Sultan began to insist on the proposal of a visit Nizam-ud-din Auliya said:

> "The house of this powerless man has two doors. If the Sultan enters by one door I shall quit by the other." On receipt of this message the Sultan decided not to give any more trouble to the saint and the relationship between the two became quite cordial.

Stories relating to 'Ala-ud-din Khalji's belief in the supernatural powers of Nizam-ud-din Auliya have come down to us. Barani in his narrative of the expedition to Warangal in 1310 has referred to the breakdown of the courier system for the transmission of news due to enemy activity. 'Alauddin's anxiety for the army under Malik Na'ib led him to depute Qadi Mughithuddin of Bayana to the saint with a request to disclose the exact position of the army through his miraculous powers. The saint's reply indicating the success of the army of Islam and further victories in future allayed the fears of the Sultan. It was indeed a strange coincidence that Malik Na'ib's report of the victory at Warangal reached the Sultan at the close of the same day.

The following description by Barani makes it clear that 'Alauddin reposed great confidence in the supernatural powers of Nizam-ud-din Auliya.

"In seeing the numerous victories and conquests and the achievement of many affairs according to his heart's desire, Sultan 'Alauddin used to say that every victory and conquest which the standard of Islam attained during his age and every matter relating to the welfare of the subjects of his empire and every measure of good government and conciliatory policy which was to be found in his dominion, were due to the benedictions and blessings of Shaikhu'l Islam Nizam-ud-din Ghiyathpuri."

Later writers have also testified to the high esteem in which the saint was held by the people of the age. To quote Nizam-ud-din Ahmad: "....the success which crowned 'Ala-ud-din's aims and objects, and the wonderful works he accomplished by his exertions and endeavours have been deemed by many to be nothing less than miracles, and they have attributed their achievement to revelation and inspiration....while others have thought that the safety and happiness of the people were due to the auspicious existence of Shaikh Nizam-ud-din Auliya." Similarly, Badaoni also mentions that some held that the peace and security of 'Alauddin's reign were due to the unbounded blessings of the Sultan-ul-Mashaikh Nizam-ud-din Auliya. These observations can be interpreted as showing the tremendous moral and spiritual influence which the Shaikh exercised over the people.

With the accession to the throne of Qutb-ud-din Mubarak Shah, who offered a striking contrast to his father whose wonderful capacity for organisation and leadership he lacked, there was a deliberate attempt to disturb the equanimity of Nizam-ud-din Auliya. Cruel, arrogant and vindictive, this unworthy successor of 'Ala-ud-din visibly lacked a sense of proportion and he indulged in 'the grossest licentiousness and the most disgusting buffoonery.' It is not at all surprising that such a monarch should have the impudence to pick up a quarrel with the saint. Diauddin Barani has provided us with an explanation for Qutbuddin Mubarak Shah's hostile attitude towards Nizam-ud-din Auliya. The fact that Khidr Khan, the Sultan's elder brother, had been one of the most devoted disciples of the saint led Qutbuddin Mubarak Shah to look upon Nizam-ud-din Auliya with suspicion and fear. It was suspected that the saint might he implicated in a plot against the Sultan to place his disciple on the throne. It may be noted here that no other reason has been adduced by contemporary or later writers who have simply followed Barani in this matter. In this context it is worth noting that the jealously of Shaikh Zada-Jam, who intended to set himself up as a rival to Nizam-ud-din Auliya, might have something to do with the lowering of the prestige of the saint in the estimation of Qutbuddin Mubarak Shah who, it was said, had obtained the throne through Shaikh Zada-Jam's prayers. Barani has given us a graphic account of the sad episode of the strained relations between Qutbuddin Mubarak

Shah and the saint:

> "He (Sultan Qutbuddin) began to speak ill of Shaikh Nizam-ud-din and openly declared his hostility towards him. The Maliks of the palace were forbidden to visit the Shaikh at Ghiyathpur. And often in his state of intoxication he used to make the impudent statement that whoever would bring the head of Nizam-ud-din would be rewarded with a thousand gold tankas. One day Sultan Qutbuddin met Shaikh Nizam-ud-din at the hovel of Shaikh Diauddin Rumi...but he showed no consideration to the dignity of the Shaikh, did not respond to his salute and took no notice of him. With the purpose of creating a rival he brought Shaikh Zada-Jam, an enemy of Shaikh Nizam-ud-din, and made him a favourite of the court. Then he summoned Shaikhu'l Islam Ruknuddin from Multan to the city of Delhi."

Hamid bin Fadlullah, better known as Jamali, would make us believe that the intensity of the persecution of Nizam-ud-din Auliya by Qutbuddin Mubarak Shah led me former to send Amir Hasan Dihlavi, his disciple, to Shaikh Diauddin Rumi with a request to use his influence with the Sultan so that he might not be disturbed any longer. But it so happened that Shaikh Diauddin Rumi was laid up with an attack of colic and the message could not be delivered to him. He succumbed to this illness and thus ended all hope of any betterment in the relations between the Sultan and the saint through the intercession of Shaikh Diauddin Rumi. Qutbuddin Mubarak Shah's vanity as well as his vindictive nature stood revealed when he ordered Nizam-ud-din Auliya to attend the royal court in person at the beginning of every lunar month. To this insolent demand Nizam-ud-din Auliya replied, "I live a retired life and I do not go anywhere. As it has been the practice of my spiritual masters not to associate with monarchs I should on this ground be excused." Afraid of the Sultan's wrath for non-compliance, the disciples of the saint tried to persuade him to obey the royal orders. But they failed to create any impression on the serene temperament of the darwesh. Muhammad Bulaq in his biography of Nizam-ud-din Auliya has represented the saint as having said on this occasion to one of his disciples, 'Izud-din 'Ali Shah, thus, "Your stay in peace. Last night I dreamt that a horned bull attempted to kill me. I caught hold of both his horns and threw him down on the ground and he was killed. By the will of God, the Sultan will not be triumphant over me." In fact this dream came to be translated into reality when Qutbuddin Mubarak Shah was murdered by the followers of Khusrau Khan. However, it was not the fault of the Shaikh that his prediction turned out to be true. Any suspicion about a link between the Shaikh and the followers of Khusrau Khan can be dispelled by a reference to this dream. If the Shaikh had anything to do with this foul deed it is unthinkable that he would have divulged the contents of the dream lest it be interpreted by implication as proof of his complicity in the murder of Qutbuddin Mubarak Shah. It may also be noted here that there is not to be found in the contemporary or later chronicles even the slightest hint about the Shaikh's involvement in the incident.

On the accession to the throne Khurasan Khan, the usurper, tried to secure the moral support of the saint by lavish distribution of wealth. Most of those who had accepted the gift had prudently kept the money is deposit to restore it when called upon to do so. Jamali in his *Siyaru'l 'Arifin* refers to Shaikh Nizam-ud-din Auliya as the recipient of a sum of five hundred thousand tankas. It has also been recorded that the saint distributed the entire amount among the needy the deserving persons.

While tracing Nizam-ud-din Auliya's relations with his contemporary sultans one finds the most eventful days of his career during the reign-period of Ghiyath-ud-din Tughluq when matters came to head. It appears that from the very start the first ruler of the Tughluq dynasty did not pull on well with the Shaikh. The reasons for estrangement between the two were many and various. The fact that Ghazi Malik in his struggle against Khusrau Khan under the slogan "Islam in danger" did not get the moral support of Nizam-ud-din Auliya partly explains his attitude towards the saint which was anything but friendly. In order to replenish the exchequer depleted by the reckless expenditure of Qutbuddin Mubarak Shah and Khusrau Khan, the very first thing that Ghiyath-ud-din Tughluq did was to force many to refund the amount that his predecessor has distributed among them. Nizam-ud-din Auliya, who had already spent the whole amount in charity, could not refund it. The saint's reply in this regard was: "It was public property which had gone to the deserving ones. I have not spent a single farthing of it on my account." It may be asked as to how the saint, who was free from worldly temptation, could condescend to accept the gift from the usurper, Khusrau Khan. No better explanation of the principle on which the saint acted on such occasions can be given that by quoting his own views on "Income and Expenditure" expressed in some of his conversations recorded in *Fawa'id-u'l-Fuad*: "The acceptance of money and expenditure is governed by some conditions. The receiver ought to receive it in a lawful way and spend it on the deserving ones....A man should not beg anything from anybody; neither should he express a desire nor think in his mind that so and so would give him a certain thing. But if a thing is offered to him without being asked and hoped for, then it is lawful for him. A certain great man has said that he never asked for a thing nor did he ever entertain and hope receiving anything from any person, but whoever would voluntarily offer him a thing he would accept it even if the donor was a Satan."

However, the fact remains that the Shaikh's inability to refund the amount annoyed the Sultan. From that time onward Nizam-ud-din Auliya remained 'a marked man' and excuses for the worsening of the relations between the two were not rare. Ghiyath-ud-din Tughluq, a puritan monarch, did not approve of the performance of the Sama' (ecstatic dance accompanied by music) in the Shaikh's monastery. It may be noted here that the rigid followers of the established religion regarded this form of devotion as unlawful. Fully aware of the Sultan's aversion to such things, the rival and jealous Shaikhs began to instigate him against Nizam-ud-din Auliya whose liberal outlook and delight in music they denounced as contrary to the canons of orthodoxy. While recording the discourse in the year of Ghiyath-ud-din Tughluq's accession to the throne (720 A.H.), Amir Hasan Dihlavi refers to the accusation made by the saint's enemies for performing Sama'. According to Firishta, Nizam-ud-din Auliya was summoned by the king to appear before an assembly of divines and scholars to explain his conduct. The saint successfully held his own against his adversaries, quoting many *hadithes*, in support of the legitimacy of the Sama'. Convinced of the legality of the Sama' the Sultan let him go free. To quote Hajiuddabir who has described the scene on the basis of *Siyar-ul-'Arifin*: "When the Sultan heard this he was struck with remorse for having troubled Shaikh Nizam-ud-din Auliya. Then he rose and advanced towards him and kissed his hands with great courtesy and humiliation. Then he sent him back, bidding him farewell amidst profound apologies."

It appears that the Sultan's dislike for the saint could not be fully obliterated even after this incident. This may be corroborated by a reference to his subsequent conduct. It is not unlikely that Ghiyath-ud-din Tughluq became jealous of the tremendous moral and spiritual influence which Nizam-ud-din Auliya exercised over the people. To make matters worse, Ulugh Khan (later known as Muhammad bin Tughluq), son of Ghiyath-ud-din Tughluq, was found to be imbued with great faith in, and unbounded respect for, the Shaikh. When the Sultan came to know of the fact that Nizam ud-din Auliya had enrolled among his followers such person as Ulugh Khan, his strained feeling grew more tense and he saw in the Shaikh a great political danger. It is pertinent to note in this connection what Ibn-Batutah has recorded on this subject. *The Rehla* has mentioned Ulugh Khan's frequent visit to the saint, Nizam-ud-din Auliya, to pay him respect and to implore his blessings. The saint was subject to spells of ecstasy during which he lost all control of himself. The prince asked the saint's followers to contact him during one of those ecstatic fits. On being informed accordingly, he rushed to the saint who was still in a trance. On this occasion Nizam-ud-din Auliya is said to have prophesied in his ecstatic trance: "We accord you the scepter." Obviously reports of incidents like this, when carried to the Sultan, must have resulted in making him suspicious of his doings of the Shaikh.

On his return journey from Lakhnauti to Delhi, Ghiyath-ud-din Tughluq ordered the saint to quite Ghiyathpur by the time he entered the capital. Alarmed at the wrath of Ghiyath-ud-din Tughluq, the disciples of the saint warned him of the Sultan's approach to the capital. To this Nizam-ud-din Auliya, a man without malice and without fear, gave a memorable reply, "Hanuz Delhi dur ast," i.e., 'Delhi is yet far off,' and so it proved to be. As it happened, Ghiyath-ud-din Tughluq met with sudden death through the collapse of a new pavilion constructed for his reception at Afghanpur near Tughluqabad, and he could not reach Delhi. This prophetic utterance of the saint has since become proverbial. It is used to indicate the difficulties which have to be surmounted before arriving at the destination, or 'the futility of an incompetent person attempting any task.'

It was the saying of Nizam-ud-din Auliya which led some western scholars to implicate him in a conspiracy to murder Ghiyath-ud-din Tughluq. Prof. Mahdi Husain, on the other hand, has given us a different interpretation on the basis of Husam Khan's *Tarikh-i-Bahadur Shahi*. He would make us believe that "by means of the above mystical phrase...he (the saint) conveyed to the emperor that there would be no further meeting between the two and that he, Muhammad Nizam-ud-din, would leave the world before the emperor reached his destination." In fact Nizam-ud-din Auliya died before the Sultan's return from Lakhnauti and Ulugh Khan incurred his father's displeasure by carrying the coffin on his shoulders. The prophetic utterance of the saint, as Dr. R.C. Majumdar says, "may also be taken to indicate some sort of conspiracy to kill the Sultan before he could actually reach the capital city. But many writers are of opinion that even if there were any such conspiracy, Nizam-ud-din Auliya had probably nothing to do with it."

In this connection it will be convenient to bear in mind the fact that innumerable utterances of the saint foretelling a future are extant. It behoves one not to read into Nizam-ud-din Auliya's saying more than what he wanted to convey. Again, it is not fair to find fault with the saint if his prediction came out to be true. There is nothing on record to suggest that he did anything to make the prediction a reality. Chroniclers, contemporary or later, have not implicated the saint in the murder of Ghiyath-ud-din Tughluq. If the western scholars had access to any other source of information which led them to cast suspicion on the saint, they should have enlightened us on it. In the present state of our knowledge we find it rather difficult to incriminate the saint on mere suspicion.

People of every rank and position craved for the blessings of Nizam-ud-din Auliya with the firm belief that he could guarantee bliss and happiness in this life and the life hereafter. Criminals and malefactors are usually superstitious and prone to atone for their misdeeds by paying homage to some saint or pir. That, indeed, is not a proof of the saint's being an accomplice or encouraging them in their reprehensible conduct. If they made offerings out of their spoils, Nizam-ud-din Auliya would accept only to spend them in charity. It was not the saint's fault that many princes and nobles also chose to become his disciples. In the absence of any incriminating evidence he must not be held responsible for any subversive political movement of the day in which the princes and nobles who happened to be his disciples, were involved. By way of illustration it may be pointed out that even such a ghastly deed as the political murder of his disciple, Khidr Khan, could not elicit any public denunciation from the saint. Again, the struggle for power between the followers of Khusrau Khan and those of Ghazi Malik under the slogan 'Islam in danger' found the saint as indifferent as ever. These are some of the facts which prove that the saint was unconcerned with the political convulsions of the day. It is highly significant that the hostile Sultans could not make out a case against Nizam-ud-din Auliya, accusing him of having dabbled in politics.

Indeed the character of saint is above all suspicion. He occupies a prominent place among the spiritual benefactors of mankind. Quite in keeping with the style of Sufi saints this darwesh of sterling qualities could never be tempted by material gain. Despite grave provocation he preferred not to deviate from the pat chalked out by his preceptor, Shaikh Farid-ud-din Ganj-i-Shakar. In the opinion of the latter concentration of heart is the vital point in Sufism and it can be achieved only by abstention from the prohibited means of livelihood and association with kings.

Shaikh Nizam-ud-din Auliya represents a great spiritual force in the history of medieval India. According to him, the ultimate object for which man was created was to love God. On this point Nizam-ud-din Auliya's words as quoted in *Siyaru'l Auliya* are as follows: "The followers of the Tariqat (the way) and the Huquiqat (the reality) agree that the main purpose and objective of man's creation is the love of the Supreme Being." In his view the love of God implied also the love of humanity without which the former would be incomplete. He spared no pains to inculcate this ethical ideal in the minds of his followers. *Siyaru'l Auliya* of Amir Khurd contains the following saying of Nizam-ud-din Auliya: "O Muslims! I swear by God that he holds dear those who love him for the sake of human beings, and also those who love human beings for the sake of God. This is the only way to love and adore God." These words bear eloquent testimony to the saint's deep attachment to the idea of universal love. How noble was his concept of life is manifest from his own utterance:

> "A Muslim must abstain from doing harm of any kind to anybody; he must also abstain from every sin and should protect his eyes, tongue and hands from an undesirable act; he should direct his eyes and tongue towards the truth and keep glorifying Allah steering clear of every doubt that might develop in his mind...The heart is a mirror which is in itself clean; but sins cover it with dust which can only be removed by repeating the names of Allah and His Prophet Muhammad."

Shaikh Nizam-ud-din Auliya's actions were actuated by a spirit of universal love for mankind in general. In fact he dedicated his whole life to the service of humanity.

Barani seems to have given us a fairly accurate idea of the tremendous impact of Nizam-ud-din Auliya's noble presence on the character of the people and the morale of the society in the following description:

> "All people, believing in him, tried to emulate him in devotion and virtue. Men and woman, young and old, low and mean, servants and slaves, and even small boys had begun to offer their prayers regularly. Rich and benevolent persons had constructed in several pleasant spots between the city and Ghiyathpur terraces with thatched roofs and had wells dug there. The terraces were supplied with large jars full of water, clay jugs and mats, and keepers and reciters were posted there so that people coming from or going to the monastery of the Shaikh may not be inconvenienced in making their ablutions at prayer times. In each of these terraces one saw crowds of people offering prayers.

> Perpetration or talk of crime had declined among the people, and they talked mostly of religious things...There was no quarter in the city where after twenty days or a month there was no gathering of the pious listening to Sufistic music and weeping in ecstasy. Sultan 'Alauddin himself, with all his family, had great faith in the Shaikh and the hearts of all classes of people were inclined towards virtue and piety. Never did the name of wine and women, crime and sin, gambling or other vile practices, profane the lips of people during the latter portion of 'Alauddin's reign. Most of the students, nobles and great men who attended upon the Shaikh were seen to be busy in the study of books on Sufism or the Islamic law."

If every a fraction of what Barani has started is to be believed, the would indeed be no mean achievement on the part of Shaikh Nizam-ud-din Auliya who tried in his own way to make the world a better place to live in.

AMIR HUSAINI

Amir Husaini was one of the outstanding personalities of the seventh and eighth centuries of Hijra. An account of his life and writings deserves a place in the cultural history of medieval India. He was at once a great sufi, a renowned poet, a prolific writer and an acknowledged thinker in moral philosophy. His contemporaries, both in and outside India, held him in great esteem on account of his rare qualities of head and heart. He had a distinguished place in the sufistic and literary circles of Iran and Khurasan, and was highly praised by the Iranian intellectuals and men of learning, including Daulat Shah Samarqandi and the well-known sufi poet Mahmud Shabisteri.

He left a number of sufistic treatises both in prose and poetry which are highly commendable and deserve to be studied.

With the passage of time his fame faded out and his name fell into oblivion. It is therefore worth while to assess the work of this great scholar whose contribution to the intellectual history of his period is so remarkable. None of his books, the manuscripts of which are abundantly available in all the big libraries of the world, have so far been scientifically published. Whatever, the early biographers have said about him in confusing and often contradictory, and the scholars have not been able to get a clear idea of his life as yet. His biography, as preserved in the records, is a confused mixture of fact and fiction. Only recently a noted Iranian scholar, Dr. Farugh-i-Hikmat, introduced Husaini to the literary circle of Iran through a learned article published in *Mujall-i Rahnuma-i-Kitab*, in which he tried to determine the place of Husaini in the realm of poetry and mysticism. The learned writer deals with Husaini's qualities as a poet and writer, but he has not been able to present a coherent biography of Husaini. The present writer will make an effort to give, in the following pages, a careful account based on Husaini's own writings rather than on confusing and contradictory information supplied by the anthologists.

The full name of Husaini was Shaikh Rukn-ud-din b. 'Alam b. Abil Hasan Al-Husaini, also known as Amir Husaini or Sayyid Husaini. His contemporaries honoured him by the title of Fakhr-i-Sa'adat. His father's name was 'Alam, as is evident from his own writings in which he calls himself the son of 'Alam. 'Alam was a native of a small place named Gurdiv in the vicinity of Ghor, and belonged to a respectable family of Saiyeds. He and his family lived by trade and seemed to be well-to-do.

Husaini was born in Gurdiv in the year 671 H., as is evident from *Nuzhat-ul-Arwah*, the famous mystical work of Husaini which was written in the year 711 H. In this book Husaini mentioned his age as forty years while making the following observation :

> O thou! It is the evening of life; and thou hast attained the age of forty; and yet thou hast not released thyself from thy ignorance. Look here: the vicissitudes of earthly life have held thy mind in their grip; and thy feet are not disentangled from worldly avocations.

Thus deducting forty from seven hundred and eleven, we can safely say that Husaini was born in the year 671 H.

An authentic record of his early life and the different stages of his education are not available in the existing sources. However, it appears from his own writings that he was well versed in all branches of knowledge current in those days. His knowledge of the various branches of learning, considered essential in his time, was exhaustive and thorough. He succeeded in developing his individual style both in prose and poetry, and wrote in a quite forceful, direct and clear manner, on various subjects like mysticism, ethics and philosophy. His scholarship and training in sufistic discipline were acknowledged by all his contemporaries.

After completing his educating, Husaini joined his father in the profession of trade, and this gave him an opportunity to make frequent visits to the city of Multan, which was in those days a great centre of spiritual learning and was specially renowned as a seat of activity of the Suhrawardia saints. His association with the learned society of Multan made a deep and lasting impression on his mind and later on played a significant role in shaping his character and ideas.

Living, even though for a short period, in an atmosphere filled with mysticism, Husaini could not remain uninfluenced by it. He developed an extraordinary passion for mysticism and gradually became indifferent to material prosperity and luxurious life which his trade involved.

It was, however, after the death of his father that Husaini gave up all his worldly possessions and set out for Multan in search in Divine light.

A difference of opinion exists among the anthologists about the identity of the spiritual guide of Husaini. According to Dr. Farugh-i-Hikmat, Jami was the first to write about Husaini and the subsequent writers have merely followed him. Jami says:

From his book "Kanz-ur-Rumuz" (store-house of secrets) it appears that he was a disciple of Shaikh Baha-ud-Din Zakriya.

But he adds that, according to some other authorities, he was a disciple not of Shaikh Baha-ud-Din Zakriya but of Shaikh Rukn-ud-

Din Abul-Fath, son of Sadr-ud-Din 'Arif and grandson of Baha-ud-Din Zakriya. Shaikh Jahangir Ashraf Samnani, the author of *Lataif-i-Ashrafi*, borrows the very words and adds the following:

> "It is related by the spiritual guide that some people of Multan have been reported as saying that Hazrat Shaikh (Baha-ud-Din) gave one of his daughters in marriage to Hadrat Mir Husaini. On this ground Shaikh `Iraqi and he, these two personages now related together, wrote two famous books, i.e., the *Lam'at* and the *Nuzhat-ul-Arwah*, in the same city (Multan). This books had the privilege of having been perused by the Shaikh..."

Later anthologists, like Daulat Shah and Lutf 'Ali Adar, mention him as a disciple of Shaikh Shihab-ud-Din Suhrawardi (d. 632 H.). But the majority of trustworthy writers, such as Shaikh Jamali, Firishta and others, are unanimous in calling him a disciple of Shaikh Zakriya.

The conclusions drawn from the statements of the author quoted above are briefly as follows:

1. That Husaini was a disciple of Shaikh Shihab-ud-Din Suhrawardi or Baha-ud-Din Zakriya.
2. That he completed his four books *Nuzhat-ul-Arwah, Tarab-ul-Majalis, Kanz-ur-Rumuz* and *Zad-ul-Musaferin* under the supervision of one of these Shaikh who read these books and praised them.
3. That there was an intimate relationship between 'Iraqi, Auhadi Kirmani and Husaini.

But all these conclusions appear incorrect and misleading from the historical standpoint. Husaini was born in 771 H., and hence the first two, namely, Shaikh Shihab-ud-Din (d. 632 H.) and Baha-ud-din Zakriya (d. 666 H.), could not have been Husaini's spiritual guides for the latter was born after the death of both of them. The third mystic of this order, Shaikh Sadr-ud-Din 'Arif (d. 676 H.), was alive when Husaini was born, but his death coincides with the fourth year of Husaini's age. He could not, therefore, have got the opportunity of being inspired by Sadr-ud-Din 'Arif. We therefore, have no other alternative than to admit that he was, in reality, a disciple of Shaikh Rukn-ud-Din Abul-Fath (d. 735 H.), the grandson of Baha-ud-Din Zakriya. This is fully supported by Jami who says," "It is related that Husaini was a disciple of Shaikh Rukn-ud-Din Abul-Fath. The holy Prophet appeared to him in vision and advised him to take Husaini under his instruction. The Shaikh accordingly gave Husaini spiritual training." This statement is further strengthened by the evidence that *Nuzhat-ul-Arwah* and *Zad-ul-Musaferin* were written in 711 H. and 729 H. long after the death of these two Shaikhs, viz., Shaikh Shihab-ud-Din Zakriya and Baha-ud-Din Zakriya. Hence, there is no ground to support the view that these books had been studied by the said Shaikhs, as is stated by the above anthologists. 'Iraqi and Auhadi Kirmani died in 688 H. and 697 H., respectively, when Husaini must have been passing through the early stages of training and instruction.

All these discrepancies on the part of Jami and others arose mainly due to the ignorance of the year of Husaini's birth. The incomplete copies of *Kanz-ur-Rumaz* were also responsible for creating a misunderstanding. Being a devout sufi of Suhrawardia order, he was spiritually attached to three early mystics of this order, namely, Shaikh Shihab-ud-Din Suhrawardi, Baha-ud-Din Zakriya and his son Sadr-ud-Din 'Arif. He has composed verses in praise of these mystics as well as in praise of his own spiritual guide Shaikh Rukn-ud-Din Abul-Fath, in his book *Kanz-ur-Rumuz*. But the later scribes of the said book have mentioned only the first of sometimes the first two spiritual guides and thereafter proceeded to the real topics, and hence Jami and others considered those two as the spiritual guides of Husaini. The verses, however, clearly show that the poet is writing after the death of all of them.

> In the firmament of religion he is the pole star;
> In truth, he is the chief of the chiefs.
>
> In effulgence of his light (of knowledge) of devil and ignorance is obscured;
>
> For the world calls (knows) him Shihab-ud-Din (meteor of religion).

The Ka'ba of truth and purity is prosperous on his account;
The city of Baghdad has become the second Yathrab on his account.

May his shrine every remain the fountain of light!
May his time be in the Hereafter spent in the vision of God!

He is the chief of the seven kingdoms (universe);
the chief of the Aulia (saints).

He is in communion with the Prophet;
and is the companion of the Great God.

He is the object of pride for the Muslims;
and 'Baha' for the religion and sharia'.

His chaste life is the fountain of truth and conviction.
When he departed from us, he like the phoenix, took rest in the Heavenly nest.

Sadr-i-Din is a treasure prized by God;
the nine heavens are but a single dish on the dining carpet of his generosity.

The Elixir is one drop of ocean (knowledge);
Like Khidr, he has acquired knowledge as gift of God.

His utterances are a series of esoteric knowledge;
his reputation is both acquired and hereditary (ancestral).

The manuscript consulted by the writer of these lines did not contain the verses describing the praise of Baha-ud-Din Zakriya and Sadr-ud-Din 'Arif; it only contained verses devoted to Shaikh Shihab-ud-Din Suhrawardi. Firishta has, however, quoted the verses in praise of two former Shaikhs. But he has left them incomplete, as they end with the following verse:

What ever message wisdom had conveyed to my heart was given the name of *Kanz-ur-Rumuz* by my spiritual guide.

We can therefore easily presume that before this verse and after the praise of Shaikh, Rukn-ud-Din Arif, there should be a few lines in praise of his own Shaikh, Rukn-ud-Din Abul-Fath, who had already suggested the name of the book as *Kanz-ur-Rumuz* and that these lines which have been ignored either by the scribe or by Firishta himself.

Husaini's arrival at Multan and the duration of his stay there cannot be ascertained in terms of exact date, but a few facts may help us to make an estimate which might be nearer the truth.

Shaikh Jamali and Firishta assert that for the first time Husaini came to Multan with his father in connection with this business and there he came to be introduced to the Shaikh of Multan. Though both have refrained from giving the year of their arrival, still this difficulty is overcome by the information supplied by Dr. Farugh-i-Hikmat to the effect that Husaini's *diwan* contains a eulogy in praise of Jalal-ud-Din Khalji. Jalal-ul-Din ascended the throne of Delhi in the year 689 H., and Husaini was seventeen or eighteen years old at that time. Therefore, it would be reasonable to maintain that Husaini come to Multan for the first time with his father at this age. According to the usual custom of the age, the visitors and traders invariable frequented the monasteries of the saint. Husaini's father must have, therefore, visited the holy Shaikh's Khanqah where Husaini got introduced to the Shaikh to seek his blessing. It is also possible that his father was already a devotee of this order. It was, however, Husaini' first brief visit, and after four or five years, towards the close of Jalal-ud-Din's reign, Husaini migrated to Multan for good. He became the full-fledged disciple of the Shaikh, and spent a considerable part of his life at the shrine of Multan in meditation and mystical training.

The sources of evidence, i.e., *Gulshan-i-Raz* and a eulogy devoted to Ghiyath-ud-Din Kurt that is available in his *diwan*, help us to determine the period which Husaini passed at Multan before he finally moved to Herat. Husaini placed some questions relating to mystical topics before the author of *Gulshan-i-Raz* and the latter gave a reply in the said book. We find the following verses in it:

It was the month of Shawwal of the 717 H., when a king and

> benevolent messenger on behalf of the people of Khurasan appeared before me saying: A pre-eminent saint is famous at that place, who, by virtue of his abilities, is brilliant like the sun; who, by virtue of his insight, is a world of life and (living) body and who is the leader of the devout and known as Saiyad Husaini. He wrote a letter regarding spiritualism and sent it to the spiritualists.

The verses clearly indicate that Husaini was at Khurasan in the year 717 H., when Ghiyath-ud-Din Kurt was the Ruler of Herat, who ruled from 706 H. to 729 H. Hence, we shall not be far from the truth if we assert that Husaini probably left Multan a little earlier than 717 H., and that the period of his stay at Multan may, therefore, he calculated to be about 15 years, falling between 695 H. and 716 H. or 717 H.

Again, we have to steer clear of the confusion statements of the biographers in regard to the date of Husaini's death. Jami in his *Nafhat-ul-Uns* gives the date of his death as 16 Shawwal, 718 H., and this has been followed by other anthologies, namely, *Majalis-ul-Ushshaq* and *Riyad-us-Shu'ara*. Daulat Shah, however, places his death in 719 H., *Haft Iqlim* in 717 H. But all these statements must be taken to be wrong, in as much as the work *Zad-ul-Musaferin* was composed in 729 H., as is evident from the following verse that occurs at the end of the book:

> In the 729th year of the Hijri era the compilation of this book was completed.

The verse bears testimony to the fact that Husaini was alive upon 729 H. and that he was fifty-eight years old at that time. He must have, therefore, died long after 729 H.

Husaini was a devout mystic absorbed in divine meditation not concerned with what was happening around him. He bore a very high moral character, which is evident from his complete detachment from the court life. He was very indifferent to the praise of worldly people, so much so that in his works we find only two kings casually mentioned at two places. His character has been well depicted by Dr. Farugh-i-

Hikmat, and some lines of his writing deserve to be quoted.

> He exchanged implicit obedience for reason, and the limping and feeble conjectures for exalted thinking. He abstained from evil company and retired into seclusion. He shut the door against his friends and strangers. He spent the rest of his days in piety, integrity and high thinking. And till the end of his life he dedicated himself to educating people of his time by his mature and accomplished writings. For this reason his writings are free from eulogy regarding high ranking orthodox persons of the Sunni sect, which was the general practice in those days. His writings as a whole were characterised by wisdom, liberalism, having the glaring tinge of the religious thoughts of his predecessors....

Husaini was a prolific writer and left a number of books, both in prose and poetry. Dr. Hikmat is of the opinion that most of his works were burnt by the Mongols. Of his prose works two were very famous, namely, the *Nuzhat-ul-Arwah* and *Tarab-ul-Majalis*. One of his books, which was apparently in prose, is lost. Of his poetical works much has come down to us.

1. *Kanz-ur-Rumuz*, 2. *Zad-ul-Musaferin*, 3. *Sawalat-i-Gulshan-i-Raz*, 4. *Sinama*, 5. Diwan containing lyrics, eulogies, quatrains, tarji's and tarkib bands.

Now we shall deal briefly with some of his works, specially the *Nuzhat-ul-Arwah, Tarab-ul-Majalis, Kanz-ur-Rumuz* and *Zad-ul-Musaferin*.

1. *Nuzhat-ul-Arwah*: Nuzhat-ul-Arwah is probably Husaini's earliest work which was composed in India at Multan in 711 H. The author was forty years of age on the occasion of the composition of the said book.

This mystical treatise is very popular and a fairly large number of MSS of the treatise are to be found in Indian and foreign libraries. The popularity of this book may again be judged by various commentaries on it, the most detailed of which is one by 'Abd-ul-Wahid Ibrahim

Husaini Bilgrami which was completed in 985 H.

The *Nuzhat-ul-Arwah* is divided into twenty-nine chapters dealing with the nature and rule of spiritual lie. It is a prose work but intermixed profusely with verses from his own writing as well as from the writings of the other poets. The author deals with all the aspects of spiritual love in a very abstract way and illustrates them by anecdotes and sayings of holy men. The style of this book is ornate and highly florid, though the sentences are not long and involved. The author is so fond of rhetorics that he is difficult to be understood. The central ideas of the book are generally concealed under the thick veil of literary and artistic artifices and it is not always easy to grasp each of the twenty-nine chapters. The admixture of so many verses which bear symbolic value makes the matter worse, for instead of illustrating the ideas, they complicate them, though the lines by themselves in most cases are not intricate the difficult to understand. The abundant use of Arabic quotations also contributes towards making the style rather difficult.

2. *Tarab-ul-Majalis*. This is another elaborate sufistic work on metaphysical and ethical matters which is divided into the five chapters.

3. *Kanz-ur-Rumuz*: This mystical work is in the form of mathnawi on the religious duties of Islam from the sufistic standpoint. Its style is plain, lucid and vigorous quite contrary to the prose works of the author. It was a popular poem and MSS, of it are found in various libraries of the world.

In this poem Husaini praises sufis of his order whom he regards his spiritual guides.

4. *Zad-ul-Musaferin*: This book is a sufistic mathnawi in imitation of Sanai's *Hadiqat-ul-Haqiqa*. It was composed according to Husaini's own exposition in 729 H. It is divided into eight Maqalas. The first deals with the various divine attributes and ends in giving counsel to the seeker of truth. The second deals with human excellences and virtues which have been illustrated by suitable anecdotes.

It was also a very popular poem and wrongly attributed to Husain

Wa'iz Kashifi under whose name it was published in Neval Kishore Press in 1291 A.H./1877 A.D.

Of the many scholars who have made a critical study of Husaini's lik. The name of Dr. Farugh-i-Hikmat deserves to be specially likely ιd. His study of Husaini's books is so deep and the conclusions visits 7y him are so exhaustive that there remains very little for scholars of lesser experience to add to them. Dr. Hikmat pays a glowing tribute to husaini's contributions to mysticism, philosophy and religion. In this respect he ranks him with Sa'di and Maula-i-Rum. He holds Husaini in great esteem for his treatment of the subject-matter and his mode of expression.

4

Syed Muhammad Al-Husaini Gesudaraz

MOTASIM A. AZAD

Syed Muhammad al-Husaini Gesudaraz, a well known Chishti saint of the Deccan, was twenty-second in the line of descent from the Prophet of Islam. 'Abdu'l Hasan al-Jundi from whom he claims descent in the twelfth generation arrived in Delhi from Khurasan. He was laid to rest in the premises of *Masjid-e Anar* (Delhi). The ancestors of our saint were popularly known as *Sadat-i daraz gisu* (Syeds with long locks) in Khurasan. His grandfather Syed 'Ali and his father Syed Yusuf al-Husaini *alias* Syed Raja, author of *Tuhfatu'n Nasa'ih* and *Mathnavi-e Raja*, were both disciples of the great saint Shaykh Nizam al-Din Auliya of Delhi.

Syed Muhammad Husaini Gesudaraz was born on 4th Rajab 721 A.H. 30th July, 1321 A.D. in Delhi and spent his childhood in that city and in Daulatabad. Both these cities were then great centres of Muslim political, social, cultural and religious activities in Asia. Delhi was not only the capital of the Tughlaq dynasty but was also the abode of countless scholars, saints, administrators and artists. There were nearly two thousand *ribats, khanqahs* in Delhi and the disciples of Shaykh Nizam al-din, 'Auliya who earned renown for their piety and learning like Shaykh Nasir al-din Chirag-e Delhi, Amir Khusro, Maulana Sharif al-din, Maulana Taj al-Din, Qadi Abdu'l Muqtadir, Shaykh 'Ala al-Din Nili and Burhan al-Din Gharib also lived there. It was in 727/1327 that Syed Muhammad Husaini accompanied his father to Daulatabad, which has just become the capital of the Tughlaq dynasty. A number of the disciples of Shaykh Nizam al-Din 'Auliya and

Burhan al-Din Gharib, had already preceded them there. It was in such an atmosphere of piety, learning and mysticism that he grew up. Abu'l Farid Minallah Husaini states that his father Syed Yusuf used to spend most of his time at Daulatabad in the company of great saints [illegible]ke Shaykh Burhan al-Din Gharib and Shaykh Babu and it is most [illegible] that Syed Muhammad used to accompany his father in these [illegible] There is no doubt that he was with his father when the latter visited the famous saint Shaykh Babu, who, seeing the young Syed Muhammad, remarked , "I see in him the qualities of a scholar and a mystic."

Syed Muhammad Husaini had his early education under his maternal grandfather and studied *Nahw* in Arabic grammar as well as *Quduri* in jurisprudence even as a child. In 731/1331 he lost his father and a few years later in 735/1334 his mother decided to settle down in Delhi with her children. Soon after reaching Delhi he, along with his brother Syed Chanda Husaini, became the disciple of Shaykh Nasir al-Din. The latter advised him to take up arduous practices involving long hours of prayers, meditations and *dhikr*, at the same time living an austere and ascetic life. He was also required by his *pir* to continue his education in the traditional learning of Islam, which he did under the guidance of Syed Sharf al-Din Katheli, Maulana Taj al-Din and Qadi 'Abdu'l Muqtadir. As it was not possible to meditate with the high concentration prescribed by the tenets of his silsilah he found a peaceful room in *Hazirah* of Shir Khan Jahan Panah, where he continued to live for the next ten years. Shaykh Nasir al-Din once visited his young disciple in the *Hazirah* and offered him a few coins by way *of nadhr*, which was most unusual on the part of *pir* and an unprecedented privilege to a *murid*. Shaykh Nasir al-Din was very pleased with the rapid and remarkable progress made by his protege in the sufi path, which reminded him of similar attainments of the great saints in the past. It is likely that these events took place before 757/1356 as Shaykh Nasir al-Din honoured him with the *khilafat* in that year.

Syed Muhammad Husaini was only 36 years old when three days after the death of his *pir* he assumed the high office of his *pir's* successor and extended his hand for *baia'th*. At forty he got married at the instance of his mother and continued to deliver lectures and conduct discourses in his *khanqah.* He always observed strictly the tenets of the *Shari'ah* and Samani reports that while he was still living in Delhi, the reputed scholar in exoteric knowledge, Maulana Nasir al-Din Qasim, who had studied under Maulana Mu'in al-Din 'Imrani, became his disciple. When Mu'in al-Din 'Imrani heard of this development he asked his student how a scholar like him could become a *murid.* Maulana Nasir al-Din replied that while he had become a scholar under him he actually became Muslim under Syed Muhammad.

Syed Muhammad Husaini Gesudaraz spent twenty-one years (736-757/1336-1356) as a disciple of his *pir*, and forty-four years (757-801/1356-1398) as the spiritual successor of the latter at Delhi, and migrated to the Deccan in 801/1398 when he was 80 years old. On his way he visited several places and finally arrived at Daulatabad in 803/1400 and at the request of Feroz Shah Bahmani settled down in Gulbarga, the Bahmani capital. After spending twenty-two years he died there in 825/1425, where his mausoleum still stands.

On his arrival in Gulbarga he found the situation completely different from Delhi, as the king, Feroz Shah Bahmani, like his ancestors, from the inception of the dynasty was in full sympathy with the sufis. This policy may not have been entirely disinterested and may have been influenced by the desire to win the support of religious leaders to his political aims. The king accorded Syed Muhammad a royal welcome and constructed a *khanqah* for him just opposite his palace outside the Gulbarga fort. While the early Chishti saints of the Deccan strictly observed the traditions of the silsila, Syed Muhammad Husaini could not follow the same at Gulbarga.

Gesudaraz as an Scholar and Author

Syed Muhammad Husaini Gesudaraz was an erudite scholar and a prolific writer. He was deeply versed in the Qur'anic studies, in tradition, jurisprudence, theology and sufism. He had intensive knowledge of Arabic, Persian, Hindawi, Deccani and Sanskrit languages. In one of his works he states that he had studied Sanskrit works and knew Hindu mythology. Syed Muhammad Husaini had made a thorough study of the following subjects:

(a) *Tafsir al-Kashshaf*—on the Qur'an,
(b) *Al-Hidaya*—on jurisprudence,
(c) *Mashariq al-Anwar*—on the Prophetic tradition,
(d) *Usul al-Bazdawi*—on jurisprudence,
(e) *Mukhtasar al-Quduri*—on jurisprudence,
(f) *Miftah al-'Ulum*—on philology,
(g) *Kitab al-Misbah fi al-Nahw*—on philology,
(h) *Al-Kafiyah*—on syntax,
(i) *Al-Risalah al-Shamsiyah*—on logic.

Apart from these works be must necessarily have delved deeply in the sufi literature available in India at that time. This is supported by the fact that he himself compiled commentaries on many classical sufi works. From this is obviously follows that the several sufi treatises available in India must have influenced his thought. Abu'l Qasim al-Junaid (d. 298/910) of Baghdad seems to have been the model for Gesudaraz. Besides him, he mentions several other sufis in his works like Najm al-Din Kubra, Jalal al-Din Rumi, Farid al-Din 'Attar and Ibn 'Arabi. Although *Fusus al-Hikam* of Muhiyial-Din ibn 'Arabi (d. 638/1249) immensely influenced his doctrines, nevertheless Gesudaraz maintained a critical attitude towards Ibn 'Arabi's concept of ontological unity of All-being, (*Wahdat al-Wajud*).

In Gulbarga, Syed Muhammad Husaini established a *madrasa* for advanced learning at his *khanqah*, in which education in various branches of Islamic thought was imparted not only to the elite of Gulbarga, but also to those coming from other parts of the Bahmani kingdom and from elsewhere in India. Syed Muhammad himself taught *Hadith, Tafsir, Suluk, Kalam,* and *Fiqh* to his sons. Qadi Raju and Shihab al-Din also studied *Multaqit* and *Qutu'l Qulub* under the saint. Maulana Abu'l Fath along with Syed Asghar Husaini and Syed Ahmed took lessons in the commentaries on various sufi tracts written by Gesudaraz and Malikzada 'Izz al-Din studied *'Adab al-Muridin*. Syed Yadullah Husaini took lessons in *Misbah* and later on started studying *Kafiyah*. In 806/1403 Maulana 'Ala al-Din came from Gwaliar to study *Tamhidat-e 'an al-Qudat* and *Fusus al-Hikam* under Syed Muhammad Husaini. The way in which this institution was run and the knowledge which it spread were a source of pride and inspiration to the people and possibly engendered envy in the heart of the ruler of the state, as the ninety year old saint continued to win the hearts and minds of the people.

Mir Vali al-Din is of the opinion that Syed Muhammad Husaini was the first Chishti sufi who put the *Ilm-e Sina* (esoteric knowledge) into the *'Ilam-e Safina* (exoteric knowledge). Our saint himself states, "Every one who traverses the path to God receives a particular gift: God has bestowed on me the gift of explaining His secrets." At another place, he writes, "The qualities of a Jurist, Sufi, Syed and Sunni in their totality are found in very few persons: God has bestowed on me all these qualities."

According to one tradition, Syed Muhammad Husaini was the author of one hundred and five works, while Syed Minallah is of the opinion that he wrote one hundred and twenty-five works. His biographers Samani and Wa'izi have listed thirty-six and forty-seven books, respectively. As a large number of his works are available either in manuscript or in published form in various libraries of India and London, it is obvious that the list given by his biographers is incomplete. However, it is difficult to ascertain the exact number of works written by him and the following are some of his more important treatises:

I. Exegesis:
- (i) *Tafsir-e Multaqit.*
- (ii) *Hawashi-e Kashshaf.*

II. Hadith:
- (i) *Sharh-e Mashariq al-Anwar*
- (ii) *A Persian translation of Mashariq.*

III. Fiqh:
- (i) *Sharh al-Fiqh al-Akbar.*

IV. Tasawwuf:
- (i) *Sharh-e 'Awarif al-Ma'arif* (Arabic and Persian)
- (ii) *Sharh-e Ta'arruf.*
- (iii) *Sharh-e Adab al-Muridin.* (Arabic)
- (iv) *Adab al-Muridin.*
- (v) *Fusus al-Hikam.*

(vi) *Sharh-e Tamhidat.* (Persian)

(vii) *Sharh-e Risalah-e Qushayriyah* (Persian & Arabic)

(viii) *Hawashi-e Qutu'l-Qulub.*

(ix) *Haza'ir al Quds or 'Ishq Nama.*

(x) *Jawaher al-'Ushshaq.*

(xi) *Athmar al-Asrar.*

(xii) *Khatima.*

(xiii) *Maktubat.*

(xiv) *Majmu'a-e Yazdeh Rasail*

(xv) *Siyar al-Nabi.*

(xvi) *Anis al-'Ushshaq.*

(xvii) *Malfuzat*—Samani mentions four *Malfuzat*. But only one, compiled by his eldest son Syed Akber Husaini under the title *Jawami' al-Kalim*, exists.

Two more works in Deccani language *Mi'raj al-'Ashiqin* and *Shikar Nama* are also attributed to him but there is no convincing evidence to establish that these were actually written by him.

Although most of Syed Muhammad Husaini's works are in the form of commentaries, one cannot underrate the originality of his thought, particularly his unique attempt at all times to bridge the gulf between the *Shari'a* and the *Tariqah*, which existed at the time as a consequence of the age-old differences between the *Ahl-e Shari'at* and the *Ahl-e Tariqat*, which prevailed throughout the Islamic world and which had acquired more emphasis in India.

Gesudaraz and Feroz Shah Bahmani

Which 'Ala al-Din Hasan Bahman Shah was the founder of the Bahmani dynasty which was established in 747/1347, his successors Muhammad Shah I, Feroz Shah and Ahmad Shah Wali Bahmani were the founder and organisers of its social and religious institutions. Both the founder of the kingdom and his immediate successor had profound respect for the sufis and had ardent affection and respect for Shaykh Siraj al-Din Junaidi, Shaykh Zain al-Din Daulatabadi and 'Ain al-Din Ganj al-'Ilm (treasury of knowledge). These sufis played a significant part in the political, religious and cultural life of the early Bahmani period.

Feroz Shah Bahmani, eighth in the line of the Bahmani rulers, ruled for twenty-five years (800-825/1397-1424) and it was in this period that Syed Muhammad Husaini Gesudaraz lived twenty-three years of his life in the capital of the Bahmani kingdom, Gulbarga. It was also during this time that a large number of immigrants from Persia, Iraq and Iran made their way to the Deccan, as is evident from family names like Sistani. Tabrizi Mazandarani and Kirmani. After ascending the throne. Feroz Shah conferred the title of *Khan-e Khanan* on his younger brother Ahmad Khan, appointed Mir Fadlu'llah Inju as *Wakil us-Saltanat*, and Maulana Lutfullah Shirazi as *Na'ib Wakil us-Saltanat*.

The king like his predecessors had profound respect for sufis, scholars and men of high intellectual calibre and was himself a profound scholar. He was keenly interested in the problems of *Fiqh*, both *Shia'* and *Sunni*, and subjects like *Qur'an, Tafsir, Hadith* and *Kalam*. He respected also other religions and had read Old Testament as well as New Testament. He had sound knowledge of Arabic, Persian, Turkish, Kanari, Marathi, Gujrati, Bengali and Telugu languages. It was the ruler's broad outlook in all matters and his desire to have eminent scholars around him that attracted the 'ulama of Iran and Iraq like Maulana Lutf al-Din Sabzwari Hakim Hasan Gilani, Syed Muhammad Garzuni and other learned men to his kingdom.

Feroz Shah's inclination towards Shi'ism is evident from the adoption of the concept of *Mutt'a* as suggested by Mir Fadlu'llah Inju, against the advice of the Sunni 'ulama at his court. He was the first Bahmani sultan to give his daughter in marriage to Shams al-Din Muhammad Inju, who was later appointed governor of Daulatabad. Accordingly, it is difficult to find out what he felt about the *Ahl'e shari'at* or the *Ahl-e Tariqat* but there is no doubt that the immigrants from Iran and Iraq, the majority of whom were Shi'ites, did influence his thought profoundly.

It is difficult to find out the exact reasons which prompted the king to invite the saint to settle down permanently in his kingdom. It is quite possible that the extraordinary popularity which the saint enjoyed with his subjects may have influenced him and it is also possible that by this time he may have become tired of the endless disputes and rivalries of the *Sunni* and *Shia'* 'ulama at his court. These experiences might have caused him to yearn for a personality far above such petty and trivial differences, who combined in himself the whole range of the esoteric and the exoteric knowledge with the deep insight and compassion of a mystic of the eminence of Syed Muhammad Husaini.

The king extended a warm welcome which drew them closer to each other and inspired mutual confidence. However, this did not last long and the relation became more strained in the subsequent years, possible for several reasons, one being the wide and unprecedented popularity of the saint among the people, which might have made the king apprehensive; the sharp differences between the *Ahl-e Shari'at* and *Ahl-e Tariqat* and the not inconsiderable influence which the *Shi'a 'ulama* exercised on the king may have been a contributory factor. Samani reports as incident which helps one in understanding the change in the attitude of the king towards the saint.

He states that Maulana 'Ala al-Din Gawaliari came to Gulbarga in 806/1403 to take lessons in *Fusus al-Hikam* of Ibn 'Arabi from Gesudaraz and this gave the 'ulama, who had profound antagonism towards Ibn 'Arabi, a chance to persuade the king to find out how Syed Muhammad Husaini explained the deviations of Ibn 'Arabi's thought from *Sharia'*. Feroz Shah deputed Khwaja Ahmad Dabir, a trusted and learned scholar of his court, to enquire from the saint what he thought of the matter under dispute, but instead of submitting his report to the king, Ahmad Dabir became the disciple of the saint and probably resigned from the court service. This might have irked Feroz Shah and alienated him from the saint. The antagonism between the two in its early stages was purely on an intellectual plane and the formal relations between the two continued to be marked by mutual respect until 810/1407. In that year Feroz Shah marched against Vijayanagar and achieved a glorious victory, which resulted in a long era of peace between the two kingdoms and in a matrimonial alliance. This produced a feeling of superiority and pride in the mind of the king. At first irked by the tremendous popularity of the saint which made vast crowds gather around him, the king issued an order to the saint to change his residence to some place outside the city as the noise created by the large concourse of people was a source of disturbance to him. The saint immediately complied with the king's order and moved to the place where his tomb now stands. Most of the historians of the Bahmani period associate this change in his place of residence with the event of the coronation ceremony of Hasan Khan, the king's eldest son, in 318/1415. In view of the facts stated above Sved Muhammad Husaini must have changed his place of residence between 810/1407 and 812/1409. One external evidence of this change is the death of the saint's eldest son Syed Akber Husaini, in 812/1408. The shrine of the latter stands exactly opposite to the shrine of Syed Muhammad Husaini.

In 818/1415 Feroz Shah appointed his son Hasan Khan as his heir-apparent and after the former coronation ceremony sent the prince to call on Syed Muhammad Husaini for the latter's blessings. The saint on receiving the prince remarked, "The crown was decreed to descent to his brother Ahmad Khan by the will of Providence; it was in vain for him to bestow it on another." Thus not only did the saint refuse to accept the king's choice of the heir-apparent but actually preferred another member of the royal family for the honour. This reflects the serious differences between the spiritual leadership and the temporal power.

In course of time a very close and intimate relationship seems to have developed between Ahmad Khan and the saint, Syed Muhammad Husaini. In 820/1417 Feroz Shah again invaded Vijayanagar, much against the wishes of the saint, and was badly defeated and it was only Ahmad Khan who finally succeeded in driving out the Vijayanagar army from the kingdom. This must have further helped Ahmad Khan is the bid for the throne. Soon after this the nobles of the court reminded the king of the close and intimate relations between Ahmad Khan and the saint and Feroz Shah remembering the prediction of the saint, ordered his brother to be blinded. On hearing this, Ahmad Khan along with his son 'Ala-al-Din rushed to the *khanqah* of the saint for succour. On seeing the two the saint removed the turban from 'Ala al-Din's head and divided it into two. One half he tied on Ahmad's head and the other half on the head of 'Ala al-Din and then extending his hand over them predicted sovereignty to both. The royal army sent in pursuit of the two was defeated by Ahmad Khan with the help of Khalaf Hasan Basari and the former assumed kingship. A few months later both Feroz Shah and Syed Muhammad Husaini died.

Deviations from Chishti Traditions

Syed Muhammad Husaini Gesudaraz during his stay of twenty-three years in Gulbarga devoted most of his energy to the establishment and organization of the Chishti order in the Deccan. The character of the *khanqah* which became active with the establishment of the Bahmani kingdom, especially during the first phase, culminating in the death of Gesudaraz, is in sharp contrast to its earlier character and its role in North India, which was passive vis-a-vis the state. The *khanqah* in the Deccan became highly active under the early sufis of the Deccan and Syed Muhammad Husaini. The change implied a clear deviation from the established traditions of the early Chishtis. The most plausible factor might be the new situation with which the sufis and the rulers had to deal in the Deccan. The Bahmani rulers appeared to be apprehensive 'about the security of their newly established empire during the first fifty years and in order to secure mass support of their subjects, had to seek the backing of the sufis, while the latter saw in this an opportunity of achieving their social and religious goal through the patronage of the kings.

Another important deviation within the *khanqah* institution which came to surface in this period was in respect of the issue of spiritual succession. The history of the Chishti order from its inception in India shows that none of the early Shaykh right upto Shaykh Nasir al-Din Chiragh of Delhi ever nominated any of their family members as their spiritual successor. Syed Muhammad Husaini, however left a will appointing one of his sons as his successor, thus making the succession hereditary.

Syed Ali Tabataba'i and other authors clearly state that Feroz Shah Bahmani, on Gesudaraz's arrival in Gulbarga, presented him *jagirs* by way of *nadhr* through an official farman, but there is a difference of opinion whether the saint accepted these *jagirs* or not. Wa'izi categorically states that the saint did not accept the king's gift and said:

> "Our Shaykhs did not accept any such income, I too shall not accept."
>
> Wa'izi further states that he saint once remarked:
>
> "I do not want that my sons, relatives and friends bring any part of such income to me."

It is also said that the saint often spoke against persons who accepted royal bounty and never consented to accept a part of such income. However, his sons and grandsons later accepted a large number of such grants in the shape of *jagirs* and cash grants.

Institutions after his Death

Soon after the saint's death the splendid intellectual and spiritual edifice developed during his stay in Gulbarga started disintegrating. There were many reasons for this, perhaps the most important being the controversy started by the family members to be the heads of the order (sajjada nashin) and the acceptance of *jagirs*, cash grants, royal titles, etc., by the sons and grandsons of Gesudaraz. Syed Ali Tabatba'i specifically states that after the death of the saint, Ahmed Shah Wali Bahmani did not have any faith in the *Masha'iqs* of the Deccan and hence he did not have any liking for them. The events relating to the spiritual succession soon after the death of the saint not only damaged the prestige and image of the family in the contemporary society, but the sultan lost all hopes in the spiritual attainments of the successors of Gesudaraz. The latter's basic concept of spiritual pursuits was replaced, soon after his death by the mundane desires of his descendants for acquisition of *jagirs* and other worldly possessions and there was not one among them who could match the high intellectual or spiritual attainments of our saint or his eldest son, Syed Akber Husaini with the inevitable result that the institution which he had done so much to set up, soon lost all hopes of every gaining the popularity which it once enjoyed.

5

The Contemporaries of Mawlana Muhammad Sadiq Kashmiri

DR. MUHAMMAD SALEEM AKHTAR

[Abstract: The following information, however, about his contemporaries, which is mainly gleaned from his own works, besides placing him in the right perspective, throws invaluable light on the social milieu and the mood of his times.]

A cursory glance at the hagiographies will reveal that *sufi* hospices and convents, if on the one hand they provided a rendezvous for the Muslim elite and intelligentsia, on the other were islands and oasis of mental peace and spiritual solace for the huge masses of the underprivileged and the downtrodden in society. The *khanqah* of Khwajah Muhammad Baqi Bi'llah was apparently no exception to this rule. Sadiq Kashmiri who, to quote the *Mujaddid,* called himself a *pir parast* (worshipper of the preceptor), must have come across a large cross-section of people in the *khanqah* of his *pir*. Moreover, his close contact with such distinguished scholars as Shaykh 'Abd al-Hqq Muhaddith Dihlawi, whose students spread from Kashmir to Lahore and Bihar; and his spiritual ties with such prominent *khalifahs* of Khwajah Baqi Bi'llah as Shaykh Taj al-Din Sanbhali, Shaykh Husam al-Din, Miyan, Shaykh Ilahdad Amrohagi and, last but not least, Shaykh Ahmad Sirhindi, cannot have been ineffectual in extending the range of friends and acquaintances. Moreover, he had acquired an early taste for the company of the learned; that too would have done much to help him cultivate relations with countless contemporaries. But unfortunately, out of negligence or sheer modesty, as with other aspects of his life, he has not left us any detail in this regard.

The contemporaries of Sadiq Kashmiri can be divided into three main categories :

(1) *Khalifahs* of Khawajah Baqi Bi'llah and their followers;

(2) Other devotees and disciples of Khwajah Baqi Bi'llah; and

(3) Miscellaneous: *Sufis,* scholars and poets.

1. KHALIFAHS OF KHWAJAH BAQI BI'LLAH AND THEIR FOLLOWERS

(i) Shaykh Taj Sanbhali

The seniormost companion of Khwajah Muhammad Baqi Bi'llah, Shaykh Taj al-Din Sanbhali, was actually a disciple and *Khalifah* of Sayyid 'Ali Qiwam's *Khalifah,* Shaykh Ilah Bakhsh. It was during his wanderings in India before settling in Delhi that Khwajah Baqi Bi'llah met him for the first time in the company of Shaykh Ilah Bakhsh in the vicinity of Sanbhal. Shaykh Taj wished to have the Khwajah initiated at the hands of his preceptor, Shaykh Ilah Bakhsh, but the Khwajah could not make up his mind. Nevertheless, he was deeply impressed by the piety and devotion of Shaykh Ilah Bakhsh and the sincerity of Shaykh Taj. Thereafter the Khwajah left for Transoxiana: Meanwhile Shaykh Ilah Bakhsh died, and when the Khawajah repaired to Delhi Shaykh Taj went there and joined his company. He was the first among the companions of the Khwajah who were allowed to enrol disciples and guide them in the Naqshbandiyah order. After his investiture as *Khalifah*, he went back to Sanbhal, but continued to visit the Khwajah at regular intervals.

Shaykh Taj was endowed with a unique ability to transform others. And according to Sadiq Kashmiri, whomsoever he graced with his attention was overtaken by rapture and the qualities of self-annihilation appeared in him instantaneously. After the death of Khwajah Baqi Bi'llah he set out on a journey of India and Kashmir, and subsequently went to the Hijaz. There also he travelled extensively, propagated the Naqshbandiyah order and deputed his *Khalifahs* in Mecca, Medina and the Yemen. He sent them to some distant Arabian islands too.

Ultimately he settled in the Hijaz and enjoyed much respect and reverence among the natives. He was alive at least until the compilation of the *Tabaqai-i-Shahjahani,* of Muhammad Sadiq Kashmiri, in 1048/1638-39.

His son-in-law, Sayyid Mahmud Amrohagi, who came from a noble family, was also a very brilliant young man. He had attained proficiency in external sciences at a relatively young age. Impressed by his virtues, Shaykh Taj gave him the hand of his daughter and spared no effort to add lustre to his intrinsic qualities. But before he could see the results of his labour, Sayyid Mahmud died in 1037/1627-28.

Shaykh 'Abd al-Rahman was another brilliant and favourite disciple of Shaykh Taj Sanbhali. When Shaykh Taj returned to Sanbhal after his investiture, Shaykh 'Abd al-Rahman was one of his first disciples, and he soon astonished his preceptor with his rapid strides in the mystical path. The excited Shaykh informed Khwajah Muhammad Baqi Bi'llah that a very bright young man had fallen into his trap: 'Come yourself and bring that brilliant young man along', was the Khwajah's reply. Accordingly, the preceptor and the novice both set out for Delhi to see the Khwajah. The Khwajah was also impressed by the capabilities of the young neophyte and bestowed on him special favours which, in turn, made him all the more firm in his devotion to the Naqshbandiyah order. At the time of the compilation of the *Tababat-i-Shahjahani* Shaykh 'Abd al-Rahman was leading a life of isolation in Sanbhal.

(ii) Khwajah Husan al-Din

He was born in 977/1569-70 at Qunduz in Badakhshan and came to India with his father, Qadi Nizam al-Din Badakhshi, in 983/1575-76. Qadi Badakhshi, whose forefathers had long been associated with the Timurid kings and had performed meritorious services under them, was received with open arms by Akbar. He conformed on him the title of Qadi Khan, which was consequently changed to Ghazi Khan. By the time of his death in 993/1584-85, the Qadi had become one of the favourite courtiers of the Emperor. After his death, Akbar extended his patronage to his son, and, in keeping with the established norms of the court, bestowed on him a *mansab* of three hundred as a first step to future promotion. Abu 'l-Fadl offered the hand of his sister to the young *mansabdar* and by the time Khwajah Husam al-Din was dispatched to the Deccan expedition with Khan-i-Khanan 'Abd al-Rahim Khan, he held the rank of 1000. However, the grandeur of the imperial camp and court could not hold his attention for ever. It was during his stay in the Deccan that the transformation came about and, bidding farewell to mundane pomp and show, he hastened to Delhi and, despite opposition from Abu 'l-Fadl, became a disciple of Khwajah Muhammad Baqi Bi'llah. Baqi Billah in the course of time invested him with the *khilafat* of the Naqshbandiyah order but, except on one occasion, he never enrolled disciples. In 1012/1603 when Khwajah Baqi Bi'llah fell ill, Khwajah Husam al-Din was the only senior *Khalifah* who was present at the *khanqah.* So he served his preceptor during his lifetime and arranged his obsequies after his death. The burden of running the main *khanaqah* in Delhi and bringing up the children of Khwajah Baqi Bi'llah also devolved upon him.

Sadiq Kashmiri, who cherished a very deep regard for Khawajah Husam al-Din has bestowed lavish encomiums on him, both in the *Kalimat al-Sadiqin* and the *Tabaqat-i-Shahjahani,* which reflect his strong faith in the latter's spritual powers. Out of the many letters that he received from the Khwajah from time to time, Sadiq Kashmiri has reproduced two in the *Kalimat.*

Khwajah Husam al-Din died at Akbarabad in 1043/1633. His body was brought to Delhi and was buried near the tomb of Khwajah Baqi Bi'llah. Sadiq Kashmiri composed the following chronogram on his death.

Sufi Gada 'Ali was a close associate of Khwajah Husam al-Din. Actually he was a devotee of Mulla Yar Muhammad Fathpuri and was employed in the army, where he held the rank of *ahadi.* Subsequently, he relinquished the government job, took to a life of indigence and resigned himself to the care and company of Khwajah Husam al-Din at Firuzabad, in Delhi. No matter whether he was in government service or not, he did not change his routine of contenting himself with the bare necessities of life and distributing everything else to the poor.

He died in 1040/1630-31 and was buried beside the tomb of Khwajah Muhammad Baqi Bi'llah, near Qadam Sharif. Sadiq Kashmiri recited the following chronogram on this occasion :

(iii) Shaykh Ilahdad Amrohagi

He was one of the trusted disciples of Khwajah Muhammad Baqi Bi'llah and his association with the Khwajah went as far back as the latter's first visit to Lahore, before finally settling down in Delhi. Shaykh Ilahdad was known for his severe ascetic austerities. During a period of five or six days he would consume a negligible amount of victuals; otherwise he was almost continually in a state of fasting, meditation and self-scanning (*muhasibah*). The Khwajah viewed the mystical achievements of the Shaykh with approval, as was illustrated by the fact that Gangohi. He had also benefited from the benedictions of several other saints, including Shaykh Kamal Qadiri Kaythali. Having committed the Holy *Qur'an* to memory at an early age, Shaykh Ahmad commenced his formal education under the patronage of his father. For higher studies, however, he went to Sialkot and sat at the feet of scholars as renowned and distinguished as Shaykh Kamal Kashmiri, Shaykh Ya'qub Sarfi, and Qadi Bahlul Badakhani. At the age of seventeen the returned to Sirhind, fully proficient in all branches of knowledge, those which call for the excercise of the reasoning faculty and those which depend on the memory, and set himself the task of teaching and imparting instructions to his students. Around the age of twenty he went to Agra and mixed with the intellectual when the former decided to go back to Transoxiana, during his stay in lahore, he entrusted his disciples to the care of Shaykh Ilahdad. While in Delhi also, the maintenance of the Naqshbandiyha *khanqah* and the upkeep of its inmates was Shaykh Ilahdad's responsibility. At the time of the compilation of the *Tabaqat-i-Shahjahani,* in 1048/1638-39, he headed the Naqshbandiyah *khanqah* and was the only surviving senior companion of Khwajah Bazi Bi'llah.

The relations between Miyan Shaykh Ilahdad and Khwajah Husam al-Din were very warm and cordial. Whosoever approached the Khwajah for initiation or wanted to learn *dhikr* and meditation, the latter would refer him to Miyan Shaykh Ilahdad. Among his disciples Mulla Mubarak

Kanbu, of Delhi, occupied a very prominent position. He was a distinguished scholar and in learning and erudition was a peer of Shaykh Muhammad Mudarris Dihlawi. The Mulla had learnt at Akbarabad the sciences that were not usually taught at Delhi. After the acquisition of worldly knowledge, he developed a taste for mysticism and became a disciple of Shaykh Ilahdad. He led a saintly life in Delhi, where he died in 1040/1030-31.

(iv) Shaykh Ahmad Sirhindi

The most prominent of the Khwajah's disciples and *khalifahs* was Shaykh Ahmad Sarhindi Kabuli Faruqi, generally known as *Muj-i-ddid-i-Alf-i-Thani,* the Reviver of the Second Millenium. He was born at Sirhind, in the Punjab, on the 14th *Shawwal,* 971/26th May 1564. His father was deeply read in traditional as well as speculative sciences, and was a disciple of Shaykh Rukn al-Din elite of the Capital, including Shaykh Abu'l-Fadl and his elder brother, Shaykh Faydl, whose eclectic tendencies, however, did not strike a favourable chord in the Shaykh's heart. When his stay in Agra was prolonged, his father, Shaykh 'Abd al-Ahad also followed him, but before long the father and son were back in Sirhind, busily teaching and writing treatises and tracts on theological and polemical subjects. Meanwhile, the Shaykh perpetually profited from the spiritual graces of his father and obtained from him permission to enrol disciples in the Chishtiyah and Qadiriyah orders. In 1007/1599, his father breathed his last and the following year Shaykh Ahmad set out for the pilgrimage (*Haj*). On reaching Delhi, he was attracted to the company of Khwajah Muhammad Baqi Bi'llah. The Khwajah received him very courteously and, contrary to his practice, asked him to put off his journey to the Hijaz and stay with him for a month or at least for a week. The Shaykh agreed to stay for a week, but hardly two days had elapsed when he felt impelled to perform penitence at the hands of the Khwajah and the acquire the Naqshhbandi ordination from him. Seeing him eager the Khwajah responded favourably and imparted to him the method of Naqshbandi *dhikr,* and thereby ushered in a new era of spiritual solace, peace and tranquility in his life. The Shaykh stayed for three months at the Naqshbandi *khanqah* and then returned to Sirhind. Before his departure, the Khwajah, besides giving him a complete code of ethics, conferred on him the robe of *khilafat* and allowed him to enrol disciples. Not only that, but as a mark of his confidence in his spiritual attainments, he transferred some of his own disciples to Shaykh Ahmad's care and supervision. Back in Sirhind, the Shaykh underwent a severe internal turmoil: a strong desire to lead a life of complete solitude and the preceptor's advice to continue with a life of academic pursuits, were in sharp contrast with each other. The latter prevailed, and he taught and trained disciples for a while before calling on the Khwajah for the second time. It was during his stay in Sirhind this time that Shah Sikandar, the grandson of Shaykh Kamal Kaythali, conferred on him the latter's spritual robe and allowed him to intiate disciples in the Qadiriyah order.

His third and last vist to Khwajah Baqi Bi'llah took place about seven or eight months before the latters' death. When the news of his arrival in Delhi reached the Khwajah, despite his frail health and weak physique, he hastened to receive his favourite disciple, half way to the *khanqah.* One day, while the Shaykh was still there and other disciples were also in attendance, the Khwajah sent for his infant sons, Khwajah 'Abd Allah and Khwajah 'Ubayd Allah. When they were brought in, the Khwajah cast an affectionate glance at them and, addressing the audience, remarked, 'They are orphans', meaning thereby that his days were numbered. How long the Shaykh stayed with his preceptor on this occasion is unknown. After his return from Delhi, he stayed for sometime in Sirhind and then, at the instance of the Khwajah, proceeded to lahore, where a large number of people were attracted to his assemblies. He was still at Lahore when the news of his preceptor's death arrived, and he rushed to Delhi, whence he went to Sirhind and lived, there until he died on 28th *Safar* 1034/10th December, 1624.

Among the works of Shaykh Ahmad Sirhindi, his letters (*Maktubat*), wherein he mainly answered questions from his correspondents and expatiated upon different aspects of mystical experience, are considered to be his *magnum opus.* The letters 106 and 107 of the first volume, 22 and 28 of the second volume, and 39 of the third volume of the *Maktubat* were written to Sadiq Kashmiri. That Sadiq entertained a very high degree of regard for the Shaykh is abundantly clear from his writings. His relations with the Mujaddid's descendants, disciples and *khalifahs* were also cordial and he noticed the following of them in the *Tabaqat-i-Shahjahani.*

(a) Khwajah Muhammad Sa'id Faruqi Sirhindi

The second son and successor of Shaykh Ahmad Sirhindi, Muhammad Sa'id Faruqi was born in 1005/1597. After the completion of his education under the care of his father, his elder brother Muhammad Sadiq (d. 1025/1616) and Mulla Tahir Lahori, by the age of seventeen he had become a scholar by all standards. He taught difficult texts like *Hikmat al-'ayn,* the 'Adudd and the Baydawi with great proficiency. He had written glosses on the *Mishkat* and his annotations on the *Hashiyah-i-Khayali* were read with interest and profit. According to Sadiq Kashmiri, he was an embodiment of perfection both in theory and practice and his main occupation was the guidance of his followers in the Naqshbandiyah order. His brother Muhammad Ma'sum was also well-known for his attainments. The relations between the two brothers were very warms and cordial. Both the them taught and imparted mystical instruction to their devotees and disciples, in a mosque situated next to their house in Sirhind, and lent splendour and grace to the virtues of piety, probity, abstinence and the fear of God. Their younger brother, Muhammad Yahya, had also completed his education and spiritual training at their feet and was counted among the scholars of his time.

(b) Khwajah Muhammad Siddiq Kishmi

He was a disciple of Khwajah Muhammad Baqi Bi'llah. After the latter's death, like so many other disciples of the Khwajah, he also passed under the spiritual supervision of Shaykh Ahmad Sirhindi. He practised a great many ascetic austerities over a long period and became blessed with full perfection in mystical flights. It was at this stage that Shaykh Ahmad bestowed on him the *khilafat* of the Naqshbandiyah order and dispatched him to Delhi. In external sciences also Khwajah Siddiq was fully accomplished and his attainments in poetry and *belles-letters* were excellent. In earlier days when he was still in military service, most of his spare time was spent in the poetical gatherings arranged by Khan-i-Khanan 'Abd al-Rahim Khan, wherein such renowned poets as Naziri (d. 1021/1612-13) and Shakibi (d. 1020/1611-12) also participated. Subsequently, when the passion for spiritualism overpowered him, he abandoned poetry altogether, came to Delhi, and made abode in the company of Khwajah Muhammad Baqi. Khwajah Siddiq died in 1050/1640-41. Sadiq Kashmiri composed three chronograms on this occasions, two in verse and one in prose. One of the versified ones is as follows :

Khwajah Muhammad Siddiq's son Muhammad Faruq, who emerged as a brilliant poet during the reign of Shahjahan, was also known to Sadiq Kashmiri. Muhammad Faruq was a very promising lad, and he made his way into the assemblies of the reputed nobles and grandees of his time at a relatively early age. Afdal Khan 'Allami is reported to have remarked that he had met with a great many scholars and poets both in India as well as in Transoxiana but he did not find any of them so versatile as Faruq. Consequently, at the instance of the 'Allami, Faruq was created a noble by Shahjahan and was deputed to the province of Kabul so that he could have an easy affluent life and devote the maximum time and energy to exercising his talents. Soon after his appointment there Faruq endeared himself to Nawwab Sa'id Khan, the governor of the province. Side by side with his literary activities, however, he paid full attention to the welfare of the local people and left no stone unturned to ameliorate their conditions. The following couplets were composed by him :

(c) Mir Muhammad Nu'man Kishmi

He was a favourite disciple of Khwajah Muhammad Baqi Bi'llah. After the death of the Khwajah he also joined the company of Shaykh Ahmad Sirhindi, who conferred on him the *khilafat* of the Naqshbandiyah order in 1018/1609-10 and ordered him to go to Burhanpur. Soon he settled in Burhanpur and became very popular among the people. He stayed there for sometime and then decided to pay a visit to his preceptor, Shaykh Ahmad, in Sirhind. During his absence all his devotees in Burhanpur rallied round his relative, Shaykh Ahmad Sirhindi's *khalifah,* Khwajah Hashim Kishmi. When Mir Nu'man got back to Burhanpur from Sirhind, he found the whole scene changed. Failing to find a sufficient following in that town, he left Burhanpur to Khwajah

Hashim and came to Akbarabad, where he was still alive at the time of the compilation of the *Tabaqat-i-Shahjahani.*

(d) Khwajah Hashim Kishmi

He was a prominent *khalifah* of Shaykh Ahmad Sirhindi. He learnt meditation and other basic teachings of the Naqshbandiyah *silsilah* from Mir Muhammad Nu'man. In 1031/1621-22, the Shaykh summoned him to Sirhind and kept him under his personal supervision continuously for two years. When he was fully accomplished in spiritual attainments the Shaykh invested him with his *khalifat* and appointed him at Burhanpur, where he died in 1041/1631-32, at the age of forty.

(e) Shaykh Tahir Badakhshi

Initially he was in the military service, but later as the result of an ecstasy, took to the life of a *qalandar.* On hearing the fame of Khwajah Baqi Bi'llah he hastened to Delhi, but before his arrival the Khwajah had already passed away. Shaykh Ahmad Sirhindi was in Delhi at that time; hence he joined the fold of his disciples. His continual occupation with Naqshbandi practices was rewarded, and ultimately he was raised to the status of a *khalifah.* After his investiture he went to Jaunpur and settled there. At the time of the compilation of the *Tabaqat*, he was still alive and very popular among the people. According to Sadiq Kashmiri, once he called on the Emperor Jahangir and impressed him favourably with his uprightness and veracity. On the accession of Shajahan he again visited the court and benefited from the imperial bounty.

(f) Mullah Tahir lahori

He was one of those distinguished scholars whom Shahjahan appointed to teach at Lahore. He learnt the external sciences from Mulla Jalal Talawi Lahori. After the completion of his education he suddenly developed a taste for mysticism and became a disciple of Shaykh Ahmad Sirhindi. He spent a considerable time in strenuous spiritual exercises before he was invested with the *khilafat* of the Naqshbandiyah order. Thereafter, he took to a life of complete detachment from the world and settled at Lahore, where he died in 1038/1628-29.

(g) Shaykh 'Abd al-Hayy Patnagi

He was a favourite disciple of Shaykh Ahmad Sirhindi. He was famous for his preseverance in the path of spiritual poverty (*faqr*) and his attainments in both the formal and the essential aspects of *sufisim.* Before his elevation to the position of a *khalifah*, he spent several years in the company of his preceptor and traversed different stages of the mystical path under his direction. He compiled the second volume of the *Maktubat* of the Shaykh. At the time of the compilation of the *Tabaqat-i-Shahjahani* he was in Patna, guiding the people in their spiritual endeavours.

(h) Shaykh Nur Patnagi

He was a disciple of Shaykh Ahmad Sirhindi. He led a very simple and austere life and was averse to any sort of association with worldly people. Although the *khilafat* was bestowed on him earlier than Shaykh 'Abd al-Hayy, he did not show much zeal and enthusiasm after his arrival in Patna. However, when Shaykh 'Abd al-Hayy was also invested with the *khilafat* and repaired to Patna, Shaykh Nur found in him a very good friend and through him became acquainted with other people also. Shaykh Nur had a smattering of *fiqh* and *hadith* and if any of the seekers after Truth approached him for guidance, he did not grudge assistance and initiated him readily.

(i) Shaykh Badi al-din Saharanpuri

Initially he was employed in the army but when he acquired the taste for mysticism he joined the company of Shaykh Ahmad Sirhindi and learnt from him the Naqshbandi *dhikr.* He also practised a lot many austerities before he was invested with the *khilafat* of that order. Thereafter he went to Saharanpur and occupied himself with the guidance of the people. Towards the end of his life, however he grew averse to social life and retired to solitude. He died in 1045/ 1635-36.

(j) Shaykh Badr al-Din Sirhindl

He was a favourite disciple and *khalifah* of Shaykh Ahmad Sirhindi. He joined his company at the age of fifteen and continually remained in his service for seventeen years. After the Shaykh's death, he compiled his biography called the *Hadarat al-Quds,* wherein he recorded three chronograms composed by Sadiq Kashmiri, at the death of Shaykh Ahmad Sirhindi.

Sadiq Kashmiri, however, does not mention him in the *Tabaqat.*

(2) OTHER DEVOTEES AND DISCIPLES OF KHAWJAH BAQI BI'LLAH

(a) Shaykh Nur al-Haqq Dihlawi

The eldest son of Shaykh 'Abd al-Haqq Muhaddith Dihlawi, Shaykh Nur al-Haqq, was deeply read in formal and essential sciences and enjoyed the full confidence of his father. He was very fond of saints and divines, but his devotion to Khwajah Baqi Bi'llah knew no bounds. The Khwajah was also very charitable towards him. Several chronograms were composed on the death of the Khwajah, but none was so steeped in emotion and marked with elegence and grace as the one composed by Shaykh Nur al-Haqq. On his accession to the throne, Shahjahan, who cherished great regard for him, appointed him the *qadi* of Akbarabad. At the time of the compilation of the *Tabaqat-i-Shahjahani,* the Shaykh still held that position and discharged his duties very conscientiously. Sadiq Kashmiri has reproduced the following verses of his in the *Tabaqat-i-Shahjahani.*

(b) Mawlana Jamal Talwai of Lahore

Mawlana Jamal, who belonged to Tala, a famous quarter of Lahore at that time, was a real prodigy. He started teaching at the age of eight. He was a pupil of Mulla Ismai'il of Uch, and had also received instruction from other teachers. He was fully conversant with the traditional as well as the speculative sciences and had a good delivery and could speak unambigously. He was renowned for his masterly exposition of different texts. According to Badayuni, the correction and arrangement of the Qur'anic exegesis *Sawati', al-Ilhani* of Faydi, was principally his work.

The Mawlana generally showed deep regard to the dervishes but towards Khwajah Baqi Bi'llah his attitude was particularly characterised by extreme deference.

(c) Mulla 'Abd al-Salam Diwi

He was one of the leading lights among contemporary scholars and was particularly celebrated for his virtuousity in *fiqh, usul* and rhetoric. He wrote a book about principles of jurisprudence which matched with *Talwih* in authenticity and was looked on as a standard work on the subject. By disposition he was modest and did not like futile wrangling and argumentation. After the completion of his education, he spent some time at the feet of Khwajah Baqi Bi'llah and greatly profited from his spiritual grace. Once he called on the Emperor Shahjahan who, out of appreciation for his sterling human qualities, conferred on him the office of the *mufie* of the royal camp. At the time of the compilation of the *Tabaqat* in 1048/1638-39, the Mulla still held that office. In his spare time he conducted classes and imparted instruction to his students.

(d) Ja'far Beg Thanagi

He was a very learned and scholarly noble, and his achievemnents were remarkable especially in calligraphy and *belless-lettres.* He served in the imperial army for several years and was included in the *mansabdars* of the Emperor Akbar. His brilliance did not fail to attract the attention of the monarch but owing to his impudence and non-conformity with the new trends of the court he soon fell into disgrace. Tired of his previous life he inclined towards mysticism, joined the company of Khwajah Muhammad Baqi Bi'llah and became one of his disciples. He practised a great many spiritual austerities and became so infatuated with his new way of life that when Jahangir, after his accession to the throne, summoned him to his court and offered to bestow on him a *mansab,* he did not accept it. He appears to have been held in high esteem in orthodox circles. He died in 1026/1617-18. Sadiq Kashmiri indicated the year of his death with the Persian phrase *Qudwah-i-Fudala.*

(e) Hafiz Jalal al-Din Ra'y of Patna

Although he was a disciple of Khwajah 'Abd al-Shahid, he also had spent sometime in the company of Khwajah Muhammad Baqi Bi'llah which did much to enhance his spiritual achievements. He was endowed with an angelic nature and enjoyed the reputation of a great divine. He died in 1037/1627-28.

(f) Shaykh Ahmad Khiri

He was an old, experienced and favourite disciple of Khwajah Muhammad Baqi Bi'llah. He died in 1045/1635-36. Sadiq Kashmiri composed the following *mnemosynon* on this occasion :

(g) Miyan Qasim Jaunpuri

A descendant of Khwajah 'Abd Allah Ansari, Miyan Qasim jaunpuri was possessed of a unique state of ecstasy, and a strange rapture characterised the whole of his life. Nevertheless, he did not let this hinder him from carrying out the obligations enjoined by the *Shari'ah.* He was a leading light of the Qadiriyah and the Chishtiya orders of his time and a great many miracles were attributed to him. There was no place whatsoever for worldly people in his heart. He was an exquisite poet and his verses were marked by elegance and grace. He died in 1039/1629-30. His son Miyan Shaykh Ni'mat Allah was given to the pursuit of Truth from his childhood. In 1007/1598-99 he came into contact with Khwajah Muhammad Baqi Bi'llah who imparted to him the secret of Naqshbandi meditation. The effect of this esoteric exercise soon became apparent in his countenance and the signs of resignation and self-effacement began to emerge in his personality. The Khwajah always looked upon him favourably.

(h) Mulla Ahmad Gujar

He had a smattering of jurisprudence and knew something about other theological sciences also. It was during his student days that he heard of the Khwajah's virtues and became his disciple, and devoted all his time to the service of his preceptor. The Khwajah also treated him affectionately. After the Khwajah's death he returned to his native place where the local population thronged around him and insisted on initiation. Nevertheless, he shunned the company of worldy people and spent his time in deserted and desolate places. He died in 1027/1617-18.

(i) Mawalana Ya'qub Thanagi

He was an outstanding, intelligent and good-natured student of

Mawlana Jalal Talawi of Lahore. After the completion of his education when he heard the fame of Khwajah Baqi Bi'llah's spiritual accomplishments, he abandoned everything and hastened to the company of the Khwajah, who initiated him into the Naqshbandiyah order. He experienced strange ecstasies and apocalypses and the Khwajah always called him a madman (*diwanah*). After the death of the Khwajah he continued to say with the sons of his preceptor until 1025/1616-17, when he went to his native place, Thanah Bhim, where he fell ill and died.

(j) Sayyid Mustafa Baghibat

A pious and holy man, he sat for years on the prayer carpet of his ancestors and helped people establish communion with God. On hearing of the fame of Khwajah Muhammad Baqi Bi'llah he bade farewell to his own sainthood, hastened to see the Khwajah, and requested him the *nisbah* of the Naqshbandyah order. His request was granted and he soon gained proficiency in that order too. When satisfied with his attainments, the Khwajah allowed him to go back and start afresh the task of guiding the people. He died on 1037/1627-28. Sadiq Kashmiri composed the following chronogram on this occasion:

(k) Shaykh Murtada Sanbhali

A disciple of Khwajah Baqi Bi'llah, Shaykh Murtada Sanbhali was experienced and scholarly. He was very fond of *sufi* aphorisms and had a special style of their narration. Sometimes he composed verses too. When he first approached Khwajah Baqi and requested initiation, the Khwajah told him that he deemed it imprudent to accept any new disciple but if he would, he could recommend him to Shaykh Taj or Shaykh Ahmad Sarhindi. Nevertheless, he did not lose hope and wrote a versified letter to the Khwajah wherein the following couplet was included.

His letter brought home to the Khwajah his sincerity of purpose, humility and modesty, and he agreed to initiate him. Soon after he was initiated. The Naqshbandiyah *nisbah* so over-powered Shaykh Murtada that he traversed the distance of months in days and attained full perfection in a relatively short time. He died in 1046/1636-37. Sadiq

Kashmiri composed the following chronogram on this occasion.

(l) Shaykh Rafi al-Din

Shaykh Rafi' al-Din bin Miyan Shaykh Qutb-i-Alam learnt the external sciences from his father but he owed his spiritual enlightenment to Khwajah Muhammad Baqi Bi'llah, who taught his mysticism. Shaykh Rafi' al-Din died in 1029/1619-20, in Burhanpur whence his body was carried to Delhi and buried there.

(m) Shaykh 'Abd al-Latif Gujarati

With two intermediaries between, he was a disciple of Khwajah Muhammad Baqi Bi'llah. He was very fond of the *Mathnawi* of Mawlana Jalal al-Din Rumi and wrote an excellent commentary on that work. He also compiled a very lucid exposition of the *Hadiqat al-Haqa'iq* which evoked great interest in the academic circles. Shahjahan conferred on him the office of the controller of salaries for the whole of his empire (*sahib tan-i-mamalik-i-Hindustan*), in which capacity he paid close attention to the welfare of the people and won over their hearts. At the time of the compilation of the *Tabaqat-i-Shahjahani* in 1048/1638-39, he still held that position.

(n) Shaykh 'Abd al-Wahid Ajodhani

He was an elderly *khalifah* of Shaykh Salim Chishti, who had met many divines, and was equally well versed in the theory and practice of *sufism*. His attitude towards Khwajah Baqi Bi'llah was one of extreme devotion and veneration. The Khwajah also showed him great respect and regard. He died in 1019/1610-11.

3. MISCELLANEOUS : THE *SUFIS*, THE SCHOLARS AND THE POETS

(i) The Sufis

(a)Shaykh 'Abd Allah Bhattah

He was an elderly Qadiri saint with a charitable disposition and a great love for the company of dervishes. He guided the people in the path of God for many years. Whoever called on him was given food and a *bahluli* by the *Shaykh.* Having heard of his fame, Jahangir summoned him to his Court. At the very sight of the emperor, the

Shaykh whispered some divine adjurations and clapped his hands. On being asked the reason for what he had done, he replied that he had prayed to keep misfortunes off. The emperor let him go unmolested. According to Sadiq Kashmiri, this was nothing less than a miracle, because very few dervishes could escape the wrath of that distrustful (*ghuyyur*) emperor. The Shaykh died in 1037/1627-28. Sadiq Kashmiri composed the following chronogram on this occasion.

(b) Shaykh Husayn Kamangar

A disciple of Shaykh Sulayman Manduwi, Shaykh Husayn kamangar was a distinguished saint and a capable scholar in his own right. During the annual *'urs* of his *pir* he visited Delhi regularly and stayed with the sons of Shaykh Sulayman. Sadiq Kashmiri, who had met him several times' reports that during the year Khusraw rose in rebellion against his father, Shaykh Husayn Jami had warned the emperor beforehand that a great calamity was in the offing. On hearing of this warning, Shaykh Husayn Kamangar conveyed it to some of the courtiers, who informed the emperor accordingly, so that when the calamity did descend he staved it off successfully. Meanwhile, Khusraw raised the standard of revolt and the whole kingdom was plunged into chaos and disorder. But soon, as prophesied by Shaykh Kamangar, the rebellion subsided and law and order were restored. The fulfilment of the Shaykh's prediction greatly enhanced his prestige, so that the king and his ministers also entered into the fold of his devotees. Shaykh Kamangar died in 1018/1609-10.

(c) Shaykh Mustafa Nanawtah

Son of Shaykh Ahmad Nanawtah he was also a disciple of Shaykh Sulayman Manduwi. He was possessed of a very pleasant disposition and had a strong yearning for the *sufi* practice of musical performance (*sama*). His conversation was suggestive of his internal anguish and grief. He was an excellent poet. Sadiq Kashmiri had met him and profited from his spiritual blessings.

Shaykh Mustafa was survived by four sons. One of them, Sayyid Sabir 'Ali, who Sadiq knew thoroughly, and who subsequently changed his spiritual robe for a courtly gown and joined the imperial army, was renowned for his altruistic nature and humane and kindly temperament.

He composed exquisite verse in both Persian and Hindi.

(d) Shaykh Arzani Patnagi

He was known for his saintly nature. Some people had great faith in his spiritual achievements and even attributed miracles to him. During the reign of Jahangir he came to Delhi and visited the saints of the town. During his sojourn in Delhi Sadiq Kashmiri met him more than once. But seemingly he failed to discern in him the many virtues for which people usually praised him. He died in Patna.

(e) Shaykh 'abd al-Wahab Bukhari

He was a distinguished notable of Delhi who was known for his good moral character and charming personality. He died in 1018/1609. Sadiq Kashmiri composed the following chronogram of this accastion.

(f) Shaykh Kamal Mutawakkil

He was a *khalifah* of Shaykh Nizam Narnawli (d. 997/1588-89) and was adorned with many virtues. His life was characterised by complete resignation to the will of God. He distributed the offerings, as and when they were received, and did not keep even a single penny for the morrow. His fondness for the musical performance (*sama*) knew no bounds and once in them, he was so overwhelmed by ecstasy and danced so violently that even the young could not hold him, though in ordinary circumstances he could not move unaided because of weakness and old age. In keeping with the tradition of his spiritual preceptors, he never showed respect to, nor expected anything from anybody. He died in 1025/1616-17 and left two sons behind, Shaykh Bayazid and Shaykh Taha. The former died in the prime of youth while the latter not only succeeded his father but also surpassed him in many ways, especially in resignation. In popularity also he left him far behind.

From the day he succeeded his father, Shaykh Taha turned his back on all worldly creatures and, in keeping with the tradition of his predecessors, never showed any respect to divines either. His son Qa'im Muhammad was also equally precocious.

(g) Shaykh Kamal Kashki

He was the son of Shaykh Haji Dihlawi Qadiri, a *khalifah* of Shaykh 'Abd al-Razzaq of Jhanjhanah and son of the letter's spiritual preceptor, Shaykh Muhammad Hasan, also known as Shah Muhammad Khayali. He sat on the prayer carpet of his father and carried on the task of the spiritual refinement of his devotees for many years. Complete detachment from the world and utter resignation to the will of God were the two hallmarks of his life. He died in 1024/1615-16. In the same year Shaykh Qutb al-'Alam, son of Shaykh 'Abd al-'Aziz also passed away. The latter was quite prominent in both esoteric and exoteric sciences. Sadiq Kashmiri sought the date of their death from the Persian phrase *'Ah! Shaykhayn-i-Dilhi.*

(h) Khwajah Khawand Mahmud

A descendant of Shaykh Baha' al-Din Naqshband, Khwajah Khawand Mahmud was one of the earliest luminaries of the Naqshbandiyah order in India. He was celebrated for his spiritual accomplishments and his devotees were spread all over Transoxiana, Badakhshan and Kashmir. His achievements in the external sciences were also commendable. He was blessed with a knack of guiding people and miracles were attributed to him. He conferred the *khilafat* of the Naqshbandiyah order on many of his disciples. He died at Lahore, in 1052/1642, and was buried near the Shalimar gardens.

(i) Shaykh Pir Mirathi

An aged saint of the Shattariyah order, with a strong penchant for ecstasy and musical performance (*sama*), Shaykh Pir Mirathi took great pains to arrange the *'urs* gatherings of his ancestors. he had met many saints and profited from their blessings. He was famous for his Hindi amulets that were believed to be very effective. He died in 1040/1630-31. Sadiq Kashmiri composed the following chronogram on this occasion.

(j) Sayyid Ahmad Qadiri

In the beginning of his mystic career he practised devotional exercises which bore fruit and he became very popular. Then he went to the Hijaz, and associated with Shaykh Muhammad Bakri. Seemingly he was quite illiterate but his knowledge of mystic niceties was so adroit that hardly any scholar would know them. Having heard of his divine virtues, Akbar grew fond of him, summoned him to his court and made him an offer of service under the crown. He welcomed the offer, joined the imperial army, and became one of the nobles of the court. Subsequently, he rose to the office of the *sadr,* which he occupied during the reign of Jahangir also. Aged and senile, in the time of Shahajahan, he requested retirement, after which he settled in Delhi, where he died in 1039/1629-30. Sadiq Kashmiri recited the following verses on this occasion.

Sayyid Ahmad Qadiri was survived by four sons. Two of them, Sayyid Hidayat Allah and Sayyid Fadl Allah, were well-educated. They were known for their charitable dispositions and most of their time was spent in the company of scholars.

(k) Shaykh Rukn al-Din

He was the quintessence of piety, purity and politeness. He led a life of complete detachment from the world and most of his time was spent in meditation and the recitation from the *Qur'an.* His benedictions were reputed to have possessed a healing effect and a capability to accelerate the fulfilment of prayers.

(l) Shaykh Sayyid Ghulam Muhammad Nanawtah

The son of Shaykh Ghulam Mustafa Nanawtah, Sayyid Ghulam Muhammad Nanawtah had a strong penchant for ecstasy and musical performance and it was under the spell of one of these ecstasies that he ultimately died in 1041/1631-32, Sadiq Kashmiri composed the following *mnemosynon* on this occasion.

(m) Sayyid Muhammad Gujarati

He traced his descent from Shah 'Alam Gujarati who was a *qutb* of his time and was celebrated for his spiritual attainments and miraculous deeds. Sayyid Muhammad was possed of many virtues and good qualities. His warm disposition and genteel manners had won him many friends which included people of all ages and from all walks of life. He was the author of many useful books and treatises. His verses were also beautiful. He died in 1042/1632-33, during the reign of

Shahjahan. He was succeeded by Sayyid Jalal Gujarati whose pre-eminence as a saint was, according to Sadiq Kashmiri, as much beyond doubt as his descent from the Holy Prophet. Miracles were also attributed to him. He appears to have been in the beginning of his saintly career at the time of the compilation of the *Tabaqai-i-Shahjahani* and according to Sadiq it looked as though he would become a lamp that would illumine the whole universe.

(n) Mir Ibrahim Husayn

A Sayyid with authentic pedigree, possessed of all the elements of formal as well as essential knowledge, Mir Ibrahim Husayn had a unique schedule in his everyday life which he stood by very scrupulously. He started his day with meditation and self-scanning (*muhasibah*) which was followed by the recitation from the *Qur'an* and the saying of prayers which continued until the middle hour between sunrise and the meridian (*chasht*). Then he started the perpetual recitation of the *Darud,* a solicitation invoking the mercy of God for the Prophet muhammad and his descendants. Having finished with it, before retiring for a siesta, he partook of his food in the company of dervishes and the poor. After the siesta was over, he renewed his ablutions and got ready for the afternoon prayer. After the prayer he sat in the company of divines and even during his association with them he made sure not to be forgetful of the Almighty for a fraction of a second.

(o) Shaykh Kamal Manduwi

He was a grandson of Shaykh Sulayman Manduwi. Shaykh sulayman fathered two sons, namely, Shaykh Dawud and Shaykh Mahmud. Shaykh Dawud died in the prime of his youth while his brother acquired full perfection under the care of his father and outlived him. On his death his son, Shaykh Kamal stepped into his shoes and took over the task of spreading the spiritual beatitude of his illustrious grandfather. He was well-known for his command of both esoteric and exoteric sciences. Especially in the latter his virtuousity was commendable. He died in 1033/1623-24. Sadiq Kashmiri composed the following two poems on this occasion.

Shaykh Kamal was survived by four sons, Shaykh Abu Muhammad, Shaykh Abu Ahmad. Shaykh Abu al-Qasim and Shaykh Abu Sa'id.

Shaykh Abu Muhammad was the eldest among his brothers and succeeded his father. Although he was a saint, he also possessed all the mundane glories and honours. His esteem was very high with Shahjahan, who conferred on him the office of the *sadi* of Delhi. By his judicious policies and even-handed dispensation of justice he fully justified his appointment to that exalted position. The fame of his generosity, magnanimity and selflessness spread far and wide. He entertained the nobility and the learned at magnificent feasts and was respected by all sections of people.

Shaykh Abu Ahmad fasted continually and was renowned for his piety and strong moral character. Shaykh Abu al-Qasim was possessed of a very pleasant nature and held a *mansab* at the imperial court. Shaykh Abu Sa'id was employed in the army. His generous nature and piety were fully discernible in his countenance. All the four sons of Shaykh Kamal were alive at the time of the compilation of the *Tabaqat-i-Shahjahani* in 1048/1638-39, and its author, who had cordial relations with that family, appears to have known each of them individually.

(p) Khwajah Abu al-A'la'

A descendant of Khwajah 'Abd Allah Ahrar, Khawjah Abu al A'la' was initially employed in the imperial army, but when divine ecstasy possessed him he turned his back on government service and became a disciple of his father-in-law, Mir 'Abd Allah Ahrari. Mir 'Ab Allah spared no effort to explore his potentialities and gradually transformed him into a perfect sufi. By the time of the compilation of the *Tabaqat* he had become so proficient what whoever approached him, came to be possessed by ecstasy and chose to stay with him voluntarily.

(ii) The Scholars

(a) Mulla Muhibb 'Ali Sindhi

Mulla Muhibb 'Ali, who flourished during the reign of Shahjahan was a renowned scholar and saint. He hailed from the Kuhbar tribe of the Chaghata 'is. His grandfather, Mirza 'Ali Beg came to India in the company of Babur Padshah and laid down his life in the battle against the Afgans. His son, Sadr al-Din later went to Thatta with the army of Humayan and subsequently settled there. Mulla Muhibb 'Ali was also born there. Although he lost his father at an early age, the Mulla did not lose hope and continued with his studies. Later on, when Thatta acceded to the Mughal empire, he came to India with Mirza 'Abd al-Rahim Khan-i-Khanan and settled in Burhanpur. At the young age of thirty years he acquired a taste for seclusion and decided to go on pilgrimage. On his way to the Hijaz, at Surat, he met with Shaykh Fadl Allah Burhanpuri who conferred on him a spiritual robe and allowed him to enrol disciples. On his return from the Hijaz, the Mulla settled at Burhanpur. When Shahjahan went on the first expedition to the Deccan, after his succession to the throne, he joined the imperial camp and accompanied the emperor.

Mulla Muhibb 'Ali was a very enthusiastic preacher of Islam. Whowever embraced Islam at his hands he took him to the imperial court and procured for him grants and monetary rewards. According to Sadiq Kashmiri, Shahjahan was so enamourred with the Mulla's enthusiasm that he decreed that whoever from amongst the infidels *(kuffar)* wanted to accept Islam should do so at the hands of the Mulla. Consequently, the Mulla converted a great many people to Islam and procured for them stipends and pensions from the imperial court. At the time of the compilation of the *Tabaquat* he was still alive.

(b) Afdal Khan 'Allami

Before his appointment as the prime minister to the emperor. Shahjahan, he was generally known as Mirza Shukr Allah, and most of his time was spent in imparting instructions to his students, in Burhanpur. He taught for several years and many of his students rose to great eminence. When Shahjahan appointed him as his prime minister *(jumlat al-Mulk)* he dedicated himself to the care and well-being of the people. His pleasant manners and axiomatic virtues were liked by everybody. Sadiq Kashmiri remarks that if the prime ministers like Nizam al-Mulk and Ibn al-'Ababd, who were celebrated for their patronage of learning, were alive in his time they would have learnt the art of administration and running the government from Afdal Khan 'Allami'.

(c) Mawlana Muhammad Fadil Badakhsi

He learnt the traditional and ratiocinative sciences from Mawlana

Sadiq Halwa'i and his contemporaries in Samarqand and Bukhar and became so distinguished in them that very few scholars in Iran, Transoxiana and India could match his attainments. In mysticism he got his initiation at the hands of Mawlaa Khwajagi Amkanagi. According to some reports, he was allowed by his precepator to enrol disciles too, but he always concealed his spirtual achievements under the guise of external sciences. He was alive at the time of the compilation of the *Tabaquat.*

(d) Qadi Aslam Harawi

Born in Herat, at an early age he left for Bukhara, whence, after the compeletion of his studies in the theological sciences, he came to India during the reign of Janangir.The latter appointed him the *qadi* of the imperial camp.This office he retained even during the days of Shahjahan and he led all the five congregational prayers in which the emperors also particpated. At the time of the compilation of the *Tabaqa*, he was the *qadi al-qudat* (Chief Justice) of India. Sadiq Kashmiri admired his piety sense of justice and his readiness to help others. According to him, the qadi was a great source of strength to the Muslims.

(e) Mulla 'Abd al-Hakim Sialkoti

He was one of the most pre-eminent scholars of his time. He recieved his early education at the feet of Mulla Kamal Kashmiri and during the reign of Jahangir confined himself to a simple and austere life in Sialkot. When Shahjahan ascended the throne, he invited the Mulla to his court and bestowed honours on him. Thereafter, the Mulla occasinally visited the court, but he mainly occupied himself with the teaching at Sialkot and Lahore where students from different parts of the country thronged to his lectures and benefitted from his erudition and scholarship. According to Sadiq Kashmiri, the Mulla entertained great regard for the *sufis* and dervishes and his attitude towards them was characterised by extreme modesty.

(f) Shaykh Abu al-Makarim

Son of Shaykh Mubarak Nagori and brother of Abu 'l-Fadl and Faydi, Shaykhh Abu al-Makarim was an orthodox Muslim. In contrast to his brothers and other members of his family, he had a strong inclination towards probity, piety and fear of God. His accomplishments were, however, mainly in the external sciences. He wrote a commentary on the *Qur 'an* in the Hanafite tradition which enjoyed great popularity. He died in 1044/1634-35.

(g) Miyan Muhammad Shakir Dihlawi

A descendant of Shaykh 'Abd al-Aziz Dihlawi, Miyan Shakir had learnt the external sciences from Shaykh Qutb 'Alam, son of Shaykh 'Abd al-'Aziz, and was considered to be one of the most eminent scholars of Delhi. He was celebrated for the purity and propriety of his disposition. But lack of courtsey and politness badly marred his personality. Nevertheless, his students were very fond of him in attendance his madrasah was unparalled in the whole of Delhi.

(h) Shaykh Muhammad Mudarris Dihlawi

We was celebrated for his erudition and learning. He exhibited extraordinary zeal for the education and welfare of his students who invariably rose to great heights and brought a good name to their teacher. His father, Shaykh Bahlul, was famous for his excellent attainments in *hadith* whereas Shaykh Muhammad Mudarris specialised in other sciences.

(i) Shaykh 'Abdal-Nabi Akbarbadi

He had an admirable knowledge of the Arabic classics and was well acomplishment in *jafr*, arithmatic and mathematics. He wrote many treatises on these subjects which were looked upon as standard works. His *tafsir* of the *Qur'an* was particularly held in high esteem.

(j) Mir Shams al-Din 'Ali khalali

He was very distinguished scholar of his time. Shahjahan appointed him in one of the *madrasahs* of Akbarabad, where he taught for a short period before his death in 1040/1630-31. At the instance of his friends he wrote a treatise in the *mathawi* of Mawlana Jalal al-Din Rumi and this, according to Sadiq Kashmiri, superseded in depth dimensions all earlier works on the subject.

(k) Shaykh Wajih al-Din

He completed his education and mystic training at the feet of his father, Shaykh Nasir al-Din , who was one of the leading saints of his time. When his father died the mantle of succession fell on his shoulders. Equipped as he was with the knowledge of the theory and practice, he discharged this responsibility with great efficiency and integrity. According to Sadiq Kashmiri, he had success written in his face.

(l) Shaykh Hamid Gujar

Shahjahan had appointed him as a teacher in one of the *madrasahs* at Lahore. He was quite distinguished in external sciences until suddenly possessed by divine ecstasy. Then he abandoned teaching and started wandering in search of saints and divines.

(m) Shaykh Rafi'al-Din Kanbu

He hailed from a family of nobles, in Delhi. In erudtion and learning he was considered to be on a par with such reputed scholars as Muhammad Mudarris and Shaykh Mubarak Kanbu. He acquried the knowledge of traditional sciences at the feet off Shaykh Muhammad Fa'id and Shaykh Mahbub Allah. He himself also imparted instuction for sometime but at the time of the compilation of the *Tababqat-i-Shahjahani* he was possessed by mystical notions, had abandoned teaching and used to spend his time in the perpetual recitation of mystical formulae on the bank of the river Jumna.

(n) Shaykh Muhammad Hashim

The son of Shaykh 'Abd al-Haqq Muhaddith Dihlawi, Shaykh Muhammad Hashim was a distinguished scholar. He was deeply read in *hadith, tafsir, siyar, tawarikh*, and *asma' al-rijal* but his attainments in the last were particularly commended by his father. Other sons of the Shaykh , namely Shaykh 'Abd al-Nabi and Shaykh 'Ali Muhammad, were also distinguished scholars. Shaykh 'Abd al-Nabi remembered the Holy Qur'an by heart and had a very sound knowledge of Arabic and Persian classics. Shaykh Ali Muhammad spent his time in academic pursuits and compiled a dictionary which was a compendium of all the earlier dictionaries.

(o) Hakim Masih al-Zaman

A notable scholar, endowed with a charitable disposition and a beautiful personality, Hakim Masih al-Zaman was equally popular with scholars and *sufis*, and lavished his favours on them equally. His poetry was of high order and according to Sadiq Kashmiri, as a physician he was comparable to Galen and Hippocrates. Nevertheless, he had no pretensions whatsoever and as far as possible, did not accept any patients. On his way to the Hijaz, on pilgrimage.

He was alive at the time of the compilation of the Tabaqat

(p) Mulla Farid Munajjim

He was a notable scholar with a sound grounding in occult sciences such a *jafr* and astrology. He wrote many tracts on these subjects. Towards the end of his life he compiled an alamanac which fully exhibited his erudition and learning. He dedicated this work to Shahjahan.

(q) Sayyid Hamaah 'Sirhindi

He had studied the science of *hadith* under *Shaykh* 'Abd al-Haqq Muhaddith Dihlawl. After obtaining permission to transmit this science to others, he went to his native town, Sirhind where he spent most of his time in teaching and other academic pursuits.

(r) Mulla Haydar Kashmiri

In *hadith* he was a student of Shaykh 'Abd al-Haqq Muhaddith Dihlawi. During his long stay at the khanqah of the Muhaddith, besides other books he studied the Mishkat and the Sahihayn also, and received permission to transmit these texts. Then he went to Kashmir and set himself to the task of spreading the theological sciences in that region. Teaching and guidance of the people occupied most of his time and he was considered to be the greatest scholar of ratinal and traditional studies in Kashmir.

(s) Mulla Abu al-khayr Sirhindi

Mulla Abu al-Khayr son of Shaykh Bayazid, a scholar renowned for his accomplishments in the art of imparting instruction, was an expert both in traditional and speculative sciences. Like his father, he was also a very skilful teacher. His lessons induced deep interest and inspiration in his students and as such, he was the most popular teacher in Sirhand.

(iii) The Poets

(a) Shaykh 'Abd al-Fattah Karnali

Son of Shaykh 'Abd al-Wahhab Dihlawl, a scholar who flourished during the reign of Jahangir, Shaykh 'Abd al-Fattah Karnali was quite well versed in poetry, prosody, rhyme, and Mu'amma. His skill in the latter was particularly remarkable. His command of language and versatality of expression were fully exhibited in his poetry and *belles-lettres.* The father and son both were excellent poets.

He died in 1044/1934-35. Since he was an old and close friend of Sadiq Kashmiri, the latter was deeply grieved at his death.

(b) Jala'i

He was a native of Delhi and was closely related to Mulla Amani Rammal, the goemancer. His actual name was Jalal and initially he used to employ the sobriquet of Jalali in his poetry. But with the passage of time, when his poetry improved and gained some lustre, he changed his pseduonym to Jala'i. His knowledge of Arabic was shallow but he had studied the works of Khaqani and some other tracts on prosody, rhyme and *mu'amma* at the feet of Khwajah 'Abd Allah.

In poetry he was a pupil of Mulla Dilbari and spent much time in his company. Subsequently he left the Mulla behind in that art. At first he was a simple soldier in the service of Nawwab Afdal Khan 'Allami, but when the Nawwab noticed his brilliance he included him among his associates. Before long he became a close companion of the Nawwab.

Jalai was alive at the time of the compilation of the *Tabaqaii-Shahjahani.*

6

Life and Works of Sayyid Ali Hamadani

AGHA HUSSAIN HAMADANI

I. Introduction

In the history of Islam in the subcontinent, the Sufi saints have played a very important role. While the Muslim warriors had to come to India with swords in their hands either to protect the helpless Muslims or to save their lands from the invasions of Hindu rulers, the Muslim saints understood of the woes of the people and gave the teachings of Islam to them as a panacea for their deliverance. The Hindu society was broken into several watertight compartments because the caste system had by that time become more rigid and the tyranny of the Brahmins over the Sudras and the untouchables had grown to intolerable extent. This division of society and the political disunity in the sub-continent paved the way for the political conquests by the foreigners.

In this state of affairs the spirit of equality, toleration and social justice propagated by Muslim Sufis began to attract a large number of oppressed Hindu masses towards Islam, which helped in creating a new society in the country. The status and influence of the Brahmins and Buddhist monks gradually declined, for their place was taken by Sayyid, Ulama, Pirs and other groups among the Muslims.

The hagiographies written by Sufis disciples are invariably shrouded in a thick fog of miracles and supernatural stories. As a result we do not get at the actuality of the time, and how in those circumstances the Sufis played a notable role. It is of utmost importance that the real contribution of these mystics should be brought to light so that we understand the part played by them and how they were able to lay the foundation of a vigorous Muslim society. A healthy society depends on the development of the individual character and in this direction the services of the mystics were of foremost importance. A number of works exist on the Sufis' philosophy which by the close of 12th century A. D. was fully developed. But it is a matter of regret that in the study of Sufi orders and Silsalas of the 13th and 14th century Indo-Pak Sub-continent, all the Tazkiras of Safi saints neglected Kashmir and hence we get very little about Sayyid Ali Hamadani in these works. In Kashmir, the influence of Sayyid Ali Hamadani has been considerable and it is possible to reconstruct an account of his activities from other sources.

In order to understand the work and philosophy of Sayyid Ali Hamadani, it is essential for us to have knowledge of the early expansion of Islam and the role of the Sufis in Kashmir. "Islam made its way into Kashmir," says Stein, "not by forcible conquests but by the gradual conversion, for which the influx of foreign adventurers both from the South and from Central Asia had prepared the ground". The influence of Islam began to be felt in Kashmir from about the middle of the 8th century, long before the establishment of Muslim rule in the country. Muslim traders and sodiers of fortune began to enter Kashmir. Kalhana records that Lalitaditya, son and successor of Vajraditya, "sold many men to the mlecchs, and introduced into the country practices which benefited the mlecchs. later Harsha employed Turkish soldiers and under Muslim influence adopted elaborate fashions in dress and ornaments. During the reign of Bhiksachara (A. D. 1120-21), Muslim soldiers were again employed and sent to attack Sussalas in Lahora.

The year of A. D. 1320 is the landmark in the history of Kashmir because Bulbul Shah, the first Sufi of Kashmir, succeeded in converting Rinchana, a non-Muslim ruler of kashmir. The story of the conversion of the ruler of the land is quite interesting and worth mentioning. Rinchana was a man of inquisitive mind and used to pay regard to learned men, Hindu and Buddhist priests. He was a follower of Buddhism. It was his habit to hold discussions with scholars of the age to know the reality of *Truth.* But none satisfied him to understand the reality of frustration and the spiritual vacuum in his life. As a result he was troubled and restless. He started weeping and praying to God to guide him to the right path. After much perturbation of spirit and constant prayers, it is said that, one night, he dreamt that some one was telling him, "Early in the morning of the next day, the first person thou dost behold is thy guide." He acted on this advice and the next morning he observed from the roof of the palace a person with his face towards the West (Ka`ba), apparently engaged in offering prayers in a manner hither to unknown to him. Rinchana at once went to this man and asked him about his name, religion and also the particular prophet whose follower he was. To those enquiries the stranger replied as under:

> "My name is Abdur Rehman ; my religion is Islam ; I worship one God who has no co-partner and I am a follower of that Prophet whose message has superseded all previous messages and commandments."

The saint next proceeded to relate several anecdotes of the Holy Prophet, together with a brief account of his mission. The king was deeply impressed by the clear and simple exposition of Islam and accepted his faith assuming Sadr-ud-Din, as his Islamic name.

This conversion in 720 A.H. (A.D. 1320) marks the second stage of the influence of Islam in kashmir. Suffice it to say that Rinchana claims our attention as the first Muslim ruler in Kashmir. This notable event increased the prestige of Islam and led to the acceptance of the new faith by some of his courtiers. In the train of Sultan's conversion to Islam, according to one tradition, ten thousand men were led to embrace Islam.

Till the arrival of Sayyid 'Ali Hamadani in A.D. 1372 Kashmir was ruled by the following Muslim Kings:

(i) Sultan Sadr-ud-Din (A.D. 1320-23).
(ii) Years of chaos and misrule (A.D. 1323-39).
(iii) Sultan Shams-ud-Din (A.D. 1339-42).
(iv) Sultan Jamshed (A.D. 1342-43).

(v) Sultan 'Ala-ud-Din (A.D. 1343-54).
(vi) Sultan Shihab-ud-Din (A.D. 1354-73).
(vii) Sultan Qutb-ud-Din (A.D. 1373-89).

It is interesting to know that during the rule of these local converted kings, Islam, the new religion, had not made any appreciable headway in the valley, even though the Sultans had been its followers. The minority of the people being still Hindu, the Muslims had nothing to distinguish them in dress, manners and customs from their compatriots. In 'Ala-ud-Din-pura for instance, there was a temple which was visited every morning by the Sultans and their Muslim subjects. These practices show that all local coverts paid lip service to the new religion Islam. Secondly, after Bulbul Shah no Sufi saint came to Kashmir. Thus Islam did not progress because there was no more conversion of the people in Kashmir until the visit of Sayyid 'Ali Hamadani in September, 1372 A.D.

The most significant event in the reign of Sultan Qutb-ud-Din was the arrival of Sayyid 'Ali Hamadani in Kashmir. It was the need of the hour that a Sufi saint should come to the valley of Kashmir to further propagate the teachings of Islam. That task was fulfilled by Sayyid 'Ali Hamadani's visit. At that time non-Islamic practices were prevalent in Kashmir society and Islam had not made any appreciable headway in the valley. 'To avert the recurrence of famine, the king performed "Yagna" in the month of Bhadra and distributed large gifts.' In contravention of the Islamic teachings, Sultan Qutab-ud-Din had two wives who were sisters. Sayyid 'Ali Hamadani disapproved of these non-Islamic practices in Kashmir and in accordance with his advice Qutb-ud-Din divorced one of his wives and adopted the dress common in the Muslim countries. It was under the influence of Sayyid 'Ali Hamadani, that, Sultan Sikandar banned all intoxicants, sati and other evil practices. Sayyid 'Ali Hamadani remained busy in Kashmir to teach Islamic ideas to the people as well as to the Sultans. Thus he commanded great influence and respect among the people.

II. Early Life of Sayyid 'Ali Hamadani

Sayyid 'Ali Hamadani was eminently suited to bring about social and religious changes in kashmir. He had had a wide cultural and educational training in his early career. His family background, education and travels through the Muslim World had initiated him into sufism. This background of the Sayyid needs to be known before we get a clear grasp of his activities in Kashmir.

The 13th century is one of the most significant period in the annals of Islam. On the one hand, the Muslim rule was established in the Subcontinent and the Muslim civilization, culture and religion developed a new dimension, on the other hand, Mongol invasions in Central Asia resulted in the decay of Muslim power and civilization. At the end of this century there was a gradual change of religious feeling amongst the Mongol settlers in Persia. According to E.G. Browne:

> "Ghazan, a ruler of II-Khan dynasty in Persia, was to make public profession of the *Muhammadan* faith and to destroy the Christian Churches and Buddhist temples which had been erected in Persia. In A.D. 1300 he even ordered that all the Bakhshis, or Mongol Priests, resident in Persia should either sincerely embrace Islam or else leave the country on pain of death".

During this period the forefathers of Sayyid 'Ali Hamadani had established their position in Hamadan. According to Lawrence Lock hart, "the 'Alavis' were a Hamadan family several member of which served as ministers under the Mongol rulers of Iran." Sayyid 'Ali Hamadani's father was the governor of Hamadan.

In A.D. 1370 the political conditions in Persia had undergone a change. Timur, the Turkish conqueror of Persia, had unleashed a policy of repression against the 'Alavi Sayyids, Percing most of them out of the country. Actually he wanted to exterminate the political influence of the Sayyids from Iran in order to conquer Hamadan. In A.D. 1386, Timur captured and destroyed Hamadan. As the political atmosphere in Hamadan was not favourable for his preaching, Sayyid 'Ali Hamadani came over to the valley of Kashmir, a place which he considered most suitable for spreading Islam in the Sub-continent.

Amir kabir Sayyid 'Ali Hamadani was born at hamadan in West Central Iran. In most of the books on Sayyid 'Ali 'Hamadani, the date of his birth is given as Monday, 12th Rajab, 714 A.H. (22 October, 1314 A.D.) but in *Khulasatul Manaqib,* a biography of Sayyid 'Ali Hamadani, it is stated that he died in 786 A.H. at the age of seventy-three years. This would place his date of birth in 713 A.H. Contrary to this, the Chronogram 'Rahmat Allah' gives the date of his birth as 714 A.H. and this confirms the first date.

The original name of Sayyid 'Ali Hamadani was 'Ali. It is commonly held that he became famous as Amir Kabir, 'Ali Sani, and Shah-i-Hamadan in history. He was called Amir Kabir because of his having a distinguished place in the long chain of eminent sufis. As his birth day was the same as that of Hazrat 'Ali, so he was called 'Ali Sani. After his stay in Kashmir, he was given the honourable title of Shah-i-Hamadan by his disciples because he hailed from Hamadan. In fact all the above surnames epitomise his basic qualities which got popularised during the life of the saint.

Sayyid 'Ali Hamadani was a Hussaini Sayyid, seventeenth in descent from Hazrat 'Ali. The genealogy of the Saint as recorded by the author of *khulasatul Manaqib* is as under :

(1) 'Ali Hamadani -b
(2) Sayyid Shihab-ud-Din -b
(3) Sayyid Mohammad -b
(4) Sayyid 'Ali -b
(5) Sayyid Yousuf -b
(6) Sayyid Sharaf -b
(7) Sayyid Mohammad Sani -b
(8) Sayyid jafar -b
(9) Sayyid Abdullah -b
(10) Sayyid Mohammad -b
(11) Sayyid Hasain -b
(12) Sayyid Abdullah -b
(13) Sayyid Zahid -b
(14) Sayyid 'Ali-Hasan -b
(15) Sayyid Zain-ul-Abidin -b

(16) Hazrat Hussain -b
(17) Hazat 'Ali.

His mother's name was Bibi Fatima. His father Shihab-ud-Din, was the governor of Hamadan, province of Iran. Though Sayyid 'Ali Hamadani was born with silver spoon in his mouth, still his family's social position least affected his childhood. In the first instance, he came under the spell of his maternal uncle, Sayyid 'Ala-ud-Din Simnani who was a learned Sufi of his age. Sayyid 'Ali Hamadani learnt Quran from his uncle and became *Hafiz-i-Quran* at an early age. He studied Islamic theology and acquired knowledge of *Tasawwuf* from his uncle. He also benefited from Shaikh Rukn-ud-Din, 'Ala-ud-Daula, Qutb-ud-Din Nishapuri and Akhi 'Ali Dausti. After staying with Mahmud Mazdaqani, he sat at the feet of Akhi 'Ali Dausti, and after the latter's death he went back to his former teacher Mahmud Muzdaqani under whose guidance he achieved perfection and was initiated into his Sufi order.

According to *Khulasatul Manaqib*, Sayyid 'Ali Hamdani was twenty-third in spiritual descent from Hazrat 'Ali, which is as under:

> " `Ali Hamadani was the disciple of Shaikh Mahmud Mazdaqani, who was the disciple of Shaikh Ala-ud-Din Daula Simnani, who was the disciple of Shaikh Abdur Rahman Asfarani, who was the disciple of Shaikh Ahmad Jazjani, who was the disciple of Shaikh Amar Yasir, who was the disciple of Shaikh Nujm-ud-Din al-Kubra, who was the disciple of Shaikh Aba Majeeb al-Sohrawardi, who was the disciple of Shaikh Aba Baqi Nisaji, who was the disciple of Shaikh Aba al-Qasim al-Jurani, who was the disciple of Shaikh Aba al-Qasim al-Maghrabi, who was the disciple of Shaikh Aba 'Ali al-Kutbi, who was the disciple of Shaikh Aba 'Ali al-Rud Bari, who was the disciple of Shaikh Aba al-Qasim Janaid al-Baghdadi, who was the disciple of Shaikh Sari Saqti' who was the disciple of Shaikh Ma`roof Kurkhi, who was the disciple of Imam Musa Kazim, who was the disciple of Imam ja'far Sadiq, who was the disciple of Imam Mohammad Baqir, who was the disciple of Imam Zain-ul-`Abidin,

who was the disciple of Imam Hussain, who was the disciple of Imam 'Ali.

In sufism, Sayyid 'Ali Hamadani attached himself to Kubriviya order. The study of the contemporary history shows that there were six main sufi orders in medieval Kashmir. These were Qadiriya, Surhawardiya, Kubriviya, Naqshbandiya, Nurbakhshiya and Rishi. But Sayyid 'Ali Hamadani did not establish any new order, although his indirect disciple, Sayyid Muhammad Nurbakhsh was the founder of the Nurbakhshiya sect in the 9th century which played an important role in the religious and literary life of Kashmir for many centuries. Sayyid 'Ali Hamadani deeply studied the current Sufi ideas. As the Chishtia order was very popular in those days; all the Chisti saints had spent their time in the service of humanity with a singleness of purpose and devotion to God. They preached the conception of all-loving and merciful God Who has shown the path of righteousness. Shaikh Mu'in-ud-Din Chisti said, "The Sufi is one who will in conformity with the Divine Will." On the other hand, Qazi Hamid-ud-Din Nagauri of Suhrawardi order discussed at length the attributes of God. Abdul Qadir Gilani, the founder of the Qadiriya order, states three circles:

> The first circle signifies *Shari'at* or God's law as revealed by His Prophet; the second signifies *Tariqat* or path of the order; the third signifies the ma'rifat or knowledge of God.

Khawaja Baha-ud-Din Naqshbandi, the originator of Naqshbandi order, permits to practise *Dhikr-i-Jali,* which is recited aloud, and also *Dhikr-i-Khafi* which is repeated in a low voice. All these Sufi orders elaborated the concept of the sovereignty of God. Sayyid 'Ali Hamadani learned a lot from these Sufi views already prevalent in his time. In order to seek the truth, Sayyid 'Ali Hamadani Continuously travelled for twenty-one years.

After the death of Shaikh Taqi-ud-Din Dausti, Sayyid 'Ali Hamadani turned towards Shaikh Mahmud Muzadaqani and humbly asked : "what are the orders for me?" The Shaikh looked at him and directed him to go on travels round the world.

Sayyid 'Ali hamadani acted accordingly and started touring extensively. He completed his education by extensive tours in different part of the world. His object in traveling was also to visit holy places then accessible to travellers and to get instructions from spiritual guides, to seek knowledge and to visit eminent sufis and shrines. According to Shaikh Shihab-ud-Din Suhrawardi :

> "The sufi was expected to meet other Shaikhs, to resist worldly pleasure, to visit historical places and to avoid running after reputation."

In *Khulasatul Manaqib,* there are references to the names of the several places visited by him such as Muzdaqan, Khutlan, Balkh, Badakhshan, Khita, Yazd, Syra, Baghdad, Rum, Mavra-in-Nehr. Sayyid 'Ali hamadani visited a hill-place at Saran-deep (Ceylon) which, according to legends, is said to have been the place where Adam and Eve met each other. Adam landed on the hill which bears his footprints. The other foot-print at Zaitoon (China) was also visited by 'Ali Hamadani.

He also went on pilgrimage to Mashhad and visited the Holy Tomb of Imam Raza. Once 'Ali Hamadani accompanied by Shaikh Mahmud Muzdaqani visited Tus. After the pilgrimage to Holy Mecca he toured the whole of Arabia. He journeyed to India, Turkistan, and Ladakh. There is a reference in *Khulasatul Manaqib*, to his having visited Rum where he stayed for forty one days. Later on he went to Badakhshan. There is a reference to Ardabil in *Rasalah Masturat.* He stopped for a short period in Masjid-i-Aqsa while going on pilgrimage to Mecca. Latif Ashrafi has referred to his travels to Qipchaq and jabl-ul-Qaf in the company of Sayyid Ashraf Jahangir Samnani. During the same tour he met Shaikh Azqani at Asfaran. In A.H. 741, he came to Kashmir and stayed at the house of Mata-hur-Sooni. He is reported to have gone on pilgrimage to Mecca twelve times on foot. It is, however, not clear as to when and from which places he started on this journey. According to Amin Ahmad Razi, Shah-i-Hamadan travelled three times over the whole world and met 1400 sufis and ulama.

During his travels through the Muslim World he was profited by meeting eminent sufis; some of whose names are given below:

1. Hazrat Sayyid Shah Wali Kirmani (d. A. H. 834),
2. Shaikh Yahya Muniri (d. A. H. 782),
3. Shaikh Mohammad-bin-Azkani Asfarani (d. A. H. 778),
4. Hazrat Makhdum Jahania Jahangusht Bukhari (d. A. H. 787),
5. Sayyid Ashraf Jahangir Simnani (d. A. H. 808).

Sayyid 'Ali hamadani obtained "Khirqah" from Shaikh Yahya Muniri Bahari (d. A. H. 782), who was the renowned sufi of the reign of Sultan Nasir-ud-Din-Mahmud. During his travels Sayyid 'Ali Hamadani had an occasion to meet Shaikh Mohammad Azkani Asfarani (d. A.H. 778) from whom he also got "Khirqah" and according to his wishes Sayyid 'Ali married with a daughter of the Sayyid, Dr. Hameed Farzam writes that Sayyid 'Ali Hamadani was invited by Sayyid Shah Niamat Ullah Kirmani, a great scholar of Kirman, (d. A.H. 834) while the former was proceeding on Haj through Kirman. But the author is silent about their meeting.

The various phases in the early life of the Sayyid have been traced above. All these experiences left an indelible impress on his life. The political instability of his family did not provide for him a cool and calm atmosphere for preaching, so he decided to go to Kashmir, a suitable place for preaching of Islam. Sayyid's early training persuaded him to lead the life of a sufi and in search of spiritual knowledge he went on travelling perpetually. This is because travelling was considered a part of sufi discipline and training. His travels through the whole Muslim world completed his sufi training and enabled him to meet eminent sufis. After completion of tours for twenty-one years, Sayyid 'Ali Hamadani remained busy in preaching for the next twenty years, (A.H. 753-773) of his life in Hamadan. During this period he guided and trained his followers and seekers of truth in the path of mysticism and wrote many valuable books i.e. *Zakhiratul Maluk, Masharabul-Azwaq, Hulul-Fasus and Al-Fatutia Sharah-i-Asma. Zakhiratul maluk* is one of the best books on ethical and political philosophy, and according to G.M.D. Sufi, "it is the best work on political ethics and the rules of good government."

III. Ethical Philosophy of Sayyid 'Ali Hamadani

Ethics in Islam is nothing but the body of injunctions laid down in the Holy Quran for the practical conduct of life and fully exemplified in the practice of the Holy Prophet throughout his life. The Quran addresses the Prophet:

"Thou has been created with an excellent character". The Holy Prophet himself says, "I have been sent to perfect moral. According to Donaldson:

> "An effort should be made to let the Quran speak for itself regarding the development that ethical consciousness which the Prophet put into it, as Muslims believe, by divine authority and in which he exhorted the believers to follow his examples."

The ethical character of the Holy Quran is shown by the following passages of the Quran:

1. "Serve Allah and join not any partners with him; and do good to parents, kinsfolk, orphans, those in need, Neighbours who are near: Neighbours who are strangers, the way-farer (ye meet), and what your right hands possess : for Allah loveth not the arrogant, the vain glorious."

II. "Those who spend (freely), whether in prosperity, or in adversity, who restrain anger, and pardon (all) men; For Allah loves those who be good.

III. "Allah commands justice, the doing of good, and liberality to kith nd kin, and He forbids and all shameful deeds, and injustice and rebellion; He instructs you, that ye may receive admonition."

The forgoing lines show that the whole of Quran is full of such injunctions and therefore Islamic ethics takes its origin from the Holy Quran. The Holy Quran lays down the foundation of a religious system on purely ethical principles, hence there is not much to distinguish between Islam as such and Islamic ethics. The moral civil, canonical, and criminal laws of Islam are not rigidly separated from one another and cannot be identified as isolated systems. The Muslims started the study of ethics along with the study of the Holy Quran.

The ethical views of Sayyid 'Ali Hamadani rest on the study of the Holy Quran and the Sunnah of the Prophet and the Sayyid keeps the Holy Prophet before him as the embodiment of the Quranic teachings. Sayyid 'Ali Hamadani quotes a Quranic verse while dealing with the Islamic ethic :

Hold to forgiveness ; Command what is right ; But turn away from the ignorant.

The Holy Prophet interpreted this verse to his followers like this:

> "The person who discords you mercilessly ; you must keep contact with him kindly ; and who denies you, the opportunity of doing good, you must sacrifice your interests on him : and who shows cruelty towards you, be faithful to him."

Sayyid 'Ali Hamadani also quotes Asama-bin-Sharik, who says:

> "That in my presence a party of Arabs asked the Holy prophet about the best thing which God has bestowed upon his creation. *Husn-i-Khulq* was the reply of the Holy Prophet."

The substance of the Sayyid's ethical views is *Husn-i-Khulq* which is derived from the third chapter of his famous book *'Zakhiratul Maluk'*; The title of the third chapter relates to *the beauties of character and nobility of conduct : the presense of balance mind in the rulers and kings in the light of the character of orthodox khalifas, who were the leaders and guides of the Muslim kings and the rulers of the people.* In this chapter the Sayyid explains his ethical views in these manners :

> "Please know that God Almighty has created the human beings on account of two reasons; The first is the appearance (*Surat-i-Zahir*) and the second is the inner self (*Sirat-i-Batin*). The appearance (*Surat-i-Zahir*) is styled creation (*Khalq*), and the

> nature (*Sirat*) is known as *Khulq* (character), and both of these have two facets of virtue and vice."

Sayyid 'Ali Hamadani draws our attention to the balancing role of both virtue and vice in the perfection of human conduct. He says that:

> "the beauty of the creation (*Husn-i-Khulq*) is not perfect without the appropriateness of all the parts like eyes, eye-brows, lips, mouth, hands, and the structure. Similarly the beauty of nature (*Husn-i-Sirat*) which is known as the beauty of *Khulq (Husn-i-Khulq*) does not reach its perfection except in the balance of virtuous qualities like knowledge, profundity, piety, generosity, courageousness, politeness, civility, humility, obedience, virtue and justice. The balancing of virtuous traits does not permit an excess or loss because once an excess or loss is committed in those virtues, the beauty of nature (*Husn-i-Sirat*) is upset. Just as excesses of extravagance and miserliness. Both those things are to be condemned. They lead to loss in the beauty and perfection of nature. The real beauty of nature is confined to a balance which is devoid of the excessiveness. The balance, as the beauty of nature, may be determined by seizing a person who is near to this balance."

In the Sayyid's explanation of balancing of virtues and vices, we come to know about two groups of human beings. The first is a group of bigoted persons and the second is that of wise persons. Sayyid 'Ali Hamadani says :

> "A group of bigoted persons, on account of the lack of insight, do not understand the meaning of this balance and consider that the beauty of nature is, entirely, dependent on saying lot of prayers and think that the evil traits of character lead to immorality and destruction of character. But this is not possible and by the instrument of prayers we cannot achieve it. It leads to a loss of time. These people on account of their foolishness tend to work in this field and turn their back to the divine *laws of Shariat.* Thus they lose themselves in a mountain of ignorance and lead

other unfortunate unknowing people to ignorance through their actions. But a group of wise people and learned scholars have actually found out that the virtues can be changed on account of excesses or losses, because if it were not so then all reformation would be useless and all the teachings of the Holy Prophet (may peace be upon him) would be fruitless, because he said : "Improve your character".

That is, to beauty your nature. Although the evil powers are destructive and have destroyed the human race, yet a man, would not be able to defend himself against destructive circumstances. But both these powers have virtues and vices and a balance has to be struck between the two to lead us to perfection."

The Sayyid also suggests various ways for balancing of virtue and vice. He says:

"The balance is actually governed by keeping in view the rule of conduct as directed by *Sharia* and the employment of these two powers should be directed according to the will of God. The people who try to receive good rewards in the next world always strike a balance between the two powers. That is why God Almighty said that the height of the perfection of those powers is achieved by striking a balance and not by destroying them completely. This fact has been explained by the example of a date and a grape, because by nurturing a date, a tree grows up just as when a seed is placed in the earth. It is like a believer who is helped by the kindness of God and he becomes a *wali* (saint)."

Sayyid 'Ali hamadani describes in detail three categories of human beings which play significant role in bringing up the evils or virtues in the heart of a person. He says:

"The human being, not accepting the influence of nurturing, belong to three categories. The *first category* is that of a child who cannot distinguish between true and false or between right or wrong. As the mirror of his heart does not distinguish between good and evil and is not covered by the darkness of evil opinions and his self is not governed by the evil thoughts, he is very quickly influenced by the sayings of his spiritual teacher which every easily reach his inner self and influence him. The *second category* is that of a human being who can distinguish between good and evil. But on account of the influence of evil he is not attracted towards doing good and does not distinguish the defects involved in disobedience. Yet he admits his fault. This category is more difficult than the previous one, because to reform him it is necessary, first of all, to destroy the evil matter from his inner self and then he may be persuaded to return to a state where he can acquire virtues. The *third category* is of a person who is brought up with an evil intention and belief. He believes the vice to be virtue and evil to be good. He takes pride in following evil. This is a most difficult category and to improve him is like digging a mountain with a nail or hammering the cold steel. His reform, according to the saying of the Holy Prophet, is like training a wolf.

According to Sayyid 'Ali Hamadani, the foundations of the highest virtues, which are the basic principles of human conduct, are ten in number and all these virtues can be gained by protecting these foundations. These are:

> "Knowledge, politeness, charity, piety, courageousness, justice, truthfulness, forbearance, nobility and faith".

Sayyid 'Ali Hamadani further says:

> "A perfect development of these virtues was attained in the personality of the Holy Prophet (may peace be upon him) and all other Prophets. Wise people and learned scholars, according to their achievement of those virtues and improvement of conduct with the spiritual influence of the Holy Prophet (may peace be upon him), had attained these virtues as much as they were nearer to the Prophet. Thus they became also favourites of God and were bestowed upon unlimited kindness."

Sayyid Ali Hamadani greatly stresses on the importance of this kind of pious men and says:

"They also led the people of their times and anybody who contravened these virtues became a devil in the garb of a human being by his deceitful actions and destructive ways. They also became a source of destruction of countries."

Sayyid 'Ali Hamadani sheds lights on the character of true believer (*Mumin*) and narrates five characteristics of a true believer, which are as under :

"Dear Reader, according to the people with enlightened mind, the beauty of nature (*Husn-i-Sirat*) lies in faith and ugliness of nature depends upon its loss. God Almighty has created a standard upon which these virtues and vices can be tested. It is said by God, anybody who is firm in love and hatred, and is patient during emotion and feelings, is a pious man. The Holy Prophet (may peace be upon him) said that the true believer faces these five hardships in his lifetime :

1. He is hated by people.
2. The *Munafiq* considers him as his enemy.
3. The devil tries to mislead him and weighs heavy on him.
4. His evil self always drags him towards evil thought and tries to keep his self on the wrong path.
5. The devil fights with him.

By bearing all these hardships he gains blessings of God and the divine honours of virtue. Sayyid 'Ali Hamadani quotes the remarks of Shaikh Abu Bakr Waraq Trimidi who said, "Anybody who drives his reins into the evils really grows in his heart, the three of regrets, repentance, disrepute and insults." He said that:

"I ascertained that the evil thoughts of the kings lead them to be slaves of the vices and patience and piety of slaves convert them into kings. The piety means the absorption of all virtues and a pious person is he who obeys all the laws of *Shariat* (equity) and who avoids all the forbidden things. The real sign of good fortune (*Sa`adat*) is that he should be able to see all hi defects. Such people are very few in number at all times."

Sayyid 'Ali Hamadani discusses commands (*amr-bil mahr'uf*) and prohibitions (*nahi-anil-munkir*) or (*Ahkam-i-Ihtisab*) in the seventh chapter of *Zakhiratul maluk,* which is a code of rules for the Sultans. In this chapter we find the three religious functions of *momin* (bondmen) which Almighty God has conferred upon them. Sayyid 'Ali Hamadani starts the chapter with this *Ayat :*

Let there arise out of
A band of people
Inviting to all that is Good,
Enjoining what is right,
And forbidding what is wrong.
They are the ones,
To attain felicity.

According to Sayyid 'Ali Hamadani, in this verse Almighty God educates to his *momin* (bondmen) with three religious teachings. Firstly, necessity of injunction for good and forbidding from wrong; secondly it is the self sufficiency in obligation that if a single person out of a large number of people fulfils the injunction, *the obligation* for the rests *would stand eliminated.* If none of them do it, all of them would be guilty and worthy of Divine wrath; Thirdly those who fulfil it would be liable to lofty and exalted ranks of victory an prosperity according to their efforts. Sayyid 'Ali Hamandani quotes various sayings of the Holy Prophet and Khulafa-i-Rashidin to prove that Commands (*Amr-i-Mahruf*) and prohibitions (*Nahi-munkir*) is essential. He further says that such person among the creation, who devotes himself for doing it, is called *Muhtisib,* and the function, which is performed by him, is called *Ahtisab.* In this chapter, the Sayyid mentions in detail about the introduction of the department of *Ahtisab.* Though presently Sayyid 'Ali hamadani's views on the system of *Ahtisab* are not attractable for the rulers but before the establishment of police, army and courts, these opinions were beneficial for the administration of a good government, and welfare of the people.

Sayyid 'Ali Hamadani also narrates the definition of evil person and vicious traits of his character. He say:

"Those, who do not see their defects, are evil persons; and they cannot save their self from destruction. Most of the people do know their defects and also the defects of others. It is only the excess of opthalmia caused by the overpowering of carnal appetite and sexual pleasures that blinds their discerning eyes. In reality it will be the vicious traits of character, like pride, avarice, miserliness, jealousy, hatred, haughtiness, and hypocricy which are literally styled as snakes and scorpion and which will torment a person in the grave till eternity.

Sayyid'Ali Hamadani also interprets the true principles of Islam and tries to inculcate the religious spirit in the hearts of the people. His exposition of religious principles is only an aspect of his ethical system. According to him, *'Ibadat* can be performed through two ways. The first relates to moral submissions consisting of the following virtues:

(i) tauhid ; *(ii) Tawakkal ;* *(iii) Sabr ;*

(iv) Tasleem ; *(v) Ikhlas ;* *(vi) Ma'rfat.*

The second is bodily submission which is subdivided into two kinds :

1. *Huqooq Allah i.e.,*

(a) Prayer ; *(b)* Fasting ; *(c)* Zakat ; *(d)* Pilgrimage ;

(e) Jihad.

2. *Huqooqul 'Ibad,* relating to the rights of the people.

According to the Sayyid, these religious duties or *'Ibadat* help a man to seek proximity with God, as well as to achieve nobility of character. He also sets down ten spiritual stations (*Maqamats*) which are essential for the sufi to travel along the mystic path.

I. Taubah (Repentance)

The first stage on the path of sufism is repentance which means the awakening of the soul from the slumber of headlessness, so that the sinner becomes aware of his evil ways and for past disobedience.

II. Zuhd (Detachment)

It is the renouncement of the world in order to give oneself to God.

III. Tawakkal (Trust in God)

It is an important virtue. When a sufi reaches this stage he entrusts himself and all his ways and works to God in a spirit of complete trust and surrender.

IV. Qana'at (Satisfaction)

It consists in a willing acceptance of whatever God stands since he is convinced that whatever befalls on him is a blessing for him.

V. 'Uzlit. (Temperance)

It means to prevent senses from doing any bad thing.

VI. Zikr (Remembrance)

The Sayyid attached great importance to the remembrance of God. It means forgetting everything except the remembrance of God and submissiveness to God.

VII. Tawajuh

It means that one should devote his attention fully towards God.

VIII. Sabr (Patience)

Patience is the exception of consolation from God and is the noblest and highest service.

IX. Muraqibah

In this stage, the seeker expects to reach his destination. Sayyid 'Ali Hamadani says that "with exercise of *Muraqibah,* the sufi is able to overcome all human attributes and his heart becomes the abode of God.

X. Riza (Submission to the Divine Will)

It is the last station and according to the Sayyid 'Ali Hamadani, one should have merged his own will into the will of God.

After defining the spiritual stations of Sayyid 'Ali Hamadani, we can compare these with the spiritual journey of Hazrat Data Ganj bakhsh (A.D. 1009-1072) stated in his book *Kash ful Mahjub*. Hazrat Data Ganj Bakhsh has not given any specific number of each station. He has in general terms:

> "There are several stations ; the first is repentance, the second conversion, the third renunciation, the fourth trust in God and so on."

We find that there is some resemblance between the spiritual stations of both great Sufis of Islam, and Sayyid Ali Hamadani, who was born two century after Hazrat Data Ganj Bakhsh, has certainly got benefited from the Data in sufism and explained it in clear terms. In his treatise *'Dah Quadah'*, Sayyid Ali Hamadani has observed that on the way to God there are so many various spiritual steps but all these are of three types. The first type relates to an ordinary Muslim, which consists on Prayer (*Nimaz*), Fasting (*Roza*), Citing of Holy Quran (*Talawate-e-Quran),* Zakat, Pilgrimag *(Haj),* and apparent actions (Amal-e-*Zahira*). The second type is of a pious man (*Ashab-i-Mujahidat*), purity of self (*Nafs-ka-Tazkiya*), contentment of heart (*Dil ka Tuzkiya*), Spiritual light (*Roh-ki-Durkhishani*), and perfection of inner values (*Ammarat-i-batin Ki-Tahmeer*). Third is the super type relating to only saints (*Sairn-i-Hazrat Samdiyat*). One can only attain the saintship passing through the ten spiritual stations narrated above.

> "Sayyid Ali Hamadani considers that, "no moral progress is possible without performing and reaching upon the religious duties and spiritual stations which lead a man to enrich his noble character and to become a Qutb, Ghaus, and Wali. 'Qutb or Ghaus is the orbit of the whole universe (*Khalq*), because Aqtab, Akhyar, Umad, and Awtad are the significant organs of the universal administration. As long as they are living, the cause is in progress Due to a single person like this, the whole universe exisis."

In this paragraph, Sayyid Ali Hamadani enumerates the various manifest kinds of saintship and their importance. Data Ganj Bakhsh also held that among the saints, who are manifest, there is regular hierarchy. At the lowest rank are Akhyar ; above them Abdal ; then Abrar; then Awtad ; then Nuqaba; and at the top Qutb or Ghaus. Defining the importance of the saints, Data Ganj bakhsh describes that:

> "God had made the saints to govern the universe. They are entirely devoted to His business, and do not follow any sensual affections. Through the blessing of their advent the rain falls from Heaven and through the purity of their lives the plants spring up from the earth, and through their spiritual influence, Muslims gain victories over unbelievers."

In the foregoing pages an attempt has been made to give a bird's eye view of a tremendously vast domain. We have concentrated on the most important features of Sayyid Ali Hamadani's ethical thoughts. Throughout his ethical philosophy he has stressed greatly on beautifying the nature (*khulq*) of a man, and tried to reform and upgrade the ethical values of a man and the most fundamental principle, which lies at the root of the Sayyid's philosophy, is *Akhlaq.* Again the Sayyid differentiates between two kinds of *Akhlaq.*

I. The first is appearance (*Khalq*) ;
II. The second is inner self (*Khulq*).

Both these kinds have two facets of virtue and vice. He advises a person to follow virtues for making good character and warns to avoid from vices. He quotes the example of a *Mumin* (true believer) and also enumerates his qualifications. We find that Sayyid Ali Hamadani is one of the few mystic philosophers who gave great importance to the reformation of moral values in their ethical philosophy. Al-Ghazzali has also dealt with this aspect in his ethical interpretation. It is also state by the writers that Sayyid Ali Hamadani has borrowed his view on religious philosophy from Ibn-i-Arabi. His spiritual views have been compared with the philosophy of Data Ganj Bakhsh, a great sufi of Islam. In his philosophy he recommends *Ibadaat* and acting upon these religious duties a person can make his character 'perfect'. Throughout his writings, Sayyid Ali Hamadani takes his stand upon Islamic teachings and invariably quotes from the Quran and the traditions of the Holy Prophet and Khulafa-i-Rashdeen in support of his views. Following the Quran, for example, he lays emphasis on spiritual values like repentance (*Taubah*), reliance (*Tawakkal*), (*Zuhd*) detachment, *Qanaat, Uzlit, Zikr, Tawajuh, Sabr, Muraqibah,* and *Riza.* All these important views show that Sayyid Ali Hamadani occupies a position unique in the history of Muslim religious and philosophical thought.

IV. Political Philosophy of Sayyid 'Ali Hamadani

The religious and ethical philosophy of Sayyid 'Ali Hamadani is closely associated with his ideas of state and government. The central idea of his philosophy is social justice which is derived from the fifth chapter of his book, *Zakhiratul Maluk* ; relating to the *Injunctions of Government, Kingdom, sovereignty, the rights of the public, the stipulations of governance, the dangers involved in the obligations and the necessity of justice and benevolence.*

Sayyid Ali Hamadani starts the chapter with this *Ayat.*

> "Allah commands justice, the doing of good, and liberality to kith and kin, and He forbids all shameful deeds, injustice and rebellion, He instructs you, that ye may receive admonition."

On this *Ayat* the Sayyid comments:

> "God Almighty desires His bondmen to desist from the path of injustice and cruelty and asks them to follow the path of kindliness, justice and benevolence. He also orders them to desist from the evil ways of life, particularly the kings and rulers who are entrusted with these duties and who have to look after the rights of the people."

The above interpretation of *Ayat* shows that Sayyid 'Ali hamadani has enumerated three injunctions of a good government which are as under:

(1) Kindliness; (2) Justice; and (3) Benevolence.

But in the political philosophy of Sayyid 'Ali Hamadani, the doctrine of justice takes a large amount of space, though he lightly describes benevolence and kindliness. Sayyid 'Ali hamadani says that:

> "The Prophets, the Khulafa-e-Rashidin, the kings and holders of the treasures had spent their time in this world with great patience. They tried to spread justice, kindliness and benevolence amongst the people in spite of the fact that they were not free from the dangers of governance and rule."

In support of his view, the Sayyid quotes the examples of the Prophet and Khualfa-e-Rashidin and makes the rulers aware of the importance of social justice in these words :

> "The rulers and the kings, so long as they are on the path of *justice* and *benevolence,* follow the limits of Shara`(faith) and enforce the religious laws, they are the Viceregents and chosen people of God, shadow of Almighty and the lieutenants of God."

To explain further Sayyid 'Ali hamadani quotes the sayings of so many companions (Sahabis) of the Holy Prophet. Here we only refer to Abu Hurraira who narrates the Holy Prophet as said:

> "On the Day of Resurrection, God will hold dearest and nearest only a just ruler and according to God, the most hated person on the same day would be a cruel king, who could be punished heavily."

As already stated, the Sayyid says that the ruler is the viceroy of God only if he is just and quotes the Apostolic traditions that :

> "On the Day of Judgement out of the seven sets of persons who would be allowed to enjoy the shadow of the Divine throne would be the set of the kings who have done justice."

In this connection Sayyid 'Ali Hamadani also discribes that Almighty God had sent Hazrat Adam to this world as *Khalifa-tul-Arz;* the Sayyid says:

> "the first persons who agreed to become the ruler and who tried to give the rights of people to them was Adam. The noble soul of Adam combined in itself two offices, viz., the prophethood and kingship. The kingship from Adam to the present times was given to few great prophets, like Yusuf, Musa, Daud, Suleman and Mohammad."

Quoting the example of Adam, the first ruler of the world, Sayyid 'Ali Hamadani, also mentions about doing justice in these words :

> "Dear reader ! with the exception of these it was a difficult time that the prophets, the Khulafa-e-Rashdin, the Kings and holders of the treasures had spent their time in this world with great patience. They tried to spread justice, kindliness and benevolence amongst the people, in spite of the fact the they were not free from the dangers of governance and rule."

All these ideas show that the Sayyid preaches this noble precept of justice and says that by doing justice the ruler can get a nearest place to the Almighty. Addressing to the kings and rulers in his writings, the Sayyid advises them to do justice to their subjects and reminds them that doing justice is one of the most important functions of good government. Similarly Al-Ghazzali deals with justice and explains its importance and says, "one day of justice is equal to seventy years of continuous prayers."

The commentary of the Sayyid on the *Ayat* quoted in the beginning of this chapter also points out the negative role of a king. Sayyid 'Ali hamadani warns a ruler about the dangers involved in the administration and says :

> "the rulers who deviate from the path of justice and benevolence, are not kind to the people of God, obey the evil self, and do not maintain the limits of Shara' (faith), then in reality they are the helpers of the devil and the enemy of God and the Holy Prophet. They are also the Khalifa of devil."

In these lines Sayyid 'Ali Hamadani tells to the rulers about the obnoxious consequences of injustice. He prohibits them from doing injustice while explaining their real position and purpose in this world, Sayyid 'Ali Hamadani writes that,

> "According to the dictates of the Holy Quran and Sunnah, it is known that everybody in this world is a traveller and for his arrival the stages are defined. First stage is when he is in the back (pusht) of his father, the second stage is when he is in the womb of his mother ; the third stage is when he is in the atmosphere of this world ; the fourth stage is a grave ; fifth stage is waiting for the resurrection, and sixth stage is paradise or hell. Anybody, who tries to earn the blessings of the stage of heaven or the hardship of the hell in this world, knows that the horse of his life is constantly on the move. Alas ! he does not know that every breath is like a step and every day is like a field and also every breath is like falling a brick from his age and deserting it and every step brings him nearer to his end and away from this world."

These lines show the unreality of this world and in this connection again Sayyid 'Ali Hamadani says :

> "that unreality of this world provides a way to the next world and is a house placed on the path of resurrection. He is a wise man who does not attach himself to it. He builds a house for the next world only after good deeds done in this world and is not fond of decorating it. Whatever is more than the need, it is poision and he would be just sorry in the next would by knowing that the pleasures of the world were like a dust an there was no gold or silver in it."

The above stated views of the Sayyid are the alarming singnals to the rulers who do injustice and do not observe the limits placed by the religion. Sayyid Ali Hamadani also expressed the same views in his letter addressed to a Sultan: In this letter, Sayyid Ali Hamadani tells him that worldly life is an accidental, transitory and immortal. It is also an illusive imagination and it prevents the bondmen of Almighty God from treading the path of felicity and deprives them of attaining eternal fortune (*Sa'adat*) and of earning the bliss of other world.

Whosoever is given kingdom and authority in this world, is placed in between internal bliss and perpetual misery. His perishable kingdom is a touch-stone and a measure of his designs and deeds. If he strives in the execution of his duties in the teeth of all his (worldly) attachments, and offers submission and his consent to the divine commands and prohibitions, his temporary affluence becomes the basis for his everlasting bliss. It, therefore, behoves a wise ruler that he should not neglect the state affairs ; instead he should perform his duties in his own interest. During his comptency he should seek proximity with God by means of justice and beneficence. He should not withhold his kindness and compassion from his subordinates. He should learn from the condition of the transgressers of the past.

The substance of the above letter reveals the mortality of this world and the significance of justice and benevolence. Similarly his other letters addressed to various contemporary Sultans are of great significance and all the letters throw a considerable light on the political philosophy.

Sayyid 'Ali Hamadani describes the evil traits in the character of a man which force a ruler to do injustice to his subjects. He says :

> "according to great scholars and people with insight, it is established that the souls and nature of human beings in the beginning of the creation, varied due to the differences in virtues and capabilities to absorb the lights of greatness and obeyance and for that reason the objectives and desires of the people differ and there had appeared a difference in the saying, deed, and faiths of the people. Then in the nature of a man the evil traits of character and morals, like *high-handedness, cruelty, enmity, malice, rebellion, hatred,* and *miserliness,* get stablished."

These are seven evil traits in the character of a man and those act as great obstacles for a ruler to perform the functions of the government.

Sayyid 'Ali Hamadani advocates the presence of a *sufi* reformer in a society for eradicating such evil traits and says:

> "thus the wisdom of God Almighty demands that amongst the people, there should exist the perfect reformers, so that they can correct the deeds of the rulers and the children of Adam and also could keep the learned people on the right path."

Sayyid 'Ali hamadani is the only sufi saint who had put forward the idea of a sufi reformer in a kingdom so that the could check and keep the ruler on the right path. This doctrine of this political philosophy distinguished him from other sufis who did not think of such a role of the sufi. The idea before Sayyid 'Ali Hamadani is that the reformer could keep the society free from injustice and high-handedness so that there should be no breaking away from the path of Shara' (faith) and the ruler should not behave with the people like animals and beasts.

Like the Sayyid, Plato, the Greek Philosopher, propounded a theory on the Rule of Philosophers in his book *Republic*). Book V and VI of the *Republic* bear on the rule of philosophy, where he says, "Until Philosophers are kings, or the kings and princes of this world have the spirit and power of philosophy, cities will never rest from their evils. The same views Will Durant in his book, *The Story of Philosophy,* quotes:

> "Until philosophers are kings, or the kings and princes of this world have the spirit and power of philosophy, and wisdom and political leadership met in the same man, ... cities will never cease from ill, nor the human race (473)."

This sums up Plato's views regarding the government of the ideal states and the rule of the philosopher king. A philosopher can properly comprehend all time and all existence. He searches for absolute Beauty beyond all beautiful things, absolute Good beyond all good things, he loves truth and can see the unity of all knowledge. He knows what is Justice and Beauty and Temperance and uses this knowledge to mould the character of those over whom he rules. "He has the noblest gifts of nature and makes the highest use of them." He has no room for covetousness. He is just and shows due proportion in all things. His reasons and his Wisdom are the motive and the regulative force in the ideal states. "The Philosopher King is not a mere addition or assertion, he is the logical result of the whole method on which the construction of the state has proceeded." In nut-shell, according to the Plato's theory of rule of philosopher king, is that a philosopher king is fit to guide a nation.

Similarly Abul Fazl says :

> "Whenever, from lucky circumstances, the time arrives that a nation bears to understand how to worship truth, the people will naturally look to their king, on account of the high position which he occupies, and expected him to be their spiritual leader as well; for a king possesses independent of men, the ray of Divine Wisdom, which banishes from his heart every thing that is conflicting ....."

In these lines, Abul Fazl expresses his views that the king is also a religious head.

Sayyid 'Ali Hamadani puts forward the obligations of a good government for a just ruler which should form the guidelines for a king. He states ten rules of good governance which are as under:

(i) In every case the ruler should mentally put himself in the position of contending parties.

(ii) He should fulfil the desires of those who have come to him for justice.

(iii) The ruler does not indulge in luxurious food and clothing and follow the example of Khulafa-e-Rashdin.

(iv) He should show leniency, not harshness, while practising Shara' (faith).

(v) He should try that the subjects should be contented with the rule of law.

(vi) The ruler should not be careless about the pitfalls of the state.

(vii) He should try to meet the learned and scholars as often as he can.

(viii) He should not be overwhelmed by his false sense of pride but he should do kindness to weak and needy people.

(ix) He should not be careless about the dishonesty of his servants and not appoint cruel officers on his oppressed people.

(x) He should function with care and wisdom.

Like the Sayyid, Al-Ghazali also describes these principles embodied in a chapter devoted to the art of government, the care of subjects and related matters.

According to Sayyid 'Ali Hamadani, the subjects of a state have rights over the king and unless their rights are duly respected nobody can be safe from the punishment of the next world. He states twenty rights of the public as well as the duties and functions of the executive arms of the government centred in the person of the king which are as under :

(i) He should treat equally all the Muslims.

(ii) He should not depend on the information supplied by one side.

(iii) The ruler should be just while losing his temper.

(iv) He should show equal justice and benevolence to all.

(v) He should not enter into any one's house without permission.

(vi) He should deal equally with all kinds of subjects.

(vii) He should pay respect towards elder in the meeting.

(viii) He should deal with the poor and the rich in courteous manner.

(ix) The ruler should keep in mind the justice.

(x) He should fulfil his promise.

(xi) He should try to conciliate in the public matters.

(xii) He should not allow minor sins to be propagated in the public.

(xiii) He should not doubt in the matters of the public.

(xiv) He should not indulge in nepotism.

(xv) He should take side with the poor instead of the rich.

(xvi) He should try to eliminate the roots of poverty.

(xvii) He should try to save roads from looting and construct guarding houses where such lootings happen. After catching the robbers, they should be dealt with heavy punishment.

(xviii) He should construct inns and bridges.

(xix) He should arrange for building of mosque in each city and appoint Imams giving them stipends.

(xx) He should instruct his public for praying to God.

Like the Sayyid, Al-Gazzali has also stated twenty rights of the public but with slight changes.

He further states the rights, narrated above, which are only for the Muslim subjects while there are different and separate rights of non-Muslims. It is the duty of every Muslim king and ruler to safeguard the life and property of non-Muslims. He should direct non-Muslims to act upon the following rules :

(i) He should not allow non-Muslims to build new churches and temples.

(ii) The non-Muslims need not repair their old religious buildings and reconstruct the followed.

(iii) They should not prevent a Muslim traveller to stay in their churches and temples.

(iv) And if Muslim stays therein for three days they should not be careless about his meals.

(v) The non-Muslims must not indulge in any conspiracy against the Muslims.

(vi) They should not wear the dress like Muslims.

(vii) They should not prevent anyone of their relations for embracing Islam.

(viii) They should not call the names of their children like Muslims.

(xi) They should pay respect towards Muslims.

(x) They should meet and sit with the Muslims.

(xi) They should be forbidden to ride on horses.

(xii) They should not keep arrow and sword in their hands,

(xiii) They should not wear the ring on which their names are inscribed.

(xiv) They should not threat Muslims with non-Muslim habits.

(xv) They should not openly drink.

(xvi) They should wear their non-Muslim dresses.

(xviii) They should not build houses near the Muslim houses.

(xix) They should not weep loudly on the death of their non-Muslims.

(xx) They should not buy Muslim slaves.

The foregoing lines reveal that Sayyid Ali Hamadani is the only sufi Philosopher amongst the political thinkers and sufis of Islam, who has briefly discussed the rights of the subjects and define the duties of a ruler for his Muslim and non-Muslim subjects.

We have briefly explained the views of Sayyid Ali Hamadani on politics. These views have been taken from the fifth chapter of his book, *Zakhiratul Maluk,* which is the true mirror of his political thoughts and a complete code of rules for a king. but we also find some material of his political philosophy from the sixth chapter of the book narrated above. Sayyid 'Ali Hamadani, has written this reason for the writing of this book and he says, that "this book was written on the requests made by the Sultans and kings.

Social justice is the central idea of his political philosophy and this noble characteristic distinguishes him from the other sufis and scholars of Islam. He has interpreted the Apostolic traditions before the kings and advises them that Islamic laws should be followed. He has narrated the basic guide-lines of an islamic government, the rights of the people, the stipulations of governance and the dangers involved in it and the stipulations of governance and the dangers involved i it and the importance of justice and benevolence. To analyse the political ideas of the Sayyid, we may compare it with philosophy of Al-Ghazzali (A. D. 1055-1111), who was born two centuries earlier. Both Sayyid 'Ali Hamadani and Al-Ghazzali have described ten rules for the conduct of the government and twenty rights of the public. This similarity shows that to some extent Sayyid 'Ali Hamadani accepted and followed the same views on politics which has been propounded by Al-Ghazzali. But Sayyid Ali Hamadani also explains twenty rights of the non-Muslims which are not described by any other sufi of Islam. This noble contribution of the Sayyid is an improvement on the concept of Al-Ghazzali in the field of politics. These rights of non-Muslims have been borrowed from the well known agreement of Hazrat Umar Farooq, which he has made for non-Muslims (or zimis). Thus Sayyid 'Ali Hamadani's greatness consists in having successfully added a new chapter in the duties of the rulers and the rights of the subjects which were over-looked by the other scholars and sufis of Islam like Al-Ghazzali.

The political ideas and views not only influenced the contemporary rulers but also convinced the people specially of Kashmir and generally of the Muslim world. Sayyid 'Ali Hamadani remained busy in Kashmir in teaching his political views to the people as well as to the Sultans which culminated in revolutionary and drastic changes in the valley of Kashmir.

V. THE WORKS OF SAYYID ALI HAMADANI

The Sayyid was not only a saint but a great scholar in Arabic and Persian too. He is said to have been the author of more than one hundred works on logic, philosophy, jurisprudence, political science, ethics, sufism and commentaries. The Sayyid also brought this books from Hamadan while migrating to Kashmir and established one Kutub-Khana (Library) in Khutlan and one Kutub Khana (Library) in Kashmir. His books were taught in the Madrasas as text-books. The Persian language and literature became popular in Kashmir and it replaced Sanskrit as a literary medium. As a result Persian exercised great influence on the developing Kashmir vocabulary. Shah Hamadani's influence also imparted mystic touch to Kashmir poetry and other works. A complete list of his works with annotation has been given below for scholars and readers interested in this field.

Persian Books

1. *Zakhiratul-Maluk ;* Zakhira-tul-Maluk is the best work on political ethics and the rules of good government in the Persian language. The book is the only source which helps us to come across lofty sayings and soul stirring thoughts of the Sayyid. It consists of ten chapters; which are : (1) Faith, (2) Duties of Man, (3) Virtue, (4) Rights and duties of parents, wives, husbands, children, etc.

(5) Rules of government, rights and duties of subjects, (6) Spiritual Kingdom, (7) Execution of the lawful and abstinence from the unlawful, (8) Gratitude and contentment, (9) Patience under visitations, (10) Condemnation of conceit and anger and excellence of humility and forgiveness. According to the Sayyid, this book was written as wished by the contemporary Sultans and Kings. Its title also verifies this fact. In all other books of Persian literature i.e., *Akhlaq-e-Nasiri* of Khawaja Nasir-ud-Din Tusi (A.H. 672-4), *Akhlaq-e-Jalali* of Allama Jalal-ud-Din Sherazi (A.H. 984), and *Akhlaq-e-Mohsini* of Mulla Husain Wai'z Kashifi (A. H. 914), *Zakhira-tul-Maluk* is a better work on ethics. It has been translated into four languages i.e., Urdu, Latin, French, and Turkish. Its manuscripts are available in various libraries i.e., Boldien Library, London; Central Library Tehran; Punjab University library; Bankipur Library; Aya sufia Library Istanbul; Berlin Library; India Office Library, London; Asiatic Society of Bengal, Calcutta; Cambridge University Library; and Princeton University Library.

2. *Rasalah Masharab al-Azwaq.* It is a sufistic commentary on Abu Hifs bin Al-Fariz Al-Misri's *Mamiya-e-Khamriya.* Its manuscripts are available in Punjab University Library; Central Library Tehran; British Museum; India Office Library; and National Library, Paris.

3. *Rasalah Istalahat-Sufia.* This Rasalah explains the sufic terms in a better way, and is available in the Punjab University Library.

4. *Rasalah Istalahat-Sufia.* It is quite different in meanings as well as interpretation from the Sayyid's *Rasalah Istalahat-sufia.* This treatise also explains sufic terms and expressions. It is available in British Museum London; Berlin Library; and Paris Library.

5. *Rasalaat Maraat al-Taibeen.* This twenty two page treatise was written on the request of Bahram Shah. Sultan of Badakhshan and Balkh. This Rasalah has four chapters concerning all to "Taubah".

Manuscripts of the Rasalah are being kept in the Central Library Tehran; British Museum; and Paris.

6. *Maktubat-e-Amiriyah. Rasalah Maktubat* contains Amir Kabir's letters to the various contemporary Sultans. The collection of his letters, named *Muktubat-e-amiriyah*, indicates that Sayyid 'Ali Hamadani had written twenty two letters in all to different Sultans of Central Asian countries. He addressed two letters to Sultan Muhammad Bahram Shah-b-Sultan Khan, the ruler of Balkh and Badakhshan; two letters to Sultan Qutb-ud-Din, the king of Kashmir; three letters to Sultan Ghias-d-Din, the ruler of Pakhli; three letters to Sultan Taghan-ud-Din, the ruler of Kohnar ; one letter to Sultan Ala-ud-Din, the ruler of Pakhli; four letters to Noor-ud-Din Jahfar Badakhshi; and other seven miscellaneous letters. The Sayyid had advised the Sultans particularly to do justice with their subjects in accordance with the teachings of the Holy Prophet laid down in the Holy Quran. These letters are available in Tehran Central Library; Tajkistan Library; British Museum, and Paris.

7. *Rasalah Fathia.* The Sayyid wrote this treatise on the request of Malik Sharaf-ud-Din Khyzer Shah in which he threw a light on Piety. This Fathia is found in British Museum.

8. *Aurad-e-Fathia.* It is a collection of all those Aurad which the Sayyid is said to have collected from one thousand and four hundred sufis of the age. It gives a conception of unity and his attributes. Its manuscripts are being kept in British Museum London; Leiden; Kapur Thala; Messur; Oriental Library; Asatic Society of Bengal; India Office Library, London; Paris; Iran; Libraries of Punjab University and Peshawar University.

9. *Rasalah Munajat.* It indicates the Sayyid's humble request to the All-Mighty God for His blessing. This Rasalah is being kept safely in British Museum, London, Paris, and Tajkistan.

10. *Rasalah Wardaat.* The Sayyid has explained the sufi terms in it and is available in British Museum London; National Library Tehran Central Library, Tehran University; and Paris National Library.

11. *Rasalah Hamadania.* This seven pages treatise denotes three meanings of the word hamadan; (i) It is the name of a tribe of Yamn,

(ii) It is the name of that city where he was born, (iii) The pronunciation 'Hamadania' is referred to "God". The Rasalah is available in Tehran; British Museum; and Karachi Museum.

12. *Rasalah Huqbat.* The Sayyid wrote this Rasalah on the request of Sultan Qutb-ud-Din, the then ruler of Kashmir, advising him to do justice with his subjects. Its manuscripts are being kept in Tehran and British Museum London.

13. *Rasalah Talqinia.* In this Rasalah the Sayyid has defined a sufi term 'Iradat'. It is available in Tehran National Library; and British Museum London.

14. *Rasalah Daudia.* This two pages treatise was written by the sayyid as requested by Daud, a 'Salik'. Sayyid 'Ali Hamadani greatly stresses on piety. Its manuscripts are being kept in Paris National Library; Tehran National Library; and British Museum.

15. *Rasalah Dah Qaidah.* In this treatise the Sayyid sets down ten spiritual stations which are essential for the sufi to travel on the mystic path. These are *Taubah* (Repentance), *Zuhd* (Detachment), *Tawakkal* (Trust in God), *Qanna'at* (Satisfaction), Uzlit, *Zikr* (Remembrance), *Tawajuh, Sabir* (Patience), *Maraqibah,* and *Riza* (Submission to the Divine Will). It is available in the Central Library Tehran University; British Museum London; and Berlin.

16. *Rasalah Aetqad-e-Amiriya.* In this treatise, the Sayyid states his faith and says that Islam has five organs i.e. *Tauhid Nimaz* (Prayer), *Roza* (Fasting),*Haj,* and *Zakat.* Its manuscripts are in British Museum; Paris and Tehran Libraries.

17. *Rasalah Darwaishia.* In this treatise, the Sayyid has interpreted the following *Ayat* of the Holy quran.

Besides, the Sayyid also criticises the kings of his age and says that the reign of kingdom are holding those peoples who have no knowledge of religion and who are slaves of worldy wealth. This Rasalah is available in British Museum, london; libraries of Iran, and Paris

18. *Rasalah Fatutia.* In this Rasalah, the Sayyid has discussed two sufi terms; "Akhuwat" and "Fatuwat." he also states about his line of "Fatuwat." It was published from Istanbol in 1961 and was edited by Dr. Riaz--in 1967 from Tehran University for his Ph.D. thesis. Its manuscripts are being kept in British Museum London; Libraries of Iran, paris and Istanbol.

19. *Rasalah Manamia.* This four pages pamphlet of the Sayyid explains the meanings of Sufi terms *'Alam-e-Misal Khiyal, Manam* and reality of *Rauya.* It is found in karachi Museum; British Museum, London; Libraries of Tehran, Tashkant, and Paris.

20. *Rasalah Tabqat-e-Mardum.* This Rasalah consists of two pages and defines various stages of a man through which he reaches its acme. Its description is simple, interesting and full of Quranic verses. It is being kept safely in British Museum, London; and Tehran University.

21. *Rasalah Mushkal Hal.* In this two pages pamphlet, the Sayyid throws a light on the recognition of Reality and describes various stages of 'ma'rafat.' The Rasalah is available from British Museum, London; Libraries of Tajkistan, Tehran and Paris.

22. *Rasalah Mashia Miria.* In this treatise, the Sayyid tells the methods of seeking destination and purification of soul. It is found in Paris; Tajkistan; British Museum London, and Tashkant.

23. *Rasalah Chehl Maqam-e-Sufia.* This Rasalah Chehl Maqam-e-Sufia explains forty spiritual steps for the sufistic journey on the path of Sufism. It is available in British Museum London.

24. *Rasalah Addab al-Muridin.* This six page pamphlet is connected with *Rasalah Safah-al-Addab* of Shaikh Najmuddin Kubra and consists of seven chapters. It is being kept safely in British Museum, London; Tashkant, and Paris.

25. *Rasalah Zikria.* In this Rasalah the Sayyid has narrated various groups of men, castes and human characteristics. It is available in British Museum, Tehran and Paris.

26. *Asnad Hulya Hazrat Mohammad* (peace be upon him). In this Rasalah the Sayyid implicits the bodily construction of the Holy Prophet.

It is available in British Museum, London and Tashkant

27. *Rasalah 'Aqlia.* This pamphlet consists of three chapters: Superiority of wisdom; five names of Wisdom; various kinds of Wisdom. It is interesting and impressive. It is found in British Museum, London; Iran, Tajkistan and Paris.

28. *Rasalah Muchalka.* Muchalka was a devout disciple of the Sayyid and this Rasalah indicates the devotion and affection of Muchalka to Sayyid. It is available from Tehran University Library.

29. *Rasalah Hal-al-Fasus.* It is a commentary on Ibn-ul-Arabi's *Rasalah Fasus al-Haqm.* It is available from British Museum, London; Bombay and Iran.

30. *Rasalah Haqiqat Nur-o-Tafasil An.* In this treatise, the Sayyid transpires the reality of light. It is available from Central Library, Tehran.

31.*Rasalah Insan Nama or Dar Mahrafat Soorat-o-Seerat-e-Insan.* It discusses the bodily and moral features of Man. Khwaja Ishaq Khutlani, a disciple of the Sayyid, compiled it after collecting the sayings of the Sayyid. It is found in British Museum, London; Iran, and Paris.

32. *Rasalah Minahaj-ul-'Arfin.* It consists of the sayings of Sayyid 'Ali Hamadani and recently it is published in Tazkara Shohra-e-Kashmir edited by Pir Hisamuddin Rashdi.

33. *Tarjmah Meradat Diwan-e-Hafiz Sheerazi.* In this eight pages pamphlet, the Sayyid translates Hafiz's Meradat and is published with Hafiz's Diwan.

34. *Haqiqat-e-Iman.* In this treatise, Sayyid 'Ali Hamadani shows a path of Salik through which he gets in faith. Explaining it the Sayyid

also uses the Quranic verses, Hadith of Holy Prophet and sayings of sufis. It is available in Tehran and Tashkant.

35. *Rasalah Makaram-e-Akhlaq.* This treatise was specially written by the Sayyid for his disciple Khwaja Ishaq. It is available in British Museum, London; Paris and Central Library, Tehran.

Mir Sayyid Ali etc. etc., are also included in the Persian works of the Sayyid.

Arabic Literature

1. *Asma'al-Hasana.* This ninety pages booklet indicates ninety-nine names of God, and their importance. It is found in Tehran, Tajkistan and Tashkant.

2.*Kitab Al-Movaddat Fil-Qurba.* It puts together traditions on affection among relatives. It is consisted on fourteen chapters. It was published from Bombay in A.H. 1310 and Syed Sharif Hussain Sabazwari translated and published it into Urdu from Lahore in A.D. 1961.

3. *Rasalah Al-Sab'in al-Munaqib.* It is consisted of seventy hadith relating to the superiority of Hazrat 'Ali. Its manuscripts are available from British Museum, London and Tehran.

4. *Rasalah Rauza tul Firdus.* In this treatise, the Sayyid has given the collection of Hadith taken from al-Hamadani's *Kitab-al-Firdus.* It consists of twenty chapters. It is available in British Museum, London and Tashkant.

5. *Rasalah Manazil ul-Salekin.* This treatise explains sufi terms and various stages. It consists of ten chapters and is available from British Museum, London; Tehran, and Paris.

6. *Rasalah Arba'in Amiriyah.* This Rasalah shows the forty Hadith relating to hazrat 'Ali and Abl-e-Bait. It is being kept in British Museum, London; Paris and Tashkant.

7. *Rasalah Al-Taubah.*The Sayyid discusses the reality of 'Taubah' in this two pages pamphlet, and is manuscripts are available in British Museum, London.

8. *Rasalah Khutab-i-Amiriyah.* It is a collection of two addresses of Sayyid which he made to his followers. Its microfilm is kept in British Museum, London.

9. *Rasalah Khwatariya.* In this treatise, the Sayyid describes about the various doubts of satan. It is found in British Museum, London; and Tashkant.

Other than above the Sayyid had also written *Rasalah Ulma-ud-Din, Rasalah Sifat-ul-Fuqara,* etc. etc.

From his other commentaries on Sufism, the following are very important:

1. *Rasalah Ser al-Talibin*
2. *Rasalah Nuriya*
3. *Rasalah Ma'ash al-salikin*
4. *Rasalah Kashf-ul-Haqaiq*
5. *Rasalah Israr-e-Wahi*
6. *Rasalah Silsilanama*

Besides, being a prolific prose writer, Sayyid 'Ali wrote Persian poetry. His ghazals or odes are naturally sufistic. The *Chehl Israr* is a small collection of religious and mystical poems. It is available in Tehran; British museum; London, Bankipur, Paris, Peshwar University libraries. Niaz 'Ali Khan published it from Amritsar in A.H. 1303.

VI. His Influence on Islamisation of the Society

> Professor Gibb remarks, "From the 13th century Sufism increasingly attracted the creative social and intellectual energies within the community to become the bearer or instrument of a social and cultural revolution".

The effects of such social and cultural revolution brought by the sufis are remarkable and far-reaching in the sub-continent. The unassuming ways of the mystics, their broad human sympathies, and the classless atmosphere of their 'Khanqahs' attracted one and all to come or receive blessing from them. Many persons with religious bent of mind, who could not be satisfied with the strict rules and regulations of the caste ridden Hindu Society found solace in the freedom and message of equality in Islam. Here they found a social order entirely different from their own. All lived, slept, and ate together. The sacred book was open and accessible to all demonstrating the islamic idea of 'Tauhid' as a working principle in social life, the medieval 'Khanqahs' became the spear-heads of the Muslim Culture. With the settlement of the Mussalmans in the sub-continent, conciliation and concord between the various culture-groups was not only a moral and intellectual demand but an urgent social necessity. The Muslim mystic contributed much "to liquidate social, ideological and linguistic barriers between the various culture-groups of the sub-continent and helped in the development of a common cultural outlook."

Sayyid 'Ali Hamadani commanded great influence and respect among the people because of his unique and simple views regarding religion, ethics and politics. Due to his learning and piety, he was looked upon with great reverence by all the contemporary Sultans in Kashmir. At the time of his third visit in A.D. 1383 the new religion (Islam) had not made any appreciable headway in the valley, even though the Sultans had been its followers. The majority of the people being still Hindu, the Muslims had nothing to distinguish them in dress, manners, and customs from their compatriots. In 'Ala'-ud-Din pura, for instance, there was a temple which was visited every morning by the Sultan and his Muslim subjects. To avert the reccurence of famine the king performed the 'Yajna'in the month of 'Bhadra', and distributed large gifts. In contravention of the islamic teachings he had two wives who were sisters. Sayyid Ali Hamadani disapproved of these non-Islamic practices and in accordance with his advice, Sultan Qutb-ud-Din divorced one of the sisters and retained the other. He also advised the Sultan to adopt the dress common in the Muslim countries. The Sultan paid a visit to the saint every day and held him in great respect. Sayyid 'Ali Hamadani gave him a cap, out of respect, the Sultan always wore under his crown. The subsequent Sultans followed the same practice until the cap was buried with the body of Fateh Shah according to the latter's will. It is said that someone prophesied the burial of the dynasty and it is curious coincidence that the dynasty actually came to an end with the rise of the Chaks. The influence of the Sayyid on the Sultans is also observed from the following incident. When Sayyid Ali Hamadani came to Kashmir for the first time, Shihab-ud-Din, the then monarch of the country, had gone out on an expedition against the ruler of Ohind, 16 miles above Attock. Qutb-ud-Din, the Sultan's brother, who subsequently succeeded him, was then acting for him. On hearing the news that Sayyid Ali hamadani was approaching Srinagar, Qutb-ud-Din went out with his Chief officials and received him with great warmth and respect and brought him and his followers to the city. After four months' stay, the Sayyid left for the scene of battle and persuaded the belligerents. Thus a terrible skirmish was averted. It was under the influence of the Sayyid, that Sultan Skindar banned all the intoxicants, sati and other evil practices.

He was also looked upon with great respect by all the contemporary Sultans of Central Asian countries. The collection of his letters, named *Maktubat-e-Amiriya.* shows that Amir Kabir Sayyid 'Ali Hamadani had written twenty two letters in all to different Sultans. He addressed two letters to Sultan Muhammad Bahram Shah-bin-Sultan Khan, the ruler of Balkh and badakhshan, two letters to Sultan Qutb-ud-Din, the king of Kashmir, three letters to Sultan Ghias-ud-Din, the ruler of Pakhli; three letters to Sultan Taghan-ud-Din, the ruler of Kohnar; one letter to Sultan 'Ala-ud-din, the ruler of Pakhli, (now in Hazara District), four letters to Noor-ud-Din Jahfar Badakhshi and other seven miscellaneous letters. In all these letters, the Sayyid 'Ali Hamadani had advised to Sultans as well as his followers to do justice with their subjects and act upon the teachings of the Holy Prophet laid down in the Holy Quran.

During his stay in Kashmir he found that the number of Muslims in Kashmir was very small while the majority of the population was Hindu. That the conversion of the valley to Islam was furthered by the presence of the Sayyid is undoubted. The newly converted people, of their own accord, changed the temples into mosques to consequence of their change of faith. Sayyid 'Ali Hamadani came in contact with the famous "yogin" of Kashmir, Lella Devi, who lived in the 14th century.

It was under the Sayyid's influence that she accepted Islam. In *Majalis-ul-Mumineen,* it is stated that, "She always wandered naked and was saying that she would dress her body, if she saw a man. Accidentally when one day, the Sayyid saw her, she started running by saying that that-day she had seen a man of great merit and that now she would not be naked.

Sayyid Ali Hamadani also came in contact with the other contemporary sufis of Islam. During the Sayyid's stay in Kashmir, Hazrat Makhdum Jahaniya Jahangusht, visited Kashmir in A.H. 748. Hazrat Makhdum Jahaniya Jahangusht was born in 707 A.H. and died in 789 A.H. He has a high place in the path of sufism and ranks distinguished among the sub-continent scholars of the time. But the contemporary works are silent about the meeting of both sufis.

During his visit of the sub-continent he was accompanied by Sayyid Ashraf Jahangir Sumnani (d. 808 A.H.), and met and obtained 'Khirqa' from Hazrat Sheikh Ahmed Yahya Muniri (d. 782 A.H.), according to the *Khulasa-tul-Munaqib,* Sayyid 'Ali Hamandani met fourteen hundred sufi saint of the time during his travel through the Muslim world.

In the literary field Shah Hamadan exercised great influence by his scholarly writings. He is the author of more than one hundred works on logic, philosophy, jurisprudence, political science, ethics, sufism and commentaries. *Zakhiratul Maluk* is his best work on political science and ethics which contains his ideas on government and the duties of subjects and the rulers. *Zakhira-tul-Maluk* is considered a unique book being a complete code of religious, moral and political rules. In all other books of Persian literature i.e. *Akhlaq-e-Nasiri* of Khwaja Nasir-ud-Din Tusi (A.H. 672-4), *Akhaq-e-Jalali* of Allama jalal-ud-Din Duoani Sherazi (A.H. 914) and *Akhtaq-e-Mohsini* of Mulla Hussain Wahiz Kashfi Hirati (A.H. 984), *Zakhira-tul Maluk* is a better work on ethics. The Sayyid also brought his books from hamadan while migrating to Kashmir and established one Kutub Khana (Library)in Khutlan and one kutub Khana (Library) in Kashmir. His books were taught in the Madrassas and included in the course The Persian language and literature became popular in Kashmir and it replaced Sanskrit as a literary medium. As a result Persian exercised great influence on developing the Kashmir vocabulary. Shah Hamadan's influence also imparted mystic touch to Kashmir poetry and other works.

Sayyid 'Ali Hamadani built 'Khanqahs', so as a working principle in social life. The medieval 'Khanqahs' were the spear-heads of Muslim culture. Shaikh Hamid-ud-Din Nagauri used to say that the purpose of constructing of a 'Khanqah' or a Masjid was to discipline the inner life of a man. This is no doubt true but these places had a social significance also and occupied a pivotal place in the community life of the Mussalmans. His co-workers, Mir Sayyid Haider, Sayyid Jamal-ud-Din, Sayyid Kamal Sani, Sayyid Jamal-ud-Din Alsi, Sayyid Fuknuddin and Sayyid Mohammad established hospices (mosques) all over the country which served as centres for the propagation of their religion in every nook and corner of Kashmir, and by their influence definitely furthered the acceptance of the faith of the Prophet of Arabia. The mosque of Hamadani called Khanqah-i-Mu'allah in Srinagar, which stands on the right bank of the Jhelum River on an irregular masonary foundations is a typical example of the wooden architecture of the valley. This type of mosque style became popular not only in Kashmir but also in other hill areas. Sayyid 'Ali Hamadani was responsible in reviving some well known Kashmir handicrafts. He brought seven hundred Sayyids with him who were expert in Persian Arts and Shawl weaving. During his stay for over two year he encouraged some shawl weavers to produce this fine textile. At that time ancient shaw industry in Kashmir was much in decay. Under the patronage of Sultan Qutb-ud-Din, the then ruler of Kashmir, the Persian companions of the Sayyid stimulated shawl industry.

Like other sufis of Islam, Sayyid 'Ali Hamadani took great interest in the social service of the community. He held the opinion that Muslims should limit their desires according to the dictates of religion, but they should not annihilate them like the Hindu Sadhus or Muslim Faqirs. He denounced the practice of crippling one's hands or feet, or unnecessarily inflicting bodily sufferings upon oneself, but he believed in a balanced life, a golden mean. As the sufis of islam always raised their voice against oppression and injustice, Sayyid 'Ali Hamadani never ceased exhorting the rulers to rule with justice and mildness. The just ruler, according to him, would be nearest to God on the Day of Judgment, while the severest punishment would be inflicted on the tyrants.

Shah Hamadan's influence on the society did not cease after his passing away in A. H. 786 but it was continued under the efforts of his sons and followers. A number of Muslim saints joined the group of Sayyid 'Ali Hamadani being impressed by his spiritual discipline. Nur-ud Din Jaffar Badakshi was the disciple of Sayyid 'Ali Hamadani, who was born in A.H. 743 at Rastaq Bazar, a territory of West Badakhshan. He migrated from Badakhshan to 'Ali Shah, a town of Khutlan in A.H. 773, and in the same year 'Ali Hamadani also came in Khutlan. Badakhshi, 'Akhi Haq Goi and Akhi Haji Tuti met Sayyid 'Ali Hamadani and since then Badakhshi began to attend Sayyid's meetings in the 'Khanqah.' Whenever Sayyid 'Ali Hamadani went on tour, the training and teaching were at the disposal of Jaffar Badakhshi. He is an authority on the work *Khulasa-tul-Manaqib,* a unique book of 8th century A.H. In which an overall survey of 'Ali Hamadani's life has been made. Another co-worker of Sayyid 'Ali Hamadani was Khwaja Ishaq Khutlani who entered his 'Halqa i-Iradat' in Khultan in A.D. 773. Being a resourceful man he was able to persuade his companion to come under the discipleship of Sayyid 'Ali Hamadani. When Timur Occupied the Khurasan, he did not only spare a moment to take action against Sayyid 'Ali Hamadani but also punished the Khwaja for having connection with Sayyid 'Ali Hamadani but also punished the Khwaja for having connection with Sayyid 'Ali Hamadani. Th Sayyid was so much impressed by Khwaja that he not only bestowed upon him Khirqa but also gave his daughter in marriage to him. One of closest pupils of 'Ali Hamadani was Shaikh Qawam-ud-Din Badakhshi, who accompanied his spiritual master in rest and action. Another Sufi Mir Sayyid Hussain Samnani, a follower of 'Ali Hamadani, hailed from Samnan, a city of Iran. Sayyid Hussain Samnani and Taj-ud-Din both were sent to Kashmir by Sayyid 'Ali Hamadani. Other prominent followers of Sayyid 'Ali Hamadani were:

(1) Sayyid Jalal-ud-Din Attai ;
(2) Sayyid Kamal;

(3) Sayyid Kamal Sani:
(4) Jamal-ud-Din Muhaddis;
(5) Sayyid Firuz;
(6) Sayyid Mohammad Kazim;
(7) Mir Rukn-ud-Din;
(8) Sayyid Ahmad Qureshi;
(9) Sayyid Mohammad Aziz Ullah;
(10) Sayyid Mohammad Murad;
(11) Pir Mohammad Qadri;
(12) Shaikh Suleman;
(13) Shaikh Ahmad;
(14) Sayyid Nahmatullah;
(15) Sayyid Baihiqi;
(16) Sayyid Han Posh;
(17) Sayyid Mahmood Azari Balkhi;
(18) Sayyid Muhammad Khawari.

The activities of the Sayyid's followers were not limited within Kashmir but the lands of central Asia also got influenced by their spiritual learnings.

In summing up his influence on the society we conclude that Sayyid 'Ali Hamadani was a great social reformer. He not only reformed the tone of society but also laid down the foundations of a new Kashmiri culture. He influenced the contemporary Sultans, Ulama, and Hindus through his deep scholarship and spiritual attainments. By his scholarship and literary contribution he was responsible in bringing about changes in the intellectual thinking. His social justice resulted in far-reaching influence in the society. Hence he is truely a pioneer in Islamising the society of Kashmir and consequently held a unique place in the history of Sufism and Muslim World.

VII. Conclusion

Sayyid 'Ali Hamadani was a sufi saint, devout preacher of Islam, great social reformer, scholar, philosopher, teacher and great man. Although the biographical data about Ali hamadani is very meagre but we find ample material on his thoughts and manners. *Zakhiratul*

Maluk projects a living image of Sayyid Ali Hamadani as a man of spiritual eminence, and a spiritual thinker of great profundity. We also come across lofty sayings in *Minhaj-ul-Arifeen,* embodying the Sayyid's wisdom and spiritual teachings.

Sayyid 'Ali Hamadani occupies a high rank among sufis. He was an emnbodiment of all that is best in Islam. He was initiated into sufism at the age of twelve and remained busy with it until his death. He was fortunate to have guidance from the eminent sufis of the time. In search of the spiritual Knowledge, Sayyid 'Ali Hamadani went on travels round the world because travelling was considered a part of Sufi discipline and training. His travel through the whole Muslim world completed his sufistic training and enabled him to meet eminent sufis. According to Amin Ahmed Razi, Shah-i-Hamadan travelled three times over the entire known world and met 1400 sufis and ulama. He is reported to have gone on pilgrimage to Mecca twelve times on foot. He prayed regularly and followed the injunctions of Holy Quran strictly in letter as well as in spirit. He stressed on purification, both out-ward (*Zahir*) and inward (*Batin*). The Sayyid was a thorough going mystic. He popularised sufism in Kashmir and assigned to mystics a highest place in the human society. He was an epitome of worldly knowledge and alumnii of 'Divine Spark. In his deep meditation ('Ibadat), he is said to have seen the Holy Prophet, who instructed him: 'O' son, Do not put yourself in bodily punishment, as you are already loved by God'. Sirajuddin 'Ali Khan Arzoo holds the view that Sayyid 'Ali Hamadani belongs to the early chain of chief saints. His acknowledgement in the field of spiritual knowledge is so high that no one could describe it in writing. Al-Hussain Ghiasuddin describes that Sayyid Ali Hamadani was an eminent scholar of gnosticism and secular knowledge.

Sayyid Ali Hamadani was a dedicated preacher of Islam. He fully devoted his life to the propagation of Islamic teachings and remained busy in it until his death. In this connection he visited several places like Muzdaqan, Khutalan, Balkh, Badakhshan, Khita, Yazd, Syria, Baghdad, Rum, Ceylon, China, India, Turkistan and Ladakh etc., etc. He came to Kashmir in A. H. 741 and ten thousan Kashmiris embraced

Islam. He built Khanqahs all over the country which served as centres for the propagation of Islam. The mosque of Hamadani called Khanqah-i-Mo'allah in Srinagar is one of them. He also trained his disciples like Mir Sayyid haider, Sayyid Jamal-ud-Din Alsi, Sayyid Kamal Sani, Sayyid Rukn-ud-Din and Sayyid Mohammad who preached Islam not only in Kashmir but also in other parts of the world. After the Sayyid's death his mission was continued by his followers and sons whose names are narrate above. Sayyid 'Ali Hamadani wrote letters to the contemporary Sultans of Balkh, Bukhara, Badakhshan, Pakhli and kohnar which played a great part in imparting the islamic teaching.

Sayyid 'Ali Hamadani was a great social reformer. He held the opinion that Muslims should limit their desires according to the dictates of Islam, but they should not annihilate them like the Hindu sadhus or Muslim faqirs. Like other sufis of islam, the Sayyid greatly stressed on doing justice. Social justice is the central idea of his political philosophy. In support of his ideas he interpreted the Apostolic traditions before the kings and advised them that Islamic laws should be followed. He has put forward the basic guidelines of Islamic state, the rights of the people, the stipulations of governance and the dangers involved in it. But in all he gave great importance to doing justice. The political and ethical views of Sayyid 'Ali Hamadam are co-related. In his ethical philosophy, the Sayyid gives great importance to the reformation of moral values of a man. *Husn-i-Khulq* is the foundation of his ethics and in this connection he says that God Almighty has created human beings on account of two reasons, the first is the appearance (*Surat-i-Zhir*) and the second is the inner self (*Sirat-i-Batin*). The appearance (*Surat-i-Zahir*) is styled creation (*Khalq*) and the nature (*Sirat*) is known as *Khulq*. The Sayyid also describes virtue and vice of a man but he held that the beauty of creation (*Husn-i-Khalq*) is based on the balancing role of both virtue and vice. The ethical views of Sayyid 'Ali Hamadani rest on the study of the Holy Quran and the Sunnah. His political and ethical philosophy has been compared with the philosophy of Hazrat Data Ganj Bakhsh and Al-Ghazzali.

Shah Hamadan was not only a saint but a great scholar in Arabic and Persian too. He is the author of more than one hundred works on logic, philosophy, jurisprudence, political science, ethics, sufism, and commentaries. *Zakhiratul-Maluk* is his work on political science and ethics and contains his ideas on government and the duties of subjects and the rulers. Among other prominent works of Sayyid 'Ali Hamadani in Persian and Arabic are *Rasalah Nuriyah* which is a tract on contemplation. *Rasalah Maktubat* contains Amir Kabir's letters. *Dar Ma'rifat Surat-o-Seerat-i-Insan* discusses the bodily and moral features of man. *Dar Haqa'iq Taubah* deals with the real nature of repentance. *Hal al-Nasus Ala-Fasus* is a commentary on Ibn-ul-Arabi's *Rasalah Istalahat* which is a treatise on sufi terms and expressions. *Dah qua'idah,* gives ten rules of contemplative life. *Kitab Al-Movaddat fil-Qurba* puts together traditions on affection among relatives. *Arba'een Amiriyah* is forty traditions on man's future life. *Manazil-us-Salekin* is on sufism. *Aurad-e-Fathia,* gives a conception of the unity of God and his attributes. Besides being a prolific prose writer, Sayyid Ali wrote Persian poetry. His ghazals or odes, are naturally sufistic. The *Chehl-Israr* is a small collection of religious and mystical poems. The Sayyid gave mystical touch to Kashmiri poetry and other works. The Sayyid brought his books with him from Hamadan and built one Kutb Khana (Library) in Khutalan and one Kutb Khana (Library) in Kashmir. The Persian language and literature became popular in Kashmir. Through his scholarly writings Shah-i-Hamadan brought about a new intellectual awakening in Kashmir.

He was also a pioneer in reviving some well known Kashmiri handicrafts. His seven hundred companions were expert in Persian Arts and shawl industry. Sayyid 'Ali Hamadani encouraged some shawl weavers to produce this fine textile. With the co-operation of Sultan Qutb-ud-Din, the ruler of Kashmir, the Sayyid's companions popularised shawl industry in Kashmir.

G.M.D. Sufi has fixed his date of death on Tuesday, the 5th of Zilhijja 786 A. D./A.H. 1385. After his stay in Kashmir of about two and a half years, he went to Ladakh in 783 A.H. enroute for Turkistan and returned to Kashmir in 785 A. H./1383 A.D. But he had to leave Kashmir on account of ill-health and stayed at Pakhli for ten days at the request of the ruler. There is difference of opinion about Sayyid 'Ali's death among the historians. G.M.D. Sufi claims that from Pakhli Shah-i-Hamadan repaired to the vicinity of Kunar where, after a short stay, he had a relapse on the last of Zilhijja 786 A.H. On Tuesday, the 5th of Zilhijja, he drank water several times and on the night of the same day he breathed his last at the age of 72. But P.N.K. Bamzai in his book, *A History of Kashmir,* says that while at Pakhli in Hazara District he had a relapse and passed away in 1384 A. D. On his death-bed *Bismillah-ir-Rahman-ir-Rahim* was on his lips, and this strangely enough, gives the date of his demise. The *Khazinatul Asfiya* (ii, 293) explains how it came about that Sayyid Ali was buried in Khutlan. He died in Hazara (Pakhli) and there the Pakhli Sultan wished to have him buried, but his disciples, for some unspecified reason, wished to bury him in Khutlan. In order to decide the matter they invited the Sultan to remove the bier with the corpse upon it. It could not be stirred from its place, when however, a single one of the disciples tried to remove it, he alone was able to lift it, and to bear it away on his head. Hence the burial in Khutlan. The death occurred in 786 A. H./1384 A.D. Abul Fazl says that Amir Sayyid 'Ali Hamadani died here (Bajaur near Swat) and his dead body was conveyed to Khutlan according to his will. But Babur writes :

> 'Mir Sayyid 'Ali Hamadani coming here (Kunar-with-Nur-gal in Kafiristan) as he journeyed, died two miles above Kunnar. His disciples carried his body to Khutlan. A shrine was erected at the honoured place of his death of which I made the circuit (*Tawaf*) when I came and took Chagan-Sarai in 920 A. H./1514 A. D.

Sayyid 'Ali Hamadani was a versatile genius and was one of the most remarkable and luminous personality of the 14th century Islam. His teachings were the essence of religious perfection of faith and basis for good conduct. Uncorrupted by the court life and unspoiled by wealth and power, he influenced the rank of Muslim society, improved its tones and helped in the evolution of Muslim mass culture in Kashmir. G.M.D. Sufi calls Sayyid 'Ali Hamadani, as the 'Apostle of Kashmir', on account of his contribution and work in the valley of Kashmir. Dara

Shakoh, writes in his book *Safina-tul-Auliya* that the growth and development of Islam in the valley of Kashmir had begun at the time of 'Ali's arrival. In the Encyclopedia of Islam the Sayyid has been called a sufi saint and the apostle of Kashmir. Hence, Sayyid Ali Hamadani, and his followers were responsible to spread Islamic teachings in the valley of Kashmir.

7

Shaykh Diya Al-Din Nakhshabi his Life and Persian Works

SAJIDULLAH TAFHIMI

Early centuries of Muslim rule in the subcontinent, particularly the seventh and eight centuries of the *Hijra* were of great importance for the development of Persian language and literature in this region.

After the annexation of the Punjab and Kashmir to his Sultanate by Yamin al-Dawlah Sultan Mahmud of Ghazna (388-421 A.H./998-1030 A.D.) Multan and Lahore became seats of Muslim culture and centres for the development and propagation of Persian in this region. Persian which was the mother tongue of the new conquerors became the official language of the Government. Since then Persian language made a rapid progress and many eminent scholars, including *sufis,* came into existance who wrote valuable books on various subjects in Persian.

Shaykh Diya al-Din Nakhshabi was also one of the notable mystics who led his scholarly life through the first half of the 8th century A.H. Besides being a *sufi* he was also an author and translator of several valuable books in Persian or various subjects.

Ancestors

It is rather unfortunate that no mention has been made of his ancestors or of events of his life in any book dealing with the biography of *sufi* saints. However, Muhammad Akhatar Dihlawi, an author of recent times, has linked him genealogically without mentioning his source, to Hadrat Sa'd b. Zayd (May Allah be pleased with him) a famous Companion of the Holy Prophet (May peace and blessings of Allah be on him) and one of the *'Asharah-i-Mubashsharah* (the Blessed Ten). But no other book in hand supports this statement. However, there may be some indication to this effect in Nakhshabi's own treatise entitled *Asharah-Mubashsharah* of which no copy has so far been found in famous libraries.

Name

Most of the biographers have mentioned his name as " Diya' al-Din" and some of them have recorded it only as " Diya ". The *Shaykh* himself in his works has mentioned his name as " Diya-i-Nakhshabi". For example in the preface of *Silk al-Suluk.*

From his statement, it is evident that his actual name was only "Diya' " to which later on was added al-Din to make it "Diya' al-Din."

Place of Birth

Regarding Nakhshabi's birth place there are the following two statements :

1. According to *Lughat Namah* and *The Encyclopaedia of Islam* and a few others, he was born at Nakhshab. The following verse of Nakhshabi himself, quoted by the author of *Tadhkirah al-Wasilin.*
2. According to *Nata'ij al-Shu'ara* as quoted in *Tadhkirah al-Wasilin,* he was born at Badaun. This conclusion of *Nata'ij al-Shu'ara* is based, as he says, on the fact that Nakhshabi has used Hindi words and Hindi names of medicines in this book entitled *Juz'iyat wa Kulltyat.*

In our opinion, the conclusion of *Nata'ij al-Shu'ara* on the basis stated above is not admissible, because brought up and educated in India it was but natural that Nakhshabi should use Hindi words and medical terms in his books. His *nisbah Nakhshabi* which he uses freely in hundreds of his verses scattered throughout his works is a strong proof of "Nakhshab" being his birth-place.

Date of Birth

Nakhshabi's date of birth is not known. However in view of the fact that that he has been a student of Mawlana Shihab al-Din of Mehmarah, a celebrated and erudite scholar and poet of his age, whose death too place before 695 A.H./1295 A.D. and according to *Tadhkirah al-Wasilin,* in 686 A.H./1287 A.D. It may be persumed that Nakhshabi was born in the third quarter of the seventh century A.H.

Education

Nakhshabi, most probably, received early education at his birth-place Nakhshab, and then after migrating from there, continued and completed his studies in India. But no details of his education are available. However, it is evident from the remarks of some of his biographers and also from critical study of his own works that Nakhshabi had not only completed higher education in the current branches of religious learning i.e. *Qur'an, Tafsir, Hadith, Tasawwuf,* etc., but also acquired proficiency in other fields like Persian and Arabic literature, medicine, prose writing and poetry. Besides acquiring perfection in Arabic and persian languages, he had also learnt Sanskrit language. Accord to *Tadhkirah al-Wasilin,* he also had some knowledge of music. Abundant quotation from useful mystical sayings and verses of various *Sufi* poets and narration of their spiritual experiences in his works indicate Nakhshabi's extensive and deep study of *tasawwuf* and its literature.

Teachers

Only Shihab al-Din Mehmarah of Badaun is known as Nakhshabl's teachers. According *Tadhkirah al-Wasilin* there was a close and intimate relationship between them and Nakhshabi even after the death of Mehmarah, had been seeking guidance and receiving favours from his grave.

Professional Life

After completion of studies Nakhshabi engaged himself in producing literary works in Badaun. He almost spent his whole life in seclusion and wrote valuable books an treatises in Persian on different subjects.

During his stay in Badaun, as apears from some happenings of his life described in *Juz'iyat wa Kulliyat,* Nakhshabi had adopted the profession of *Tababat* (Practice of indigerious medicine) as a means of livelihood. Besides medical treatment he also provided spiritual healing to his patients.

Initiation into the Chishti Order

Nakhshabi, as it is evident from his works, seems to have a natural inclination to *tasawwuf.* But any detailed account of this place of his life is not available. According to *Tadhkirah-i-Husayni* and *Subh-i-Gulshan,* Nakhshabi had been occasionally attending assemblies of Shaykh Nizam al-Din Awliya (d. 725 A.H.). It was the *Shaykh's* company which inspired and enabled him to have his spiritual experience and receive Divine blessing and favours. Consequently he was initiated into the Chishti order by Shaykh Farid al-Din Naguri after 730 A.H., when the *Shaykh* had migrated from Nagur to Delhi in the reign of Sultan Muhammad Tughluq (725-752 A.H./1324-1351 A.D.).

Nakhshabi remained in his service for many years and, striving hard under his his guidance, attained to high spiritual levels. *Khazinah al-Asfiya* mentions him as one of the greatest Khalifahs of the *Shaykh.*

Some biographers have confused Shaykh Farid al-Din Naguri with the famous Shaykh of Pakpattan (in West Punjab) namely Shaykh Farid al-Din Masu'ud Ganj-i-Shakar, generally known as Baba Farid (d. 664 A.H.), who was the successor of Shaykh Qutb al-Din Bakhtyar Kaki (d. 633 A.H.).

According to Sa'id Nafisi, a renowned scholar of Iran, Nakhshabi was attached to the courts of khalji emperors, specially Qutb al-Din Mubarak Shah (716-720 A.H.). But this statement, supported by none, seems to be merely based on that of Nakhshabi given in the preface of *Juz'iyat wa Kulliyat,* describing Qutb al-Din Mubarak Shah as the reigning sovereign.

Last Day and Death

Nakhshabi after leading a long secluded life, died in 751 A.H 1350 A.D. and was buried in Badaun. His tomb is situated there on a terrace by the side of the grave of Shibab al-Din Mehmarah.

His Works

Nakhshabi, as already mentioned, spent most of his life in producing literary works on various subjects. All of his known works, are basically in prose. Although Nakhshabi possessed a fine poetic taste also and all his works contain his own Persian verses, yet he has not left any seperate collection of his verses of any size. All of his works, known so far, are in Persian, and are as follows :

1 *Tuti Namah*
2 *Gulriz*
3 *Silk al-Suluk*
4 *Juz'iyat wa Kulliyat*
5 *Sharh-i-Du'a-i-Suryani*
6 *'Asharah-i-Mubushsharah*
7 *Anis al-'Ashiqin*
8 *Risalh-i-Suluk*
9 *Ladhdhat al-Nisa'*

Brief introduction of these books is given below :

1. Tuti Namah

Tuti Namah is the most popular and the best known of Nakhshabi's works. It comprises 52 tales related by a parrot describing immodesty, malice and sexual perversity of women. These tales are based on the Sanskrit *Sugasaptati*, a collection of tales about women, literally meaning seventy tales related by the parrot.

In seventh century A.H. Some unknown person had translated 52 selected tales from Sanskrit original into Persian. This translation is only known from its mention in the preface of Nakhshabi's *Tuti Namah* while referring to some one of his patrons without mentioning his name, thus:

Nakhshabi's *tuti Namah,* as appears from its preface, based on the above mentioned translation. As the earliest translation was very verbose, artless and unattractive, Nakhshabi, on the request and persuasion of the said patron, rewrote this book in an artifical style of charming ornate prose, replacing a few tales which seemed to him more obscene and unintresting by better one.

Later biographers like Sa'id Nafisi, an eminent ranian scholar, and Shaykh Muhammad Ikram (the author of *'Ab-i-Kawthar* and *Armaghah-i-Pak*) and others have mistakenly supposed Nakhshabi's *Tuti Namah* to be a direct translation from Sanskrit. But Nakhshabi's own statement in this regard indicates that it was not a direct translation from the Sanskrit original but, as already said, it was simply reproduction of the first Persian version referred to above. However, it is possible that the original *Sugasaptati* may have been before Nakhshabi.

Nakhshabi completed this work in 730 A.H./1339 A.D. and styled it, in the preface, *Hikayat al-Riwayat.* But this book, most probably in view of its contents, became known and popular with the title of *Tuti Namah* (The Book of Parrot).

Tuti Namah is one of the most popular and widely read books of the world. This is why, since Nakhshabi's death numerous translations, abridgements and selections of it have been done and widely published in several famous languages and besides printed copies, its manuscripts are seen in almost all famous libraries of the world.

Some of the well-known versions of Nakhshabi's *Tuti Namah* are as follows:

(a) Persian :

1. Abu'l-fadl Mubarak 'Allami (d. 1011 A.H. / 1602 A.D.). by command of Mughul Emperor Akbar (963-1014 A.H./ 1556/1605 A.D.), rendered *Tuti Namah* in a more easy and simple version under the same title.
2. In 998 A.H. Hamidi Lahori (d. after 998 A.H.) versified 30 tales of *Tuti Namah* and two stories of *Gulistan* of Sa'di, under the same title.
3. In 11th century A.H. an abridged Persian translation of selected 35 tales was done by Sayyid Muhammad Qadiri. This translation is the most popular of all versions of *Tuti*

Namah. Later versions and selections are mostly based on it. This translation was published in 1800 A.D. from Calcutta and in 1801 A.D. from London, and several editions from Bombay.

4. Some little known person namely 'Ibad Allah rewrote *Tuti Namah* in a very simple and insipid Persian in 1282 A.H./ 1865 A.D.

(b) Dakhkhani

1. A famous poet of the Deccan namely Ghawwasi did a versified translation of *Tuti Namah* into Dakhkhani language which was completed in 18th October 1639 A.D. and published in 1951 A.D.
2. Second versified translation into Dakhkhani language was done by another famous poet of tht language namely, Ibn-Nishati in 1076 A.H./1665 A.D.

(c) Turkish

Turkish translation of *Tuti Namah* was done by Sari 'Abd Allah Effendi in reign of Sultan Sulayman A'zam of Turkey (926/974 A.H./ 1520-1566 A.D.) and published in July 1838 A.D. from Bulak and in 1256 A.H./1840 A.D. from Constantionople.

(d) English

M. gerrans did a free translation of *Tuti Naman* in English entitled "Tales of a Parrot", and published its 12 stories in 1792 A.D. from London. It was the very first version of *Tuti Namah* in a European language which introduced the book and its author to Europe.

(e) German

(i) A German translation of 12 stories with their original text, was rublished by H. Bockhans in 1843 A.D. from Leipzing.

(f) French

According to E. Berthels "there is a French translation in MSS in Munich". But he did not mention any particulars of it including the name of its translator.

(g) Russian

E. Berthels has translated the book into Russian but it is so far unpublished.

2. Gulriz

Gulriz is a novel dealing with a ficticious love story, the main characters of which are Prince ma'sum Shah son of Tayfur Shah (King of Nakhshab) Nushlab (the daughter of fairy queen) and 'Ajab Malik (the prince of Turkistan).

No mention of this novel was made in any book till its publication in 1912 A.D. In later period, besides *Catalogue of* Persian MSS in the Library of the India Office, only a few modern biographers like 'Ali Akbar Dehkhuda, Sa'id Nafisi Sabah al-Din 'Abd al-Rahman, Shaykh Muhammad Ikram and E. Berthels have referred to this book. It appears that *Gulriz* came to be known through its publication in 1912 A.D.

'Allama 'Ali Akbar Dehkhuda, a prominent scholar of Iran has stated on the basis of *Pamus al-'Alam* (Turkey) that *Gulriz,* like *Tuti Namah,* has been translated from Hindi into Persian. But this is not correct. *Gulriz* was written in original by Nakhshabi himself as he in the preface of the book.

Gulriz was edited by 'Agha Muhammad Kazim Shirazi and R.F. Azoo from the rare manuscript which was own by col. D.D. Phillott, and was published by the Asiatic Society of Bengal, Calcutta in 1912 A.D. comprising 191 pages of text and two additional pages of introduction in English by 'Agha Muhammad Kazim Shirazi. In this brief intorduction he says:

> "The rare manuscript from which the present edition is edited, is the property of Colonel D.C. philot:..... The MS. is written in a beautiful naskh hand on Kashmiri hand-made brown paper, contains the finally executed miniature. It is bound in old embossed leather cover with the binder's name Ziauddin Pishawari, on the top. It measures 10 by 6-1/2 and contains four hundred and seven pages, eleven lines in every page. No date appears in

the MS. It appears to be about three hundred years old and is well preseized. This is perhaps the only copy existing in India. The India Office Library contains only a defective and worm eaten copy (vide Ethe No. 2852). C. Stuart in his catalogue of the late Tippoo Sultan's Library mentions a copy of this work. This work is also mentioned by W. Perstch in Z.D.M.G. XXI, p. 511.

Thirty-three headings have been given through out the book of which the following four headings have been given to four sections of the preface :

After these four preliminary sections the story, containing 29 headings, begins with

The book ends on the following short prayer corresponding to the ending of the story:

Gulriz, basically, is a prose work but considerable portions of it contain verses also, scattered throughout the book, numbering more than one thousand Persian verses and about 20 Arabic ones.

Although *Gulriz,* as already mentioned, appears at first sight, to be merely a common fliction but its importance in the history of Persian literature of the Subcontinent may be based on two main facts: firstly for being one of the oldest novels (most probably the first one) written in Persian in this subcontinent, and secondly, for its remarkably beautiful and unsurpassed style.

This novel, it appears, has not been written merely to entertain the readers. The author's aim seems to be their moral instruction and to provide them, to a certain extent, with literary, mystical, and on occasions with scientific information. This is why, the author, on certain occasions, appears to be a straight forward preacher of ethics, using abundantly Qur'anic Verses, Traditions of the Holy Prophet (P.B.U.H.), Arabic maxims proverbs and quotations and has discussed the glory of man in contrast to other creature of God specially the jinns and fairies. Medical and astronomical terms have also been used in the book which not only indicates the author's deep knowledge of these sciences, but also adds to the reader's information.

3 Silk al-Suluk

Silk al-Suluk is the second best known of Nakhshabi's works. This book is on *tasawwuf* and is considered one of the early and very significant prose works produced on Islamic mysticism in the subcontinent.

Besides an introduction containing respectively, *Hamd, Salat* and the reason for writing and naming the book as *Silk al-suluk,* the author divides it into 151 short chapters. Each chapter has been styled *Silk* and each *Silk* has been specified with serial numbers, such as *Silk 1, Silk* 2 and *Silk 3.*

First sixteen *Silks* specifically deal with mystical terms only while the *Silks* 17 to 138 comprise concise description of various topics. Including interpretation of numerous terms of *tasawwuf.* Definition and explanation of terms and subtle points of *taswwuf* have been given with clarity in the light of the Holy *qur'an* Traditions of the Holy Prophet and sayings of the eminent *sufis.*

The mysticals terms interpreted and explained in the book are as follows :

Silk 1 : Tawbah; Silk 2 : Maqam; Silk 3 : Hal; Silk 4 : Wajd; Silk 5 : Tawajud; Silk 6 : Qabd and Bast : Silk 7 : 'Um al-Yaqin; Haqq al-Yaqin, 'Ayn al-Yaqin, Muhadarah, Mushahadah Mukashafah, Haybat and 'Uns : Silk 8 : Lawa'ih, Lawami 'Tawali'Ghaybat and Hudur; Silk 9 : Mahw, Ithbat, Fana and Ecqa : Silk 10 : Talwin, Tamkin; Silk 11 : Sahw, Sukr, Jam', I'rad, Hijab, Tafasul, Salb al-Mazid, Salb-i-Qadim, Tasalli and 'Adawat; Silk 14 : Mu'jizah, Karamat, Ma'rifat and Istidraj; Silk 15 : Nafs-i-Shahwani, Ruh-i-Nurani and Qalb-i-Rabbani; Silk 16: Shukr, Du'a and Rida; Silk 18 : Al-Ghani al-salih, Al-Kafir al-Faqir, Al-Kafir al-Ghani and al-Mu'min al-Faqir; Silk 33 : Zindah, Murdah and Zindah-i-Murdah; Silk 39 : 'Ubudiyyat; Silk 41 : Yaqin; Silk 54 : Murawwat; Silk 56 : Faqr; Silk 60: Ita'at-i-Lazimah, Ita'at-i-Muta'ddiyah; Silk 64 : Zakat-i-Sari'at, Zakat-i-Tariqat, Zakat-i-Haqiqat, Zakat Wiqayay and Sadaqah : Silk

89: Mard-i-'Ali Himmat Silk 98 : Khatarah and 'Azimat; Silk 104 : 'Aqil; Silk 105 : Huzn; Silk 111: Tawadu and Mutawadi' Silk 119 : Nafs-i-Mutma'innah, Nafs-i-Lawwamah and Nafs-i-Ammarah: Silk 115 : Riyadat; Silk 118 : Mard-i-Hushyar; Silk 125 : mard-i-Kamil; Silk 126 : Zuhd; Silk 132 : Hurriyat Silk 133 : Tafakkur; Silk 134 : Kufah-i-Nashizah and Kulah-i-Latiyah : Silk 138; Bandah-i-Kha'if.

Silks from 139 to 150 contain short biographical notices and spiritual status of the following prominent well-known *sufis* saints:

Silk 139: Hadrat Uways Qarni (d. 32 or 37 A.H./653 or 657 A.D.).

Silk 140: Hadrat hasan basri (d. 110 A.H./728 A.D.)

Silk 141: Hadrat Ibrahim Adham (d. 162 A.H./778 A.D.)

Silk 142: Hadrat 'Abu Yazid Bistami (d. 261 A.H./874 A.D.)

Silk 143: Hadrat Junayd Baghdadi (d.297 A.H./910 A.D.)

Silk 144: Hadrat 'Abd Ullak Khafif (d. 371 A.H./981 A.D.)

Silk 145: Hadrat Husayn b. Mansur Hallaj (d.209 A.H./825 A.D.)

Silk 146: Hadrat Rabi'ah Basri (d.185 A.H./801 A.D.)

Silk 147: Hadrat Dhu'l. Nun Misri (d. 205 A.H./821 A.D.)

Silk 148: Hadrat Ma'ruf-i-Karkhi (d. 200 A.H./815 A.D.)

Silk 149: Hadrat Thufyan-i-Thawri (d. 161 .AH./778 A.D.)

Silk 150: Hadrat Shaqiq Balkhi (d. 194 A.H./809 A.D.)

The last *Silk* No. 151 contains short description of 426 *Mardan-i-Ghayb* with their number as under:

(i) *Nuqaba* (300 nos); (ii) *Nujaba* (70nos); (iii) *Abdal* (40 nos); (iv) *Akhyar* (7 nos); (v) *'Imad* (5 nos.); (vi) *Awtad* (3 nos.); *Ghawth* (one).

Nakhshabi briefly discussed in this book almost all important problems of *tasawwuf* in a very simple and explicit style. Eucidating minute points in a concise and brief way, he quotes profusely from the Holy *Qur'an,* traditions of the Holy Prophet (P.B.U.H.), sayings of the celebrated *sufis* and sometime Arabic verses and maxims in support of his concepts and beliefs. He makes his points more clear by narrating short stories most of famous *sufis.* It is remarkable that 151 *silks* contain about 300 stories and parables.

Nakhshabi's style in this book is charming and expressive, and it becomes more attractive and persuasive when the reader, in each *silk,* is addressed with the words (Listen, listen) or (my dear). Each *silk* ends on a beautiful *ruba'i* containing the gist of the subject discussed in it.

Silk al-Suluk has been considered as an important and authentic book of *Tasawwuf* which has been used by later writers on this subject as one of their sources. A large number of its manuscripts exist in most of the libraries of Subcontinent and also in the famous oriental libraries of the world. Original book has been published from Delhi in 1895 A.D. and 1911 A.D. Its Urdu translation has also been published from Lahore by Malik Channan Din, Alla wala ki qawmi dnkan, Lahore.

4 Kulliyat-wa-Juzi'yat

Kulliyat wa Juz'iyat is the fourth important of nakhshabi's works, written on the subjects of *tasawwuf* and medicine. This book deals with the description of forty various parts of the human body as the noblest creature of God and their physical benifits and spiritual gains.

Nakhshabi started compilation of this book in the reign of Qutb al-Din Mubarak Shah (716-720 A.H./1316-1320 A.D.) whom, in the preface of the book mentions as the reigning sovereign, and after *hamd and n't* praises him in sixty two couplets.

The book is divided into 40 sections. Each section, styled as *Namus,* contains description of the best known qualities and the excellence of distinct parts of the human body. This is why this book is also known.

The parts of human body described in the book are as follow:

1	Hair	2	Head	3.	Brain	4.	Forehead
5	Eyebrow	6	Eyelid	7	Eyelash	8	Eye
9	Tear	10	Nose	11	Cheek	12	Ear
13	Tress	14	Beard	15	Lip	16	Mouth
17	Teeth	18	Tongue	19	Chin	20	Face
21	Mole	22	Throat	23	Neck	24	Back
25	Bones	26	Arm	27	Vein	28	Blood
29	Hand	30	Finger	31	Nail	32	Breast
33	Heart	34	Soul	35	Side	36	Belly
37	Waist	38	Knee (zanu)	39	Leg	40	Foot

This book is still unpublished. However its manuscripts are available in various libraries, a few of which are as follows :

(i) National Museum of Pakistan, Karachi (Nos. NM. *1957.909/27,* NM. 1965.213 and NM. 1972.173);

(ii) Panjab University Library, Lahore (Shirani Collection ; No 1149)

(iii) India Office Library, London (No. 2034)

(iv) British Museum, London (No. Add. 26300).

5. Sharh-i-Du'a-i-Suryani

Du'a-i-Suryani (or Syriac Prayer), also known as *Surah-i-Suryani,* is, originally, a part of the holy *Zabur* (i.e. Psalms of David), and according to *Sanawat al-Atqiya* this *surch* in *zabur* is similar to *Surah-i-Rahman* in the *Qur'an.* Hadrat 'Abd Allah Ibn-i-'Abbas (May Allah be pleased with him) one of the celebrated companions of the Holy prophet Muhammad (P.B.U.H), had translated it in Arabic verses, beginning :

Nakhshabi wrote an exegesis of it in Persian in 728 A.H./1327-8 A.D.

In *Nuzhat al-Khawatir* this book has been mistakenly mentioned with two different titles-i.e.—as two separate books.

A rare manuscript copy of this tract exist in the Panjab University Library, Lahore, (Vide Shirani Collection, No. 3758/725).

6. 'Asharah-Mubashsharah

This work its known only from its mention in *Akhbar al-Akhyar, Sanawat al-Atqiya, Khazinah al-Asfia* and a few other books. But unfortunately, neither any manuscript copy of it has so far been traced out in libraries, nor any account, except its name, is avaliable in any of the sources in hand. However, its title reveals that this book might have contained the biographical notices of *Asharah-i-Muhasshshrah* (the blessed Ten).

7. Anis al-'Ashiqin

This book is known from its mention in *Fahrist-i-Makitutat-i-Shirani* according to which a rare manuscript of its exists in the Panjab University Library, Lahore (Shirani Collection, No. 4403/1352).

8 Risalah-Suluk

This treatise is also known from its mention in *Fahrist-i-Makhtutat-i-Shirani* according to which a rare manuscript copy of it exists in the Panjab University Library, Lahore (Shirani Collection, No. 4638/1588/4).

9. Ladhdhat al-nisa

This is the Persian version of the famous Indian book "Koka Shastra", dealing with sex and its problems.

The attribution of this treatise to Nakhshabi has been denied by Prof. Khaliq Ahmad Nizami in his book namely *Tarikh al-Maqalat.*

Several MS. copies of this exist in the National Museum of Pakistan, Karachi (vide Nos. NM. 1958.242; NM. 1976.47; NM. 1978.19) and Diyal Singh Trust Library, Lahore (No. MS. 386).

8

Hadrat Sayyid Jalal Mir Surkh Bukhari of Uch Sharif

MIR HASAN ALI

His Ancestry

Hadrat Sayyid Jalal Mir Surkh Bukhari was a progeny of Imam Ali Al-Naqi and a genuine descendant of the Holy Prophet Muhammad (Peace be upon him). This fact is unanimously acknowledged by all the historians and choroniclers be they Sunni or Shi'i. Qadi Nur-Allah Shustri, the famous Ahi'i Scholar and writer of the times of Emperors Akbar and Jahangir in his well-Known work *'Majalis al-Mu'minin'* has at one place, while Peaking of him, given his name as 'Sayyid Jalal'. As per the Family Tree of Sayyid Jalal available with the present writer, Sayyid lalas is a descendant of the Holy Prophet through twenty-one lines, as under :

> Sayyid Jalal son of Sayyid 'Ali Abu Mu Mu'id son of Sayyid Jalal son of Sayyid Taqi son of Sayyid Muhammad son of Sayyid Zayn al-'Abidin son of Sayyid Baquar son of Sayyid Jafar son of Styid Ahmed son of Sayyid Isma'il son of Sayyid 'Abd Allah son of Ali Asghar son of Ja'far son of Imam 'Ali Al-Naqi son of Imam Muhammad Al-Taqi son of Imam 'Ali Al-Rala son of Imam Musa Al-Kazim son of Imam Ja'far Ai-Sadiq son of Imam Muhammad Al-Baqar son of Imam 'Ali Zayn al-'Abidin son of Imam Husayn son of Hadrath 'Ali and Fatimah daughter of the Holy Prophet Muhammad (Peace be upon him).

Hadrath Imam 'Ali Al-Naqi died during internment in Samra (or Sarman Rai) on the 3rd of *Rajab* 253/254 AH. having been poisoned by the Abbasi Caliph Mu'tiz billah according to some, and was buried in the same town. On his death there was bitter feud and rivalry for succession to the 'Imamate' between his two sons Hasan Al-'Askari and ja'far Al-Hadi. The majority of the followers of the Late Imam 'Ali Al-Naqi, however, supported the Claim of the elder brother hasan Al-'Askari and ja'far could not gain much support for his claim during the life time of his brother. However, after the demise of Hasan Al-'Askari in 260 A.H. the claim of Ja'far to the Imamate made head-way and gained strength as he stated that Hasan Al-'Askari had left no issue and it is a condition for the *imam* that he should leave behind an issue on his death. As a result of this disclosure by Ja'far many of the adherents of Hasan Al-'Askari joined the ranks of the followers of Jaffer who received the title of Al-Hadi (the Guide). Those who acknowledged the Imamate of Ja'far came to be known as the Ja'fariyah'. Among those who joined the ranks of Ja'far Al-Hadi was hasan son of 'Ali son of Fadal who was one of the reliable Scholars and *muhadauthin* of the *Sh 'i.*

At the demise of Ja'far Al-Hadi his son 'Ali laid claim to the 'Imamate' jointly with his sister Fatimah as stated by Shah 'Abd al-'Aziz *'muhaddith'* of Dehli. Two sons of this 'Ali decided to migrate from their home-land Iraq, the elder Sayyid 'Abd Allah to Bukhara and the second one Sayyid Isma'il to Bhakkar in the Punjab and founded the family of *'sadat'* of Bukhara and Bhakkar respectively. The reason for their decision to migrate from their home-land Iraq is not known but it can be guessed that this was due to the uncongenial political atmosphere, the bitter sectarian rivalry and the chaotic economic and social conditions prevailing in Baghdad and Iraq at that time. The pomp and power of the Abbaside Caliphs had declined by the end of the Third Century A. H. and their Turkish Body Guards had gained complete ascendancy and mastery at the Court of Baghdad. They deposed and installed calips an the throne at their sweet will the result that there was no political stability and the people of Iraq got fed up with the consequent uncertainty and lack of peace and prosperity.

Whatever the reasons for the same it is a fact that Sayyid 'Abd Aliah migrated to Bukhara probably during the first quarter of the 4th Century A.H. and settled down in the Mohalla Sare-e-Pul (literally

Head of the Bridge) of that town. This seems to have been a happy choice, for Bukhara had become a flourishing town by that time having greatly progressed during the reign of the Samani rulers who were great patrons of art and literature and highly respected and patronized the learned, the holy men and the descendants of the Holy Prophet Muhammad (Peace be upon him. This Town built by Abu'l 'Abbas Tusi during the reign of the Abbaside Caliph Al-Mehdi (AH 158 to 169).

The atmosphere of Bukhara seems to have proved congenial for Sayyid 'Abd Allah as he permanantly settled down there and his descendants flourished and gaiued prominence during the subsequent times to such an extent that the Shah of Turan, Mahmud Shah gave one of his daughters in marriage to one of his descendants Sayyid 'Ali Abu Mu'id, the father of Sayyid Jalal, out of which wed-lock Sayyid Jalal was born. Similarly the other Shah of Bakhara gave one of his daughters in marriage to Sayyid Jalal, out of which wed-lock two of his sons Sayyid 'Ali and Sayyid Ja'far were born.

This Sayyid Abu Mu'id, who was a descendant of Sayyid 'Abd Allah through eight links as indicated in the Family Tree given at page flourished in the 7th Century A.H. and died about the year 660 AH. He is reported to have been the *'qutb'* (the greatest Saint) of Bukhara of his time. Hadrat Baha al-Din Zakaria of Multan during his stay of about four years in Bukhara in connection with higher studies is reported to have met Sayyid Abu Mu'id there and to have been introduced to his son Sayyid Jalal. Both Baha al-Din Zakariya and Sayyid Abu Mu'id are reported to have been very much impressed by each other. Sayyid Abu Mu'id is reported to have spoken highly of Baha al-Din Zakariya to his son, Sayyid Jalal on departure of Baha al-Din from Bukhara. These encomiums lavised on Baha al-Din Zakariya by Sayyid Abu Mu'id are said to have induced his son Syed Jalal to leave Bukhara and come over to Multan to join Baha al-Din as a disciple.

Eleven generations of his ancestors (from Sayyid 'Abd Allah Bukhari to Syed Abu Mu'id Bukhari) had already resided at Bukhara for about three centuries when Sayyid Jalal was born on the 5th of

Dhil Hijjan in the year 595 AH out of the wed-lock between Sayyid Abu Mu'id and the daughter of Sultan Mahmud the Shah of Turan. Sayyid Jalal is reported to have been a born *wali* (saint) and many miracles and supernatural deeds are attributed to him since his early childhood. He received religious instruction and spiritual training at the hands of his revered father. When he came of age he was married to the daughter of the Shah of Bukhara out of which wed-lock two sons Sayyid 'Ali and Sayyid Ja'far (or Sayyid Muhammad according to some) were born.

It appears that Jalal decided to migrate from Bukhara During the closing years of the fourth decided of the 7th Century of the *Hijri* era. From Bukhara he went to Najf Ashraf to pay homage to the shrine of Hadrat 'Ali. From there he procceded to the Holy city Medina. It is said that he residents of this Holy city questioned the descent of Sayyid Jalal from the Holy Prophet (Peace be upon him) and demanded clear proofs in support of his contention. It was decided that Sayyid Jalal should appeal to the Holy Prophet to vindicate his stand. So he approached the tomb of the Holy Prophet and said. "Peace be on you O my father". Reply was received from the tomb. "Peace be on you also O my son and the 'joy of my eyes' and the Lamp of all my *'Umma'*. You are from me and of my house-hold". On hearing this voice all the *'sadat'* of that town certified to his being an off-spring of the Holy Prophet and held him in great esteem and regard. From Madina Sayyid Jalal procceded to Mecca and performed the Haj ceremonies. From Mecca he went to Baghdad and from Baghdad he proceeded to wards and arrived at Bhakkar in the Punjab. His two sons Sayyid 'Ali and Sayyid *Ja'far* accompanied him in his travels from Bukhara to Bhakkar. During his stay at Bhakkar Sayyid Jalal married Fatimah the daughter of Sayyid Badr al-Din, a prominent personalty of that town, all concerned having received clear instructions in this regard from the Holy Prophet (Peace be upon him) in their dreams. But the atmosphere of Bhakkar did not prove congenial for Jalal after his marriage with Fatimah dur to the Jealously of his in-laws and therefore he shifted to Multan. At Multan Sayyid Jalal became a disciple of the famous Shaykh of Town, Hadrat Mohammad Baha al-Din Zakaria, and received spiritual training under him for some years. On completion of this spiritual training Hadrat Zakaria awarded him the *'Khirqah Khilafat'* and directed him to shift to Uch Sharif and to make it his head quarter and the future activities. Accordingly Jalal shifted to Uch Sharif n the year 1244 AD (641/442 AH) and laid the foundation of 'Muhalla-i-Bukharian' in that Town. He laid the foundation of the town of 'Jhang Sayallan' in the Punjab. Due to his missionary efforts a number of Rajpur tribes of the Punjab embraced Islam at his hands. He arranged dispatch of religious missons to various parts of the Sub-Continent for propagation of Islam. During the whole of his life time he imparted religious instruction and spiritual training to all those who came in contact with him. The number of his personal disciples (*murids*) ran into thousands.

Sayyid Jalal died at the age of ninety-five years on the 19th of *Jamadi al-Awwal* 690 AH and was buried in Uch Sharif. His tomb is situated at an elevetated place outside the Township. His annual *'Urs* is celebrated with great pomp and fervour and is attended by devotees from every nook and corner of Pakistan. Uch Sharif is about fourteen miles from the railway station of Amedpur Sharqi and is one of the most important shrines of Pakistan.

Jalal Bukhari is the founder of the Bukhari family of *sadat'* in the Sub-Continent. Every Bukhari Sayyid' claims his descent from him. His descendants are also known as 'jalali', this surname having been derived from his name Jalal.

Sayyid Jalal is known by various' surnames and titles as under :

> Mir Surkh, Sharif Allah, Abu'l Barkat, Abu Ahmed, Mir Buzrug, Makhdum-A'zam, Jalal-i-Akbar and 'Azim Allah.

Sayyid Jalal was the most prominent *'khalifah'* (spiritual heir) of Hadrat Muhammad Baha al-Din Zakaria of Multan (d. 7th of *Safar 661* Ah) and one of his very close friends.

The *Shijrah-i-Tariqat'* (chain of spiritual succession of Syed Jalal .is as under :

1. The Holy Prophet Muhammad (Peace be upon him)

2. Hadrat 'Ali.
3. Hadrat Khauajah Hasan Basri.
4. Khawajah Habib 'Ajmi.
5. Khwajah Daud Ta'i.
6. Khwajah Ma'ruf Karkhi.
7. Khwajah Sirri Sikhti.
8. Khawajah Junayd Baghdadi.
9. Shaykh Mamshad Dinuri.
10. Shaykh Aswad Ahmad Dinuri.
11. Shaykh Abu 'Abd Allah.
12. Shaykh Wajih al-din Suharwardy.
13. Shaykh Diya al-Din Abu Najib Suharwardy.
14. Shaykh Shahabu al-Din 'Umar Suharwardy.
15. Shaykh Baha al-Din Zakaria Multahi Suharwardy.
16. Hadrat Syed Jalal Mir Surkh Burkh Bukhari Suharwardy.

It appears that Hadrat Sayyid jalal himself was the founder of a new *sufi* order named '*Jalaliyah*' after his name—an off shoot of the main Suharwardia order to which he belonged—as Hadrat Shah Wali Allah Dehlavi in one of his works states that he had 'spiritual connection' (*Nisbat*) with Makhdum Jahanian in this (Jalalia) order. On a querry about this matter by the present writer Professor Doctor Ghulam Sarwar, who has conducted research about the 'awliya' (saints) of Uch Sharif, in his letter dated the 7th of November 1963 addressed to the present writer confirmed that Sayyid Jalal Bukhari was himself the founder of the 'Jalaliyah' order referred to by Hadrat Shah Wali Allah Dehlavi.

From the chapter entitled 'Bazm-i-Sufia' of the famous Book *Rahat al-Qulub'* of Hadrat Baba Farid al-Din Ganj-i-Shakr, it transpires that the Baba Sahib Hadrat baha al-Din Zakaria Multani, Hadrat Sayyid Uthman Marwandi (Known as 'La'l Shahbaz Qalandar') of Sehwan and Sayyid Jalal Bukhari of Uch were very close associates and devoted friends. They are therefore commonly known as *awliya-i-Arba'a'* (the four saints). It is however rightly pointed out by Mr. Syed Bashir Husain Bukhari that one respect the position of Sayyed Jalal Bukhari is unique among all the saints of the Sub-Continent that from his progency sprang up a large number of *'awliya'* (saints) who indulged in missionary activity and propagated Islam in the different parts of the Sub-continent—Assam, Gujrat, Kathiawar, Sarhad, Punjab and Sind.

Progeny of Sayyid Jalal: Sayyid Jalal had five sons. Sayyid 'Ali and Sayyid Ja'fer were born at Bukhara out of the wed-lock with the daughter of the Shah of Bukhara and had accompanied Sayyid Jalal througoont his travels from Bukhara to Bhakkar. Sayyid Ahmad Kabir was born out of the wed-lock with Bibi Fatimah, daughter of Sayyid Badr al-Din of Bhakkar. His fourth and fifth sons were born out of the wed-lock with Bibi, Zehra Sayyidah Sharifah whom Sayyid Jalal seems to have married after he had shifted to Uch. About his daughters nothing is known except that one daughter was given in marriage to one Muhammad son of Ibrahim who was a very pious man and was known by the title of 'Shaykh al-shyukh.' Out of this wed-lock was born Hadrat Shayakh Jalal Mujarrad of Sylhet. This daughter of Sayyid Jalal Bukhari is said to have died three months after the birta of Shaykh Jalal Mujarrad and his son-inlaw Muhammad is said to have died some years later when Shyakh Jalal Mujarrad was still a child. This Shaykh Jalal Mujarrad who was destined to become famous as a saint in subsequent years in said to have been brought up and bred by his uncle Sayyid Ahmad Kabir Suharwardy. The district of Sylhet in Assam was subjugated and brought under the rule of Sultan Shamsh al-Din Firuz Shah of Bengal with the assistance of Shaykh Jalal Mujarrad. This Shaykh Jalal died in 1340 AD (740 AH) and was buried in Sylhet. His Tomb in Sylhet is the most famous shrine of East Bengal.

Now as to the line of successors through his sons, the most famous line is through his third son Sayyid Ahmad Kabir Suharwardy, who himself was a *'wali* of a high order. The tombs of his decendants exist through-out the length and breath of the Sub-Continent and are held in high reverence by the devotees. His two sons Sayyid Jalal al-Din surnamed Raju Al Qattal achieved immortal fame as great *sufis* and *'awiiya'* (Saints). The tombs of all the three still exist in Uch. The tombs of Hadrat Burhan al-Din 'Abd Allah (surname 'Qutb-i-Alam) and Hadrat Siraj al-din Muhammad (surname Shah Alam), son and grandson of Hadrat Nasir al-Din Muhammad, son of Makhdum. Jahanian Jahan Gasht, are the famous shrines of Ahmedabad in Gujerat. The tomb of Sayyid jalal al-Din Bukhari, a descendant of Hadrat Makhdum Jahanian, exists on the bank of the river Jumna in Agra near Taj Mahal. These are only a few names from among a very large number of the escendants of Sayyid Jalal and Sayyid Ahmad Kabir whose tombs are spread throughout the Sub-Continent.

9

Tomb of Sharaf Un-Nisa Begum Known as Sarvwala Maqbara at Lahore

MASOOD UL-HASAN KHOKHAR

Lahore has been a witness to several turmoils and upheavals of foreign invasions as well as internal feuds since its very early days. The comparatively recent resurection affecting the political, social and religious life of the Punjab was the extra-ordinary ruthless role played by the Sikhs here on the decline of the Moghul Empire. The Sikhs created a serious problem of law and order throughout the province, and it was under these circumstances that in 1713 the Moghul Emperor Farrukh Siyar appointed Khawaja Abdul Rahim known to history as Abdu's Samad, Governor of Lahore. He strived hard to manage the affairs of the province and maintained law and order after quelling rebellions of Banda Bairaji, and other local chieftains like Isa Khan Munj, Husain Khan Khesghi of Qasur (1717-19), Sharaf-ud-Din Kashmiri, (1726).

Abdu's-Smad Khan married Begum Jan a daughter of his uncle, Khawaja Zakariya, and gave her the honorific title of Begum-i-Kabir. The famous Zakariya Khan was Abdu's Samad Khan's son from this wife. Besides Abdu's Samad married another lady named Sharf un-Nisa to whom was born a son named Abdullah Khan. Both the wives of the Khan were very pious like their husband. Begum Jan had wished that after her death, her ornaments should be sold and the money so collected spent on the construction of a mosque near the tomb of Shah Chiragh. Sharf un-Nisa used to recite the Quran very regularly. It has been related that she constructed a sixteen feet high brick-tower where she sat every day for an hour for the purpose. She kept in the tower a bejewelled sword alongwith the Quran. After her death, she was buried, according to her will, in the tower alongwith the Quran and the sword. A pyramidal dome was constructed over the platform. Iqbal the poet philosopher, was so much impressed with the piety of the lady that he wrote in his *Javid Nama :*

The Palace of Sharaf al-Nisa

I said, 'Yonder mansion of pure ruby
which gathers tribute from the sun,
you station, you abode, you lofty palace
whose portico the houris throng pilgrim-robed—
tell me, you who inspired the travellers to search,
who is the owner of this habitation?'
Rumi replied : 'This is the mansion of Shraf al-Nisa ;
the birds on its roof sing in the angels' choir.
Our ocean gave not birth to such a pearl;
no mother gave birth to such a daughter.
By her grave the earth of Lahore vies with heaven;
none in this world comprehends her secret.
She was all ecstasy and yearning, anguish and burning,
eyes and lamp to the governor of Punjab;
radiance of the family of Abd al-Samad,
her poverty is an image remaining eternally.
To cleanse her being wholly with the Koran,
not for one moment did she cease recitation;
at her side a double-edged sword, the Koran in her hand,
flesh, body, mind and soul drunken with God'
solitude with sword, Koran and prayer—
O happy life, passed in supplication!
When the last breath issued from her lips,
looking upon her mother most yearningly
she spoke: "If you would have knowledge of my secret,

regard this sword and this Koran.
These two forces preserve each the other
and are the axis of all life's creation.
In this world, which dies every moment,
only these two were your doughter's intimates.
Now that I take my leave I have this to say to you :
do not remove the sword and the Koran from me.
Take to your heart these words I speak;
better my tomb without dome and lamp;
for believers, sword and Koran suffice—
let this be the furniture of my grave."

The tomb of Sharaf un-Nisa now standing in a historic locality of Lahore called Begampura near the Engineering University, known after Begum Jan. During the period of the rule of Nawwab Abdu's Samad Khan and his successos, the locality was created the governor's headquarters, where several palaces, mosques, tombs and administrative blocks were built. However, many of them were pulled down during the invasions of Nadir Shah (1739) and Ahmad Shah Abdali (1747-70). One of these architectural monuments was the tomb of Sharf un-Nisa, now commonly known as Sarvwala Maqbara, so named because of its four Cypress trees created in faienee mosaic on the exterior of the tomb (Pl. I). On the west been created the entrance to the tomb. A garden in Mughal style was originally created around the tomb, on the east and north were big water-tanks augmented with fountains, while on the west was a Baradari. Nothing of this adorment is left except the ruinous tomb amidst a multitude of low and high residential buildings.

Architecturally, the tomb is rather peculiar. It is in the shape of a tower which tapers upward, Square in plan, the base of the tomb is 19 feet side. At the height of 16 feet 7 inches, a square room, measuring 13 feet side, has been constructed, which is surmounted with a pyramidal dome. The total height of the tomb is about 30 feet. The entrance has a cusped arch, 5 feet 5 inches long and 7 feet high.

The tomb is particularly significant for its two main features;

first, its height, and, secondly the pyramidal dome not very uncommon in Mughal architecture at Lahore, where we have other tombs of identical shape like that of Jani Beg who was a mason of Shah Jahan's period, the so called tombs of Zebun-Nisa, tombs of Miyan Mir and Mulla Shah Badakhshi. The dome was decorated with chevrons in glaze of blue, green and orange colours. Only traces of it remain now. The dome rests of a low drum and is crowned with a final. The parapet is decorated with a floral design border in glazed tiles on the upper and lower parts. In between this border on the face of parapet on all the four sides, an inscription has been executed on yellow tiles which reads :

(God is eternal, all the rest is perishable).

Under the drum is the projected *eve* built in bricks using the interlock joints resting on brick brackets divided in three panels of equal size on all the four sides of the tomb. The inner surface of the *eve* is plastered with *pucca* Kalai, bordered with linear design in yellow and green. The background of the panels is white enameled tiles. The central panel is bigger while those on either side are smaller. In the central panel, flower vase resting on a pedestalled dish has been created in glazed tiles in orange, green and blue, while small vases are on the other sides panels.

The four sides of the tomb passess big panels with white enameled tiles background. The panels have beautifully created four large cypress trees of glazed tiles in green. In between the cypress trees, the tulip plants in glazed tiles in blue, orange, sky blue and green colours have been depicted. The panel is bordered with beautiful nine-inch broad strip decorated with floral designs in orange, blue, green like mosaics. The panels on north east and south are still intact while on the west only trace of border are visible. Below these panels, another narrow border of 1 feet 3 inches created in glaze tiles on all the four sides. Only traces of its are visible now. The rest of the extension below it is plainly plastered in lime.

At the height of 16 feet 7 inches, the *dasa* in brick is marked on all the four sides. The cenotaph, measuring 5 feet 5 inches, is on a terraced platform in the centre of the room in north-south direction. The interor of the room has no decoration except three cypress trees, two large and one small on the northern wall. The vaulted roof and the niches are all lime plastered.

The tomb was damaged during the Sikh rule who got it opened in search of treasures, but found little of their interest. Again, to quote Allama Iqbal:

> For long ages, beneath this golden dome,
> the sword and the scriptures lay upon her shrine.
> Her resting-place, in this inconstant world,
> spoke a message to the people of the Truth
> until the Moslems did with themselves what they did
> and time's revolution rolled up their carpet.
> The man of God was mindful of other than God,
> the lion of the lord took to the trade of the fox;
> the quicksilver fire and fever departed from his heart—
> you know well what befell Punjab—
> the Khalsa snatched away sword and Koran
> and in that land Islam expired.'

The monument was, due to its historical and architectural importance, declared protected in 1912 under the old 'Ancient Monuments Preservation Act 1904,' and was placed under the control of the then Archaeological Survey for maintenance some repairs were carried out prior to this action in 1880 by the British Government. It is now a national monument of second category.

10

Hadrat Nizamuddin Aulia

M. HAFIZ SYED

Hadrat Nizamuddin whose name was Muhammad and who was universally called "Beloved of God, King of Saints," was born in Badayun in the year 634 A.H. His forefathers originally came from Borhara; first they came to Lahore, and then migrated to Bokharai. Both his father and mother belonged to a pious and saintly family.

When Muhammad was just five years old his father passed away. He was brought up under the loving protection of his mother, who was looked upon with great reverence for her piety and austere living.

Nizamuddin received his early education in Badayun. Maulana 'Alauddin Usuli invited the learned men of the time in whose presence the "turban of learning" was put on Nizamuddin's head in recognition of the fact that he had completed his education, that is, the education that was in vogue in those days.

In order to prosecute advanced studies in Islamic subjects, he migrated to Delhi with his mother and learnt several subjects from Maulana Shamsuddin Wamghani, whose erudition was recognised by King Balban, who conferred on him the title of Shamsul-Mumalik.

Nizamuddin's spiritual teacher was Baba Ganjshakr, who not only initiated him into the mystery of the spiritual life but also taught him various religious and mystical subjects in which he was considered an adept. For several years Sheikh Nizamuddin lived in the monastery of his teacher and practised the severest austerities and completed his spiritual development.

After some time he was directed by his murshid (teacher) to go to Delhi and occupy himself in devotion to God and in the service of his fellowmen.

At the time of his passing away Baba Ganjshakr willed that his staff and robe be given to his devoted disciple, Nizamuddin, as his vicegerent (khalifa).

When the Sheikh was parting with his murshid, the latter gave him a word of admonition :

(1) If ever you borrow anything from anybody you must see that you return it as soon as possible.

(2) Try to serve and please your enemies under any circumstances.

The last time when the Sheikh went to his murshid at the time of parting he blessed the Sheikh with these words : "May God keep you regenerated and spiritually elevated at all times. You would be like an ever-green tree under whose shadow people would find comfort, rest and inspiration." He further said, "Do not relax your efforts in developing more and more spiritual knowledge and insight."

When Sheikh Nizamuddin came to Delhi for the first time at his Murshid's bidding, he did not find the place sufficiently quiet and secluded for his prayer and mediation. Therefore, he had to resort to a lonely place in the outskirts of the city in order to continue his spiritual practices.

At that time the city of Delhi was the centre of corruption, debauchery and immorality. This was one of the main reasons, why he took his abode outside the city in a village called Ghyathpur. For a long time he spent his days there in great hardship and starvation. On one occasion he had to go without food for three days at a stretch.

When Sultan Jalaluddin Khilji heard that the Sheikh was passing his days in penury and poverty, he was so touched by this news that he offered to grant him a free gift of some villages so that he might be able to maintain himself from their income. But the Sheikh and his disciples thankfully declined this offer.

There is a touching story about this time of his life. For want of food he had to starve for several days. A pious and kind-hearted lady living in his neighbourhood brought him a handful of flour, which was being cooked in an earthen pot. Just when this flour was ready for use a dervish visited him and asked him for some food. The Sheikh brought the pot of the food and placed it before the dervish who having satisfied his hunger with a few morsels of it, threw the pot on the ground and disappeared after uttering these words:--

"Sheikh Fariduddin Ganjshakr endowed you with the wealth of spiritual life, and I broke into pieces the pot which was a symbol of poverty. Now you have been made the king of inner and outer life."

After this incident Sheikh Nizamuddin's indigent condition was surprisingly changed and he began to receives gifts and presents in abundance from morning till evening from his devotees and admirers. But the Sheikh was so God-reliant and contented that he would order all that he received during the day to be distributed among the poor people and would not allow anything to be kept for the next day.

It was during this period of his life that Sultan Mu'zzuddin Kayqabad built a palace near the Sheikh's village. Therefore people began to congregate in his village in large numbers, disturbing the Sheikh's peace and quiet. He decided to leave this village, but an unknown person suddenly visited him and asked him not to be disheartened with the presence of the crowd, but to carry on his spiritual mission and remain inwardly undisturbed.

As the Sheikh was living in Ghyathpur village very close to the royal palace, the ministers and the state officials visited him frequently. Some of them were initiated by the Sheikh and were the recipients of his grace and guidance. Some well-to-do citizens who were indulging in various sorts of objectionable pleasure totally abstained from evil ways and began to lead a pious life.

Amir Khusro's father, Amir Saifuddin, had joined the circle of

Sheikh's disciples. In fact, his whole family accepted him as their spiritual leader. At that time Amir Khusro was only eight years old. His parents placed him at their murshid's feet. He was an accepted disciple at this tender age. Amir Khusro was utterly devoted to his teacher and acted up to his instructions most loyally all his life. It is reliably recorded by the historians of his time that during the course of his training he kept a fast for full forty years. The Sheikh was also deeply attached to him.

Amir Khusro was not only an outstanding poet and literary man of his time, but, on account of his close intimacy with the royal family, he had built up a fortune. In the presence of the Sheikh he behaved like a mere servant.

There is a touching story about his devotion to his spiritual teacher. Once a dervish visited the Sheikh and wanted some gifts from him. But the Sheikh could not afford to give him anything except a new pair of shoes which he had at that time. While the dervish was going away he met on his way Amir Khusro and his royal party. The Amir stopped him and asked him if he had received anything from his murshid. When Amir Khusro learnt that the dervish had received a new pair of shoes from his murshid, the Amir offered to have it back from him by surrendering to him in exchange all the wealth that he was carrying with him from an expedition. He took that pair of shoes, put it on his head and carried it back to his beloved teacher.

There is also a story about Sultan Jalaluddin Khilji. The Sultan desired to have an interview with the Sheikh, but the latter declined to grant it.

Amir Khusro was away on an expedition with Sultan Muhammad Tughlaq. As soon as the news of the passing away of the Sheikh was conveyed to him, he took the king's permission and returned post-haste to the tomb of his *Peer*. He ordered whatever wealth he possessed to be distributed to the poor. After six months deep mourning he expired and was buried near the Sheikh's tomb.

During his life-time Sheikh Nizamuddin Aulia's influence was so great that people living in his monastery as well as those living within a distance of fourteen miles from there led a good and pious life and refrained from evil ways.

The author of *Seerul Aulia* says that the Sheikh subjected himself to intense spiritual austerities for thirty years. In his middle and old age he devoted more and more time to spiritual development. He kept fast all his life. Throughout day and night he used to say his prayers (namaz) four hundred times. He used to reside in the upper storey of his monastery. Even at the ripe old age of eighty he used to climb down from his room to join the congregational prayers. After morning and noon prayers he used to engage himself in giving spiritual instruction to his disciples and followers. A large number of Sufis and aspirants on the path of God-realization used to flock round him.

Although he was deeply immersed in divine contemplation and devotion, he never forgot the interest of the general public, whom he treated with the utmost consideration and whom he helped in every way.

His patience and forbearance was so greatthat even when he was ill-treated by his adversaries he invariably returned good for evil. He took special delight in imparting instruction to his disciples and in improving their moral character.

The day when his soul was about to quit his body and attain union with God, he peremptorily ordered that whatever was kept in his storeroom should be given away to the poor. Just a moment before he breathed his last, he opened his private box and bequeathed the following gifts to his disciple, Sheikh Nasiruddin Chairagh Delhi : a prayer-carpet, a clock, a rosary beed and a wooden-staff.

Then he said his morning prayer. While the sun was rising this "glorious son of religion" disappeared in the "realm of eternity."

The date of his passing away, chronicled by the historians, is Wednesday, the 18th of Rabiulawal, 725 A.H. His mausoleum is in Delhi, where all classes of people congregate every week to pay their homage to him.

Epistles of Nizamuddin Aulia

The epistles of Nizamuddin Aulia are treated by Muslim scholars as his original works. The following books may be mentioned:

(1) *Fawdul Fuwad. (2) Fadlul Fuwad. (3) Rahatul Fuwad. (4) Seerul Aulia.*

The first one was compiled and edited by Khawaja Hasan Sanjari, who was one of the most beloved disciples of the saint.

There is a story about this beloved disciple. Once the Sheikh visited the tomb of Sheikh Bakhtiar Kaki, where he saw Hasan Sanjari enjoying his life in revelry and drunkenness in the company of his pleasure-loving friends. As Hasan Sanjari had spent his early days in the company of the Sheikh in Badayun and was quite familiar with him, he composed a quatrain addressed to the Sheikh, the purport of which was that he had spent years in his company, but had not derived any benefit from him. "Thy piety has not helped me to renounce my evil ways, which are stronger than thy piety." These words touched the Sheikh's heart, who simply said, "Everything has its own time. You will have your better days." These words of the Sheikh kindled a new life in Hasan Sanjari attain who fell on his feet and from that time renounced his sinful habits and began to lead a pious life. The Sheikh accepted him as his disciple. From 707 till 719 A.H. whatever remarks he heard from his murshid's lips he committed them to writing.They were compiled in book form under the caption of *Malfuzat*. These sayings of the Sheikh were held in high esteem by the mystics of those times and even upto this day they are treated as the highest authority in mysticism.

Fadlul Fuwad was another set of epistles collected and chronicled by Amir Khusro

The third set of letters, named *Rahat-ul-Muhibbin,* was collected by an unkonwn disciple from 689 to 698, a rare copy of which is still preserved in the British Museum in London.

Khwaja Syyid Muhammad Mubarak was one of the Sheikh's disciples, who in his welknown book *Seerul Aulia* has preserved the

Sheikh's instructions along with the biographical notes of the saints of the Chishti order.

The Sheikh's Teachings

I. The true devotee of God is one who at all times bears Him in mind and loves nothing but Him and yearns for union with his Beloved. Love of God has two aspects: (1) the love of God Himself and (2) love of His attributes. The former comes from His Grace and the latter is the result of constant practice. What one has to do in this respect is to free one's mind from things other than God, and constantly occupy the mind with the thought of God. There are four obstacles in this path:

(a) The world and its passing attractions. (b) God's creatures. (c) Temptations of the lower self. (d) Satan and temptations spread by him.

The ways to remove these obstacles are these:--

(1) If you lead a sequestered life, people of the world will not disturb you.
(2) Worldly desires can be overcome by contentment.
(3) To overcome one's lower self and temptations placed before one by Satan one should sincerely pray to God to grant him strength enough to overcome them.

II. Intense Love. The dervish is a creature of God's love. Learned people follow the lead of reason. Sin is apt to be committed so long as one's love of God is superficial, but when it becomes deeper and enters the inner core of heart, sinful thoughts and acts become impossible.

III. Patience and resignation to the will of God is the *sine qua non* of success in the Path of God-realization. In face of affection and calamity, not to murmur and complain is patience. Not to be disgusted when some one is a victim of a calamity is contentment and resignation. The best example of complete surrender of God's Will is that of a dead body in the hands of one who bathes it. The Other turn it to any side he likes. So the man who has surrendered himself completely to the Will of God has no wish and will of his own. He has merged his individual will in the Divine will. Man's full and abiding faith in God comes only to those who treat this world with all its seeming attraction as worthless as the camel's excreta. One should not depend upon any one except God. Those who pretend to love God and at the same time love the world are liars.

According to Sheikh Nizamuddin, devotion to God depends upon six basic requirements:--

i) The aspirant should lead a sequestered life quite by himself. This lonely habit will help him to analyse the insidious working of his lower nature and the way to overcome it.
ii) The aspirant should see that he remains with ablution and preserves purity of body and mind. If at any time he is overcome by sleep, when he wakes up, he should perform ablution again.
iii) He should try to keep fast all the year round. If this is not possible, he should reduce his meal to a minimum.
iv) He should always try to keep aloof from everything that does not relate to God.
v) He should have intense love for anil devotion to his murshid.
vi) For the sake of God he should ever be ready to renounce everything.

There are four things from which an aspirant should abstain:--

i) He should avoid the company of rich people.
ii) Renouncing everything except God, he should occupy his mind with constant memory of God.
iii) He should wholly withdraw his attention from things other than God.
iv) He should not have even the least interest in the worldly things. When once an aspirant realises the futility and harmfulness of any desire and makes up his mind to desist from it once for all, he should never turn back and resume his old habits.

The sheikh has paid equal attention to outward morality along with the inner moral sense. He thinks that a man can develop his spiritual faculties if he eats less, speaks less and sleeps less and does not mix with the people of the world.

He is definitely of opinion that while refraining from the company of worldly people, one should not ignore what one owes to them. One should discharge one's duties and responsibilities to those with whom one comes in contact.

This leads the aspirant on to have sufficient consideration for the welfare of his neighbours, whose defects and shortcomings he should not make public.

The Sheikh has Imphasised the need for observance of the essential tenet of Islam under any circumstance. The aspirant is enjoined to say his prayers five times a day without fail, keep fast for thirty days and scrupulously keep away from all evil ways. Further he says that the aspirant on the path of God should not have the least desire to acquire such powers as may enable him to perform miraculous and extraordinary deeds.

The Sheikh permitted his disciples to hear such select music as depicts of protrays the glory and greatness of God.

11

The Life and Mission of Shaykh Ahmad Sirhindi

M. ABDUL HAQ ANSARI

The great seventeenth century Indian saint and religious reformer, Shaykh Ahmad, was born at Sirhind, now in the state of Punjab, north-west of Delhi, on Friday the 4th Shawwal 971/26th May 1564, in a family with long scholarly tradition which traced its descent from the Caliph 'Umar al-Faruq. He received his early education from his father, Shaykh 'Abd al-Ahad (927-1107/1521-1598) and memorised the Kur'an. He was then sent to Sialkot, at present in Pakistan. Here he learnt logic, philosophy and theology from Mulla Kamal Kashmiri (d. 1017/1608-9), a renowned scholar of rational disciplines; studied Hadith with Shaykh Ya'qub Sarfi (d. 1003/1544), the author of a commentary on the *Sahih* of Bukhari and a Sufi of the Kubrawiyah order; and read some advanced texts of *Tafsir* and Hadith with Qadi Bahlul Badakhshani. Sirhindi completed this education at the age of seventeen and return home.

Three years later he left for Agra, the capital of the great Mughal Emperor, Akbar (reg. 963-1014/1556-1605), and established contacts with the scholars of the court, such as the poet laureate, Faydi (954-1004/1547-1595), and his younger brother, Abu'l-Fadl (958-1011/1551-1602), a distinguished writer and an informal secretary of the Emperor. It is said that he helped the former at times in writing his commentary on the Kur'an, *Sawati' al-Ilham,* which has the unique distinction of being free from letters containing diacritic. With the latter, however, he found it difficult to carry on. For, though Abu'l-Fadl believed in God, he denied the necessity of prophecy, repudiated the Shari'ah, condemned worship as hypocrisy, regarded every religion equally bad, and pinned faith in reason. Abu'l-Fadl was not alone to have these ideas; the royal court had many others like him. Sirhindi referred to this situation when he wrote: "The people of our times question the very idea of prophecy, deny the possibility of establishing the claim of a particular prophet, and refuse to follow the prophetic Shari'ah. This trend is spreading among the people, and some who have established themselves in power are persecuting the 'Ulama' and torturing them in various ways which I would not like to mention, simply because they follow the laws of the prophets and believe in them."

At a discussion with Abu'l-Fadl, Sirhindi contested his ideas and argued the case for prophecy; the latter lost temper and abused some great scholars of Islam. Sirhindi was very much shocked and broke with him. When his father was informed of Sirhindi's disillusionment he came down to Agra and took him home. On the way he married him to the daughter of Shaykh Sultan, a member of the nobility at Thanesar, at the latter's request. Back home Sirhindi took up the study of Sufi texts like the *Ta'arruf* of Kalabadhi (d. 390/1000), the *'Awarif* of Suhrawardi (d. 636/1234), and the *Fusus* of Ibn 'Arabi (d. 638/1240) under the guidance of his father.

At an early age Shaykh 'Abd al-Ahad had sought to be initiated into Sufism by the Great Chishti saint Shaykh 'Abd al-Quddus of Gangoh (d. 991/1583), famous for his ecstasies and his faith in *wahdat al-wujud.* But the Shaykh advised him first to study the Shari'ah and the Hadith. Shaykh 'abd al-Ahad returned, took up study, visited various scholars and travelled to a number of places. When he came back, the master had died, and his son Shaykh Rukn al-Din, who was also highly ecstatic and a firm believer in *wahdat al-wujud,* guided him in the Qadiri and Chishti *tariqahs* and awarded him *khirqah.* Shaykh 'Abd al-Ahad, too, believed in *wahdat al-wujud,* but, as Sirhindi says, was not a blind follower of the doctrine. Some of its details he interpreted in his own way. Sirhindi refers in one of his tracts to a book of his father, *Kanz al-Hazq'iq,* and his biographer, Muhammad Hashim Kishmi, mentions another work, *Asrar al-Tashahhud.*

Sirhindi studied Sufi texts with his father and practised *suluk* under his direction. In his *Mabda' wa Ma'ad* he speaks of his debt to his father: "I acquired the *nisbat-i fardiyah* from my father who had acquired it from a revered Sufi, intensely ecstatic and famous for his miracles... I also developed a taste for supererogatory works (*nawafil*), particularly *nafl* prayers, from my father who got it from his teacher, a Chishti saint."

After the death of Shaykh 'Abd al-Ahad in 1007/1597-8 Sirhindi started for Hajj. On his way at Delhi he was introduced to Khwajah 'Abd al-Baqi (991-1012/1563-1603), one of the first Naqshabandi saints to come to India. Naqshabandis were noted for comparatively stricter adherence to the Shari'ah in their *suluk* and were popular in Central Asia from where the Mughal rulers had come. Khwajah 'Abd al-Baqi, commonly known as Baqibillah, had come to Delhi only a few months previously, but even in this short period he had become very popular. He persuaded Sirhindi to spend sometime with him. Within a few days Sirhindi was so much impressed that he offered himself for *bay'at,* and in a short period of two months and a half attained the Naqshabandi *nisbat,* and then the real self-annihilation (*fana' al-haqiqi*) or absolute union (*jam' al-jam'*). He continued his *suluk* till he reached the stage of post-union separation (*farq ba'd al-jam'*), which the Khwajah called "the end of human endeavour" and "the stage of perfection" (*maqam-i takmil*). The Khwajah was very much impressed by the wonderful progress of his disciple; in a letter to a friend he wrote :

> A man from Sirhind named Shaykh Ahmad has recently come. He is very learned and has great spiritual powers. He has lived with me for some days; on the basis of what I have seen of him in this period, I expect that he will be in future a lamp which will illuminate the world.

After the first meeting Sirhindi returned home, pursued his *sayr* and *suluk* as the Khwajah had suggested, and kept him informed of the visions and experiences he had. He visited the Khwajah again and spent sometime with him. When he intended to return, the Khwajah asked him to teach the *tariqah,* and gave some disciples in his charge.

Sirhindi was hesitant to take up the responsibility, but the Khwajah testified to his preparation. Sirhindi bowed and started the work. A little before the death of the master in 1012/1603, he visited him again. On this occasion of the Khwajah honoured his disciple by walking a distance to welcome him, and when Sirhindi left he entrusted his sons to him for spiritual direction.

Sirhindi has described his mystical development, at times briefly, and at times in detail. A short account of his first experience is this :

> I believed in the *tawhid-i wujudi* [i.e. *wahdat al-wujud*] from the time I was a boy. My father apparently believed in the doctrine, and used to carry on spiritual exercises on *wujudi* lines. But in spite of that he was able to maintain in his innermost self (*al-akhfa*) the state of indeterminateness (*martabah bekayf*). As the saying goes, the son of a jurist is half jurist. I knew the doctrine very well, appreciated and enjoyed it. Later on, when God brought me to Shaykh Baqibillah, and he taught me the Naqshabandi *tariqah* and attended closely to my development, the Unity of Being (*tawhid-i wujudi*) was revealed to me in a short period in virtue of following the Naqshabandi *tariqah.* I was completely absorbed in that experience, and the ideas associated with it began to pour in on me. There was hardly a truth that was not revealed to me. I was informed of profoundest ideas of Shaykh Muhyi'l-din Ibn 'Arabi's philosophy and was blessed with the experience of Divine self-illumination (*tajalli-i-dhati*) which the author of the *Fusus* had said to be the culmination of spiritual ascent, and beyond which there was nothing, according to him, except pure non-being. I also came to know in detail the truths of that *tajalli* which the Shaykh had claimed to be a privilege of the 'Seal of Saints.' I was so much engrossed in the *tawhid* and intoxicated with it that in one of my letters to the Khwajah I wrote the following two couplets which were the product of sheer intoxication *(sukr).*
>
> *This Shari'ah is, alas, the way of the blind.*
> *Our way is the way of infidels and fire-worshippers.*

Infidelity and faith are the lock and the face of that beauty.
In our way infidelity and faith are one.
This condition prolonged to months and years.

Sirhindi describes the next stages of his mystical development as follows :

> After a period, I had a new vision of things which dominated my consciousness. But I hesitated at first to revise my attitude towards *tawhid (wujudi)* in deference to, rather than in disregard for, that doctrine. I remained in a stage of indecision for a long time. At last, I was induced to renounce that doctrine. I was shown that *tawhid (wujudi)* was a lower stage, and was asked to move to the stage of *zilliyat* (i.e. the vision that things are the shadows of God and different from Him]. But I did not like to move from that stage since many Sufis were stationed there. But I had no choice. I was brought to the stage of *zilliyat* where I realised that I and the world were shadows.
>
> I wished I were not moved again from that stage of (*zilliyat*) because it had an affinity with *wahdat al-wujud* which was still a symbol of perfection for me. But it happened that God, by a pure act of grace and love, carried me beyond that stage and brought me to the stage of *'abdiyat* (i.e. the vision that man nothing more than a servant of God, that things are merely His creation and that He is absolutely other and different from the world]. At that time I realised the greatness of that stage and scanned its lofty heights. I regretted my earlier experiences, turned to God and begged for His mercy. Had I not been guided in this manner and shown the greatness of one stage after the other, I would have remained at the stage of *tawhid (wujudi)* because in my view there was no stage higher than that. God alone establishes the truth and shows the way.

These rather long passages are quoted in order to introduce the reader to Sirhindi's own account of his mystical development. This will remove, it is hoped, the doubts which some writers of our times have raised about his experiences since he does not fit in their view of Sufism.

Sirhindi has characterised the three stages of his experience in metaphysical terms: the Unity of Being (*tawhid-i wujudi/wahdat al-wujud*); shadowism (*zilliyat*) and creaturehood or servanthood (*'abdiyat*). Put in purely mystical language they represent the stages of union (*jam'*) rather non-difference (*jam' al-jam'*), separation after union (*farq ba'd al-jam'*), and absolute difference. The first two stages are common and widely attested by Sufis, but the last is somewhat uncommon though by no means rare.

Sirhindi mentions these stages time and again for two reasons: He wants first to bring home to the mystics of his day, most of whom were moving at the first stage or stationed at the second, that there is a higher stage of mystic experience at which one stops seeing that man is one with God, or that the world and God are One Being, and realises instead that God is completely different and absolutely other, that the world has nothing common with God, and that man is simply a creature and a servant. He wants to underline, secondly, that the truth of God's absolute transcendence is not for him a matter of faith which a common believer has, nor an intellectual conclusion at which a theologian arrives, but a fact of his own experience to which he was brought against his wish and expectation.

After the death of Khwajah 'Abd al-Baqi, Sirhindi settled down at Sirhind and devoted himself single-mindedly for the rest of life to some great works. He hardly left Sirhind except a few times for Delhi and Agra, and that, too for the cause he struggled for.

The first task to which Sirhindi addressed himself was to preach and popularise the Naqshabandi *tariqah.* People came to him from different parts of India, North and South, East and West, seeking spiritual guidance. He instructed them and supervised their progress, and when they had attained to a level of perfection sent them back to their native places to preach the *tariqah* there. Those who were more gifted were posted at important cities of India such as Lahore, Delhi, Agra, Saharanpur, Badayun, Jawnpur, Allahabad, Mankapur, Patna,

Mangalkot (Bengal), Burhanpur (Deccan), etc., and were asked to spread the views and the practices of the order (*silsilah*). How popular the (*silsilah*) became can be ascertained by a remark of Jahangir (reg. 1014-1037/1606-1627), son and successor of Akbar, which he wrote sixteen years after Sirhindi had started his work: "The disciples of the Shaykh have spread all over the cities and the towns of India."

The *silsilah* was not confined to India. It spread outside in Afghanistan and Turkistan, the lands of the first naqshabandi saints, and in Tabaristan and Iran. Sirhindi put his deputies (*khulafa'*) at Shadman (Isphahan), Husain Abdal (Kabul), Kishm (Badakhshan), Berk (near Qandahar) and Taliqan. He kept himself in constant touch with their work, heard from them the problems they felt or the questions which people asked them about the *tariqah,* and wrote replies and sent instructions. In these letters Sirhindi mentions the distinctive features of the Naqshabandi *tariqah,* in particular its strict adherence to the Sunnah. It avoids, he says, musical sessions (*sama'*), dervish dances (*raqs*) and *dhikr* with loud voice; it eschews austere practices and severe exercises, and observes moderation in food, drink, sleep and dress. It disparages ecstasy (*wajd*), visions (*mushahadat*) and illuminations (*tajalliyat*); censures boastful claims and ecstatic statements (*shathat*); and subjects mystical revelations (*makshufat*) to the doctrines of the Shari'ah. It holds that the goal of *tasawwuf* is neither union with God, nor participation in His attributes, but simply to obey the Shari'ah and to be a faithful servant of God. There is no stage higher than the stage of servanthood (*'abdiyat*).

The propagation of the Naqshabandi *tariqah* and the purification of the souls, however important that may be, were only a part of the task which Sirhindi had set before him. "I have not been created", he said, "for the spiritual direction of the people and their self-perfection. The purpose of my creation is different, and I have a different mission." He considered himself to be more than a *wali,* a renovator (*mujaddid*) of religion, who had been commissioned to revive Islam at the turn of its second millennium. Although he did not elaborate, there is no doubt that he had a very clear conception of his mission and what it required in his days. Judging from the work he did, we can safely say that his mission was to criticise unbelief, heresy and false doctrines, and reaffirm faith in prophecy, revelation and the religion of the Prophet; to condemn evil, disobedience and innovation, and revive piety and adherence to the Sunnah; to oppose anti-Islamic forces and powers and restore Islamic institutions and laws. Sirhindi used all his powers of mind and heart to achieve these ends. He wrote books and tracts wherein he attacked erroneous ideas and practices among all sections of society—masses, scholars, Sufis and statesmen—, explained what is true faith and right piety and defended them on grounds of the Kur'an, Sunnah, reason and sane Sufi practices. He wrote letters to important personalities in every walk of life, in colleges (*madrasahs*), cloisters (*khanqahs*), army and government, urging them to reform the views and practices of the people under their influence, realising the great responsibility which God has placed on their shoulders in this regard. He sent to them his emissaries, and travelled to see them personally when he considered it helpful. He used the network of his disciples spread over the whole of India and outside India to urge people to give up false beliefs and evil innovations, to follow the Shari`ah and adhere to the Sunnah of the Prophet. He got several copies of his letters (the medium for the propagation of his ideas) made and disseminated them among the people. In the following pages the present writer shall review briefly the work Shaykh Ahmad Sirhindi did.

A section of the society, small in number yet quite influential, was that of the scholars at the royal court. The present writer has already mentioned Abu'l-Fadl; besides him there was his father, Mulla Mubarak Nagawri (d. 1001/1593), who initiated Akbar into heterodoxy, Fath Allah Shirazi (d. 997/1588), who headed a committee to examine the rationality of the Shari'ah, Sharif Amuli, whom Akbar deputed later in Bengal to preach his new religion, just to mention a few. These people had learned Greek philosophy and acquainted themselves to some extent with Indian thought mostly by their contact with Hindu pundits at the court. They objected to the belief in prophecy and revelation, and denied the need for a Divine Shari'ah. To counteract this trend Sirhindi wrote his first book *Ithbat al-Nubuwwah, (Defence of Prophecy)* when he was at Agra. After a brief mention of the situation at the court, which has already been quoted, Sirhindi enters into a detailed discussion of the nature, function and necessity of prophecy, and the method to establish the claim of a particular prophet. He upholds the possibility of a super-rational way to knowledge by referring to the phenomena of dream and mystic *kashf,* and underlines the need of prophetic revelation by showing that human reason is incapable of establishing truths beyond the world of perception, and that the mystic *kashf,* which is another alternative, is not infallible, especially in view of the fact that such revelations vary from one mystic to another. The only reliable source is the prophetic *wahy.* So far as the establishment of a particular claim to prophecy is concerned, Sirhindi bases his argument on the life, message and the work of the prophet, in addition to the miracles that he performs. In the case of Muhammad (peace be upon him!) his argument centres on the Kur'an, his exemplary life, the perfection of Shari'ah and its impact on society. The *Ithbat al-Nubuwwah* is a concise, cogent and forceful work on the subject. In this and other theological discussions scattered over many of his letters Sirhindi draws upon the whole theological tradition of Islam, above all the Maturidi *kalam* prevailing in Central Asia. But one also comes across many fresh insights and new arguments, particularly in discussions on the essence and attributes of God, freedom of will and responsibility for belief in God before revelation, not to mention his theosophical doctrine of *wahdat al-shuhud.*

Along with prophecy the honour of the Companions (*sahabah*) of the Prophet was also under attack. A campaign of vilification was launched by the extremist Shi'ahs throughout the country with renewed vigour, following the revival of similar activity in Iran, against the first three caliphs for depriving 'Ali, as they said, of the right of succeed the Prophet, and against 'A'ishah, Talhah, Zubayr and Mu'awiyah who opposed and fought 'Ali afterwards. Those who supported these Companions were also cursed; this amounted to the condemnation of the entire community of Companions except a few members of 'Ali's house and his supporters. The campaign at the Agra Court was carried out by Shi'ah scholars headed by Qadi Nurullah Shushtari; in the south it was led by the successors of Burhan Nizam Shah (1508-53) who had recently employed hundreds of people in order to abuse the Companions and kill those who opposed them; in the north, Kashmir was another centre for this campaign. The scholars at Agra came out with a book refuting the criticism levelled against them by the Sunni scholars of Central Asia (*Ma Wara' al-Nahr*), and vindicating their own position. This book was being projected as a great achievement and was used to strengthen the campaign.

Sirhindi reviewed this work in his book, *Radd-i Rawafid,* and substantiated the Sunni position. In it and the other letters dealing with the subject, Sirhindi tries to show that the Shi'ah practice of condemning and vilifying the Companions of the Prophet is mistaken, degrading and disastrous. First of all, it is not true that the Prophet nominated 'Ali to succeed him, and the so-called *ahadith* mentioning his nomination are forged. Second, it is against the known practice of the first three caliphs to violate the Prophet's decree, as it is against the dignity of 'Ali to subject himself to their authority and falsify thereby his claim, if the prophet had nominated him. Third, if the Shi'ah position is accepted and the Companions are condemned, it would seriously affect the credibility of the Kur'an which they had collected, and undermine the authenticity of the whole corpus of Hadith which they had transmitted; it would further discredit the work of the Prophet who spent his whole life instructing men who *en masse* violated the will of their leader. In the case of the Companions who opposed 'Ali later on, Sirhindi states clearly that in their feuds the truth was with 'Ali, and his opponents were in the wrong, but their opposition was due to an error in judgment, as many scholars have pointed out, regarding the right course of action, rather than caused by personal motives. Hence, they deserve not to be condemned, but to be excused. If anybody thinks that this explanation clears Talhah, Zubayr and 'A'ishah, but not Mu'awiyah whom Sirhindi would not except, even then the practice of vilification against him after his death is degrading, particularly when he had rendered a number of enviable services to Islam.

Sirhindi's *Radd-i Rawafid* was well received; an indication of its popularity is that almost a century later, a scholar of Waliyullah's calibre chose to write a commentary on it and popularise its ideas.

The life of the Muslim masses was ridden with *Shirk* and *bid'ah* (unauthorized innovation) due to their contact with the polytheistic religions and cultures of India. Ignorant of their faith, muslims participated in the religious rites of the non-Muslims, and prayed to their idols and Gods for various purposes; women, in particular, sought their protection against diseases such as small pox. They joined Hindu festivals such as *rakhi* and *dipavali,* and celebrated the latter by lighting lamps, cooking rice and sending it as a present in coloured pots to relatives and friends as the Hindus used to do on that occasion. The influence of Indian culture has spread to other classes, too; a poet of great talents at the court of Khan-i-Khanan in Deccan, for instance, had adopted *kufri* (the lover of *kufr*) as his poetic name (*takhallus*).

The other cause of the religious degeneration of Muslim masses was the influence of ignorant and misguided Sufis. On their bidding they made votive offerings (*nadhr*) to saints (*masha'ikh*) and offered sacrifices on their graves. Women usually fasted in the name of Sufi teachers, even their wives, and observed various rituals in this connection. For instance, they would not break their fast except with the food they collected by begging, even though they did not need it. Both men and women made special efforts to celebrate the tenth day of Muharram, the fifteenth night of Sha'ban, the twenty-seventh day of Rajab, and the first Friday night of the same month, which they called *Laylat al-Ragha'ib,* and offered *salah* (prayer) in assembly considering it to be a highly meritorious act.

Most Sufis held musical sessions (*sama'*), indulged in spiritual dances (*raqs*) and celebrated the birth of the Prophet; even the sons of Sirhindi's preceptor did not mind attending to music and songs on Thursday nights. They cared more for *dhikr* and *fikr* (contemplation) than *fard* and *sunnah,* indulged in spiritual exercises such as *arba'inat* (a special course of forty days to supererogatory acts), and neglected prayers in assembly (*ba jama'at*), even the weekly prayers on Friedays. The novices had developed strange ideas about their masters: they believed that they had power to deprive them of their spiritual attainments if they became angry, and secure God's pardon for their misdeeds if they were pleased.

Those who subscribed to *wahdat al-wujud* cared little for the

Shari'ah. They believed that the goal of the Shari'ah was to attain knowledge; hence if any one realised the truth of *wahdat al-wujud,* he did not have to perform the duties of the *Shar'*. Some of them disparaged *salah* because it differentiated between God and the servant; others equated resurrection with the Sufi experience of *fana'* (annihilation) and denied judgment and punishment. Some even loved to gaze at beautiful faces and hear sweet voices, because they were the manifestations of the Eternal Beauty.

Sirhindi referred to these ideas and practices in his letters and denounced them as *shirk* (associationism), *kufr* (infidelity) and *bid'ah* (innovation). He urged upon Sufi teachers and *masha'ikh* to discard these evil practices and reform their lives. To a Sufi teacher at Thaneshwar, for instance, he wrote:

> To delay the *'isha'* prayer till the second half of the night in order to make the *salat-i tahajjud* easy, is highly objectionable; it has been condemned as *makruh-i tahrimi* by the Hanafi *fuqaha.'*.. This practice must be stopped and the earlier prayer must be repeated...you should never recommend the water that you have used in ablution (*wadu*) to the people for drinking; because the water spilt in ablution is dirty according to Abu Hanifah. The *fuqaha'* have forbidden its use...I have come to know from a reliable source that the disciples of your deputies (*khulafa'*) prostrate before them, and are not satisfied with simply bowing their heads. This is reprehensible, and should be strongly condemned and forbidden.

Sirhindi did not distinguish between good and bad innovations: he denounced every innovation (*bid'ah*), provided it belonged to the field of religion. In a letter to a disciple he explained his views as follows :

> You have asked how is it that I forbid *dhikr* with loud voice and condemn it as *bid'ah,* but do not condemn many other things which had not existed at the time of the Prophet such as the shirt open in front (*libas-i farji*) and pyjama. Please note that the acts of the Prophet were of two kinds: those that were performed as

> *'ibadah* (an act of worship) and those that were done as *'urf* and *'adah* (habits and customs). The acts which were done as *'ibadah,* we consider deviations from them to be evil innovations, and condemn them strongly, for they are innovations in religion (*din*) and must be rejected. But the acts which were done as part of habit and custom, we do not regard deviations from them as innovation, and do not proscribe them for they do not belong to religion (*din*); their existence or disappearance depends upon the custom of society under than religion.

If we review the practices which Sirhindi has condemned as *bid'ah* we find that the innovators introduce things into religion (*din*) which have no textual support, which change the relative priorities among the rules of the Shari'ah which increase the importance of a thing beyond what the *Shar'* has itself provided, and which specify time, place and ways for doing things which have been commended by the *Shar'* but without those specifications. Every *bid'ah* Sirhindi says, changes the recommended course of doing things and replaces the Sunnah.

Sirhindi laments that the 'Ulama' of the time who are the guardians of religion and whose duty is to save the masses from *shirk* and *bid'ah* are themselves involved in those practices. "The world is drowned", he says, "in the sea of *bid'ah* and delights in its black acts; the 'Ulama' of our times have become the preachers of *bid'ah* and destroyers of the Sunnah. No one has the courage to speak against *bid'ah* and revive the Sunnah. Most of the 'Ulama' lead people to *bid'ah*, and prove that they are commended and desirable."

The 'Ulama' did not stop at *bid'ah,* they moved to change the very face of religion. One *'Alim,* for instance, who was the highest authority on religion in the country, issued a *fatwa* saying that the Hajj was no longer incumbent as the journey to Makkah was unsafe. Other 'Ulama' at Lahore ruled that charging interest was legal; still others came out with the verdict that prostration before the king for honour was quite proper. One "crown of the gnostics" (*taj al-'arifin*), using his insight into *wahdat al-wujud,* supported this verdict on the ground that "the king was one with God, nothing less." The cousin of another gnostic ruled that shaving one's beard was perfectly in order because the inhabitants of Paradise were said to be beardless youths.

Sirhindi deplores these acts as sheer distortion of religion and condemns their perpetrators. He calls them the robbers of religion (*lusus-i din*). His wrath is particularly directed to the 'Ulama' of the court who shared the responsibility with heretics like Mulla Mubarak and Abu'l-Fadl in leading Akbar astray. Superficial and incompetent, they could not defend Islam against the free-thinkers; self-seeking and narrow-minded, they discredited religion by fighting between themselves and condemning each other as *fasiq* and *kafir*; and corrupt and mean, they degraded themselves by using their authority to amass wealth.

Sirhindi appealed to the God-fearing 'Ulama' of the country to realise their responsibility in the situation, and to condemn the evils which had infected the life of the masses and damaged the image of Islam. He warned that any complacency in the matter would be disastrous. To an *'Alim* at Lahore, for instance, where some scholars had legalised interest on the plea of need (*ihtiyaj*), he wrote a long letter wherein he refuted their arguments at length, and urged him to realise his duty of enjoining good and forbidding evil (*amr bi'lma'ruf wa nahy 'an al-munkar*). In another letter which he wrote to Mulla Ahmad Barki (d. 1026/1617), his deputy at Berk, he urged: "Try to spread the knowledge of the Shari'ah and the rules of *fiqh* at places where ignorance prevails and *bid'ah* rules, and do it with the same concern and love which, by the grace of God, you have for your friends... Prepare yourself for the task and discharge the duty of enjoining good and forbidding evil which you have towards the people there, and do it only for the pleasure of God."

In 987/1579, some scholars of the royal court prepared a testimony (*mahdar*), got it signed by others and presented it to Akbar. They testified that Akbar was "the most just, most knowledgeable and most God-fearing", that, as such, he ranked above the *mujtahids,* and that he had the authority to rule in matters in which they differed. Armed with this testimony, Akbar did within the next two decades three things which had far reaching consequences for Islam and Muslims in the subcontinent. He launched a new Divine Religion (*Din-i Ilahi*), drafted by Mulla Mubarak and his illustrious son Abu'l-Fadl. He and his loyal scholars entertained the idea that since Islam had completed a thousand years of its life (the natural life-span of a religion!), it ought to be replaced by a new religion. This Divine Religion was so formulated that it incorporated creeds, rites and practices from every religion—Hinduism, Zoroastrianism, Buddhism and Christianity—except Islam. Its details are very interesting, but the present writer shall not discuss them. For, except its original authors and a few more disciples, in all eighteen, no one took the religion seriously, and there are indications that the head-priest, the Emperor himself, ceased to be serious about it afterwards. It is also worth noting that Sirhindi who counteracted Akbar's other measures, took no notice of this new religion. As religion it proved a total failure; however, it succeeded in highlighting the religious degeneration and scepticism of the age.

Second and more important, Akbar gathered at his court men who criticised, flouted and ridiculed Islamic beliefs, practices and personalities. Originally, he started seeking for truth in different religions, but the ambitions of some self-seeking scholars and the rivalries of narrow-minded 'Ulama' turned the quest into a campaign against Islam. Faith in God was retained, but every other belief, life creation of the world, existence of the angels, resurrection of the body, revelation or prophecy was rejected. Eternity of the world and transmigration of soul were instead affirmed. The life of the Prophet was criticised; his name was expunged from individual names; *salah* and other rites were flayed, and injunctions concerning lawful (*halal*) and unlawful (*haram*) acts were ridiculed. Things did not end there: those who refused to comply and dared to object were humiliated, imprisoned or exterminated.

Third and most important, Akbar acted to change the laws and institutions of the country based on the Shari'ah. He abolished *zakat* and *jizyah;* withdrew the prohibition of drinking and gambling; forbade marriages between cousins allowed in the Shari'ah; prescribed polygyny, but ironically enough, removed censor on prostitution; banned slaughter of cows; prohibited killing of animals on many specific days of the year; dropped the name of the Prophet and Companions from Friday sermons; discontinued the Hijri calendar; introduced new coins marking the new millennium; discouraged the study of Arabic and islamic disciplines; stopped or reduced government aid to Arabic/theological schools; and did not seek to fill the ecclesiastical posts which fell vacant.

The effect of these measures was that Islam ceased even to be a religion among other religions: it was constricted and castigated. The revival of Hinduism in northern India by the followers of Chaytanya made the conditions worse. At several places the life of Muslims was threatened, mosques were demolished, and the observances of Islamic rites obstructed. Sirhindi laments the situation in several letters: "In the earlier generation non-Muslims freely performed their religious rites in Muslim towns, but Muslims could not practise Islam; if they dared, they were put to death." "The non-Muslims of India are not afraid to demolish mosques and erect temples in their place. For instance, in Kurukshetra there was a mosque and the tomb of a saint. They have been demolished and in these places a very big temple has been erected. Moreover, non-Muslims openly carry out their rituals, but Muslims are powerless to fulfil the Islamic injunctions. During Ekadashi, Hindus fast and strive hard to see that in Muslim quarters no Muslim cooks or sells food on these days. On the other hand, during Ramadan they openly prepare and sell food, but owing to the weakness of Islam, nobody can interfere. Alas, the ruler of the country is one of us, but we are in such a miserable state."

Towards the end of Akbar's reign a struggle for succession between his sons ensued. Salim secured the support of some influential officials of the court who resented Akbar's religious policies. He promised to defend the Shari'ah, and ascended the throne under the name of Jahangir after his father died in 1014/1605.

Sirhindi was delighted to hear about Jahangir's accession. But he was not sure if Jahangir had the will to carry out the promise, or knew the way how to do it. He therefore made it a point that Jahangir's commitment to the Shari'ah was strengthened and that he got proper advice in the matter. He was also apprehensive of opposite elements that had by no means disappeared. With this reading of the situation he started to write to the officials close to Jahangir to tell him the plight of Islam and Muslims in the country and impress upon him the need to act promptly. To the Sadr-i Jahan (d. 1027/1618), who had tutored Jahangir before and enjoyed his confidence as the highest religious authority, he wrote: "Now that things have changed and the hostility of the people has subsided, it is the duty of the leaders of Islam, the *Sadr-i Islam* and the 'Ulama' of Islam that they work for the implementation of the Shari'ah. The institutions of Islam which have been demolished must be quickly restored; delay is not at all good, it makes us very uneasy...If the king is not enthusiastic to implement the rules of the Prophet (peace be upon him!), and if his confidants also excuse themselves and like to pass their days in peace, life will become difficult and miserable for Muslims who have no means." To Khan-i Jahan (d. 1040/1630), another official of the court, he wrote: "Since the king listens to your words and gives them weight, it would be really great if you could explain to him briefly or in detail, as you like, the beliefs of the *Ahl-i Sunnat wa Jama'at.* Please inform him of the doctrines of the People of Truth (*Ahl al-Haqq*) and look for every opportunity to talk about Islam and the Muslims, defend the tents of Islam and condemn infidelity and heresy." When Jahangir desired to have four 'Ulama' to advise him, he wrote to Shaykh Farid, who played a leading role in securing the throne to Jahangir, to persuade him to have only one God-fearing and competent *'Alim,* lest rivalries between the 'Ulama' disgust him as they had disgusted his father earlier.

Sirhindi also urged upon the high officials in the provinces to do what they could in their own spheres. He wrote letters to Shaykh Murtada (the Governor of Gujarat), Qulich Khan (the devout Viceroy of Lahore), Lala Beg (the Governor of Bihar), 'Abd al-Rahim Khan-i Khanan (the Commander-in-Chief of Deccan), and many other top-most dignitaries. He called them to spread the teachings of Islam, to defend the faith, to abolish unIslamic laws, to restore Islamic institutions, and to suppress anti-islamic forces. He told them of the great reward that awaited them in the Hereafter even for any small thing they would do, because they would be doing the work of the prophets.

Six years after his accession Jahangir married Nurjahan, who because of her beauty, culture and great talents established unlimited ascendancy over her husband, and by getting her brother appointed as premier, and her father an important member of the court, secured full control of the government. With her ascendancy the extremist Shi'ah elements at the court started working against the Sunnis. As Sirhindi exercised considerable influence on the Sunni section, they turned against him. They impressed upon Jahangir that because of his great following throughout India, his contact with officers at the court and in the provinces, Sirhindi posed a threat to the kingdom. On the other hand, the Sufis whose ideas and practices Sirhindi had condemned and whose *masha'ikh* he had criticised were not happy with him. When some of his over-enthusiastic disciples began extolling his mystical attainments and publicised his visionary experiences, they came out to denounce him openly. A letter that Sirhindi had written sixteen years previously, wherein he had mentioned that in a vision he went beyond the stage of Abu Bakr, aroused strong condemnation from various quarters. Some even called him an infidel (*kafir*) deserving to be killed.

In 1028/1619 Jahangir called Sirhindi and asked him to explain the charges levelled against him. In his *Memoirs* where he records the episode, he says that he was not satisfied with Sirhindi's answer, and to chastise him and to pacify public sentiments he ordered for his imprisonment. Other sources say that Jahangir was satisfied with Sirhindi's answer, but since he did not prostrate in honour when he entered the court, Jahangir sent him to jail.

Sirhindi bore the sufferings of the prison with patience; he neither regreted his action nor made any effort to secure release. Believing that the trial would not have happened had God not allowed it, he took it as a way of the Lord to bring him closer to Himself. He continued his work in prison with the same vigour as he did outside. Impressed by his life and preaching, hundreds of non-Muslim convicts repented of their past deeds and embraced Islam.

A year later, Jahangir set Sirhindi free, called him to the court, honoured him with a robe, returned his property, and offered him one thousand rupees. He gave him the option to go home or stay with him in the camp. Sirhindi preferred the camp, for it provided him the unique opportunity to preach to the king and the people around him. In various sessions which he had with Jahangir, he read out the Qur'an to him, explained its message, discussed the principles of faith, and elaborated the rules of the Shari'ah. This seems to have had its effect. A year later when Jahangir conquered the fort of Kangra he showed unusual enthusiasm to enforce some Islamic laws in that quarter. He forbade the same year the practice of marrying Muslim girls to non-Muslims in Kashmir. He reintroduced the Hijri calendar, engraved an Islamic emblem on coins, rebuilt the mosques that had been demolished, and encouraged Arabic and Islamic learning.

Sirhindi remained three years at the camp, accompanied the king on several campaigns and visited many places. By this time his health had started failing. He returned to Sirhind, reduced his contacts, and devoted himself to *dhikr* and prayer. On 28th Safar, 1034/10th December, 1624, he breathed his last to meet his Lord.

What has been discussed above offer only an outline of Shaykh Ahmad Sirhindi's mission concerning *tasawwuf* and its relation with the Prophetic Islam. For the first time in the history of Sufism, a mystic of his calibre has analysed mystic experience, elucidated the nature and characteristics of its different stages, and assessed their value and significance. For the first time again, a Sufi of his eminence has clearly distinguished between the prophetic way and the saintly way to God, and has judged the latter in the light of the former. With an unusual boldness, Sirhindi reviews the whole history of Sufism and identifies what ideas and practices are within the bounds of the Shari'ah and what must be condemned as aberrations. Nothing deters him from censuring any personality, however great, if he or she said or did anything that goes against the Shari'ah. He particularly subjects the philosophy of *wahdat al-wujud* to searching criticism, and censures its consequences to Islamic beliefs, values and practices. Last and nor least, he expounds a theosophy in place of *wahdat al-wujud* that would agree with the highest mystic experience of difference (*farq*), on the one hand, and the Islamic Shari'ah, on the other.

This work as Shaykh Ahmad himself thinks is his best contribution to the renovation of Islam in India though it has been little studied and far less appreciated.

12

Baba Farid Ganj-I-Shankar and his Mystical Philosophy

MOHD. NOOR NABI

A man lean and thin, wearing tattered clothes, living in indigent circumstances and residing under a thatched roof, starts for Juma 'prayer in the nearby mosque. As he steps out of his house, people eagerly rush towards him, kiss his hands and encircle him. No sooner does he manage to come out of this circle than he finds himself encircled by another group. He gets rid of one circle to be enmeshed into another and this process goes on until he reached the mosque tired and worried. As he finishes his prayer, people kiss his hands in overwhelming numbers.

This man is Shaikh Farid-u'd-din Mas'ud, popularly known as Baba Farid Ganj-i-Shakar. He was born in1175 A.d. at Kahtwal and died in 1265 A.D. at the age of ninety in Ajodhan, present Pakpattan.

Baba Farid's mother, Qarsum Bibi by name, was a lady of fervent piety and penitence. It was the lap of his mother from where his education began. She generated that spark of Divine love in him which lasted throughout his life and which later developed and dominated his entire personality. From the very beginning of his career in Kahtwas he became well-known for his intense devotion and piety. Shaikh Bahau'd-din Zakriyya, the founder of Suhrawardi order in Multan, expressed his desire to see him at that time.

Shaikh Jalal-u'd-din Tabrizi, an eminent disciple of Shaikh Abu Sa'id Tabrizi and a close associate of Shaikh Shihabu'd-din Suhrawardi, on his way to Delhi heard about him and came to Kahtwas to meet him. He offered Baba Farid a piece of pomegranate, which he could not eat at that time due to his fast. After the departure of the Shaikh, Baba Farid found a seed of the pomegranate, lying on the floor. He picked up that seed and ate it at the time of Iftar. This brought a sudden spiritual illumination in him.

At the age of 18 after finishing his education at Kahtwal Baba Farid proceeded to Multan for higher studies. There he committed to memory the entire text of the Qur'an. It was at Multan that he met Shaikh Qutbu'd-din Bakhtiyar Kaki, the Khalifa and successor of Shaikh Mu'in-u d-din Chishti, popularly known as Khwaja Gharib-i-Nawaz, in a mosque at whose feet he surrendered for his spiritual discipline. When Shaikh Qutb-u'd-din left Multan for Delhi Baba Farid accompanied him and in Delhi he engaged himself in prayer and mortification. When Khwaja Ajmeri happened to visit Delhi, he made enquiries about Baba Farid and seeing him remarked, "Baba Bakhtiyar! You have caught a noble falcon which will not build his nest except on the holy tree of the heaven. Farid is a lamp that will illuminate the silsilah of dervishes."

Baba Farid enjoyed the unique privilege in the Chishti Order of being initiated both by the director (Pir, Shaikh Qutb-u'd-din) and the director of his director (Shaikh Mu'in-u'd-din Chishti).

Baba Farid led a life of piety and penitence. He was proud of his poverty (faqr) and observed continuous fast. At Ucch he performed the Chilla Ma'kus by hanging head downwards in a well, suspended from the boughs of a tree. It is the general opinion of the Indian Shaikhs that no saint has excelled Baba Farid in his devotions and penitences. The devotion and penitence of Baba Farid reminds us of the devotion and penitence of Shaikh Bayazid Bistami.

According to Shaikh Nizam-u'd-din Auliya, it was a pathetic and thrilling scene to see Baba Farid in his prayer. When alone in his room he would lay his head on the ground for hours and recite, (I die for Thee and I live for Thee).

Baba Farid was a living embodiment of all the moral virtues which he preached to his disciples and visitors. His excellence was the excellence of his character. There was a complete unanimity in his thought, words and deeds. He had a lovable and affectionate nature—truthfulness, honesty, sincerity, love and devotion were the chief traits of his personality. His private life was a perfect mirror of his public life. There was a complete absence of hypocrisy. He had a very sympathetic and tender heart. He always tried to console the hearts of aggrieved people. He spent his long life in lifting the humanity from the quagmires of sin and superstition.

Baba Farid's monastery (khanqah) was open to all irrespective of caste and creed. Rich and poor, official and non-officials, old and young, Hindus and Muslims were received equally in a cordial way. A stream of visitors flowed to the monastery every day, but Baba Farid never got tired of it. He attended to the problem of every visitor individually and tired his best to remedy his grievances. He furnished the society of his day with an infinite moral force which removed the social, ideological and linguistic barriers between the various cultural groups of India. He, for the first time, sowed the seed of emotional, cultural and linguistic integration which later on flourished and as a final shape we have the Hindustani culture and Hindustani of Urdu language.

Delhi, at the time of Baba Farid, was a great centre of Muslim culture. Many refugees from Central Asia had settled there. They generally aspired for mundane honour and position. Allurements of court life had drawn them to Delhi. Baba Farid, too, breathed in that atmosphere for a short time. His fame and popularity spread in Delhi like wild fire. But Baba Farid was not hankering after worldly grandeur and honour. He was in search of truth and solace for the suffering humanity. Therefore, he left Delhi and migrated to Hansi. He used to deliver sermons at Hansi. Very soon he attained popularity there. He shifted to Kahtwal and from Kahtwal he came to Ajodhan, where he settled permanently. Very soon in Ajodhan the period of self- discipline came to an end and the seclusion (uzlat) was changed into association (suhbat). The door of the Khanqah was opened and every one was allowed to visit him without any discrimination. Shaikh Farid -u'd-din devoted his long life there to enhance the moral and spiritual condition of the society. His humanity, sublimity of character and spiritual calibre helped in spreading the fame of the Chishti Order to distant places.

Baba Farid possessed all those qualities of head and heart which are needed for the expansion of any silsilah. He made Sufism a mass movement. Sufism took root in the life of the people and became more and more Indianised in its character and expression. There was a vital difference of approach between the orthodox theologians and the sufis. There was no place in the heart of a theologian *(Alim-i-zahir)* for sinners or misery-stricken people. A theologian was just like a lawyer or a judge who was talking simply in terms of virtues and vices, punishment and reward, Muslims and infidels. But sufis, on the other hand, took Islam to the masses. In doing so they exclusively emphasised the moral training and building of conduct and character. They dealt with the problems of suffering humanity at a personal level. Whenever, any aggrieved person or sinner came to Baba Farid, the latter welcomed him with affection and warmth of emotion. He consoled his tormenting heart and tried his best to pacify him. As a new babe gets consolation in the lap of its mother, so the visitor, either suffering from the worldly or spiritual trouble or conflict, used to get solace and peace of mind in the company of Baba Farid. Baba Farid trained a number of disciples and khalifas who spread the Chishti silsilah in different parts of the country. And it can be rightly said that though Chishti silsilah was founded in India by Shaikh Mu'in-u'd-din Chishti, it was popularised in Delhi by Shaikh Qutb-u'ddin Bakhtiyar Kaki. But the credit goes to Baba Farid who made it a mass movement and with his effort and with the effort of his illustrious khalifa and successor, Shaikh Nizam-u'd-din Auliya, it spread in every nook and corner of the sub-continent.

Writing a paper on Baba Farid is, no doubt, a tempting task, but the great difficulty is the difficulty of the sources of material. Baba Farid himself did not write any book. The statement of Shaikh Nizam-u'd-din Auliya in *Fawa'id-ul-Fu'ad* and of Shaikh Nasir-u-din Chiragh-i-Delhi clearly prove this point.

It is alleged that *Fawa'id-us-Salikin* is a collection of the conversations of Shaikh Qutb-u'd-din Bakhtiyar Kaki compiled by Shaikh Farid-u'd-din Ganj-i-Shakar and *Rahat-ul-Qutub* is a collection of the conversations of Shaikh Farid-u'd-din Ganj-i-Shakar compiled by Shaikh Nizam-u'd-din Auliya. But the above two books are pure and simple fabrications. I have examined the contents of these two books in my book *Development of Muslim Religious Thought in India,* and have shown that the books are a fabrication. Credit is due to authors of *Fawa'id-u'l-Fu'ad, Khair-u'l-Majalis* and *Siyar-u'l-Auliya* who have recorded the conversations of Shaikh Nizam-u'd-din Auliya and his Khalifa and successor Shaikh Nasir-u'd-din Chirag-i-Delhi and their Khalifas through which we come to know the thought of Baba Farid.

The Bani of Baba Farid Incorporated in Adi Granth

Sometimes in the 16th century Guru Nanak met twice Shaikh Brahm (Shaikh Ibrahim), the twelfth in the line of descendants of Baba Farid. The Guru held spiritual colloquies with him. The Shaikh presented a collection of shalokas alleged to have been composed by Baba Farid in local dialects. The Guru must have gone through these shalokas very carefully and cautiously. The message of broad humanitarianism based on forgiveness, non-injury, consolation of the aggrieved heart, fear of the consequences of evil action, love of God and humanity, transitoriness of the worldly riches, grandeur and honour, importance of death as a deterring factor from oppression, tyranny, sin and pride and cultivation of higher moral values, is the theme of these shalokas. This message of Baba Farid is really a universal message rising above differences of sect, creed, community, colour and race. It has a great moral force which ennobles a man and prepares him for the vision of God. Guru Nanak, who was a seeker of truth, must have been attracted by this message and that is why he included these shalokas in the Adi Granth which later on were incorporated in Guru Granth. It cannot be said conclusively that the words used in the Bani are exactly the words of Baba Farid; but as far as the matter is concerned, it is in perfect harmony with the teachings of Baba Farid as we find in *Fawa'id-u'l-Fu'ad, Khair-u'l-Majalis* and *Siyar-u'l-Auliya.*

Let us now formulate his mystical philosophy.

Conception of God

Baba Farid had a unique personality, unique in the sense that he was a profound scholar of theology, a very good speaker and, last but no least, a man of great mystic vision and gnosis (*ma'rifat*). Therefore, his conception of God was not merely a scholarly presentation or an outcome of logical reasoning but it was the expression of his deep religious meditation and intuition. God for him, was a living reality having an all embracing personality present in his intellectual, ethical and mystic experience. It was not the God of Deism who after the creation became aloof from the universe and left the universe to go on mechanically, nor was it the God of Pantheism who Himself mainfested in the universe and became immanenet in it, but it was the God of Theism who was both Transcendent and Immanent.

Baba Farid felt as if God was always in his presence. While offering prayers, he seemed to be communicating with Him. The brother of Baba Farid, Shaikh Najib-u'd-din Mutawakkil, asked him one day. "People say that when you pray you hear God saying. I am present my 'Abd (Creature); is it so? "It would be presumptuous to say 'yes' to his query," replied Baba Farid. Baba Farid did not want to be oblivious of Him even for a single moment. One day he was walking a little distance with the aid of a stick. All of a sudden he threw away the stick and became restless. When the reason was asked, he replied that he was reprimanded because he was depending on something other than God. God for Baba Farid was omnipotent. It was his firm belief that He was the only bestower. Recommending the case of a certain person to Sultan Ghiyath-u'd-din Balban, he wrote: "I put his case first before God and then before you. If you award him something, you will be thanked for it because you are the agent for this award, but god, in the real sense, is the only bestower; if you refuse it, then you are helpless in this matter, because God is the only refuser." He, in the *Khilafat-Namah,* which he gave to Shaikh Nizam-u'd-din Auliya, says, "God alone deserves all praises. He is the first and the last, the Manifest and the Hidden, whomsoever, He elevates none can bring him down and whomsoever He throws down, none can elevate him. None can bring to light what He has concealed and none can conceal whatever He has revealed."

All the above statements of Baba Farid clearly show that God, for him, was a living Reality having an objective existence. He was in personal contact with Him and he had a firm conviction that God was always in his presence. This consciousness of the Divine presence was a guiding and stimulating force for his practical life which made him a citizen of that universal society in which God is the supreme creator and the entire humanity—nay the entire universe-is His humble creation.

Love of God

The *summum bonum* of life, in the opinion of Baba Farid, is the attainment or the realisation of God, as expressed in the verse, "In both the worlds thou alone art the object that I cherish."

For the attainment of this cherished end he prescribed the path of love. He attached so much value to love of God that he used to greet his visitors with these words, "May God give you pain (*dard*) of love." He had great admiration for the individual who was intoxicated with the love of God. He called such a person a `Faqir' (mystic-dervish).

The learned men (*'Ulama*), according to him, are nobler than the common people, but the faqirs are the noblest of all. The faqirs occupy the same position in relation to the learned men which the full moon occupies in the constellation of stars.

A true devotee, in the opinion of Baba Farid, is one who is the love of God. He says, "Those alone are true devotees whose heart is sincere in love with God. The ones whose heart is belied by their tongue are false, inconstant. The true devotees soaked in God's love are ever in ecstasy of realisation; Those indifferent to Him are a burden on earth. The true devotees are those whom God attaches to Himself, Blessed is their birth; truly fruitful their life,"

"Lord, I seek shelter in Thee
Thou alone the bestower of forgiveness,

Grant to shaikh Farid the charity of
Thy devotion."

The above Bani of Baba Farid incorporated in Adi Granth, p. 588, truly depicts the attitude of Baba Farid towards God and the importance of love and devotion to God. Baba Farid categorically says that love of God and greed cannot go side by side.

"Farid, Love of God and greed go not together
With greed love is rendered impure
Such love is frail as leaking straw roof against rain."

Love of God begets the union with God and for the union with God purification of the heart from the evil desires, control of the emotion and passions and performance of noble deeds are but indispensable.

Baba Farid says:

"Listen man, shouldst thou ennoble thyself, Then mayst thou have union with the creator and have true bliss; whoever is for God, the world will be for him."

Baba Farid also emphasises the Grace of God. He is but categorical in his statement that it is only through the grace of God that Union (with God) is possible.

"To one separated from her Lord, what comfort? Through His grace alone my she find union."

He further says:

"God in His grace may join me to holy company. As I look around, God alone I find my succourer.

Baba Farid as a Humanist

Baba Farid was a great humanist. The entire mission of his life was to remove the pain and miseries of the suffering humanity and to provide a man with that vigour and energy with which he may face the ordeals of practical life and lead a life of peace, progress and solace in this world and the world beyond.

The humanism of Baba Farid was not in complete tune with the humanism preached by great medieval thinkers, such as Anselm (1033-1109 A.D.), Abelard (1079-1142 A.D.) Aquinas (d. 1274 A.D.), Duns Sotus (d. 1308), etc. The humanism of these thinkers was too much other-worldly. "Only as a member of a superhuman and supernatural society, of the kingdom wherein God is king, could man hope to attain the full fruition of his rational nature," was the motto of the medieval Humanism. Baba Farid, on the contrary, emphasised the earthly life, the life with family members in society, the goodness of which would make the life afterwards or the eternal life comfortable and pleasant.

It was also not in perfect agreement with the views of the prophets of humanism in France both in the age of the Revolution and after, the ideal of Condorcet, the saint Simoniams, Auguste Comte (d. 1789 A.D.). etc. Humanism, in their opinion, was conceived as the "simplest of philosophic standpoint, the aim of which is the preception that the philosophic problem concerns human beings striving to comprehend a world of human experience by the resources of human minds."

Baba Farid against the claim of the above humanists categorically asserts that the resources of human minds, i.e., the scientific reason, are limited in nature. Scientific reason has no access in the spiritual realm. The problems of spiritual realm can be grasped only by inspiration (kashf) and gnosis (ma'rifat), i.e. by intuition.

As far as the 20th century movements in Humanism such as Pragmatism, Marxism and Existentialism are concerned, these movements, too, basically differ from that of Baba Farid.

Baba Farid does not agree with the basic proposition of the pragmatist that a man is the measure of all the premises. He differ from Marxism on the point that matter is the only reality and that there is no place for God in the creation, maintenance and working of the universe. He does not agree with the motto of the existentialist that "there is no other universe except the human universe, the universe of human subjectivity." This relation of transcendence as constitutive of man (not in the sense that God is transcendent, but in the sense of self-surpassing) with subjectivity (in such a sence that man is not shut up in himself but for ever present in a human universe) is called existential humanism.

It is but obvious that Baba Farid does not conceive the transcendence and subjectivity in the sense in which it is conceived by an existentialist. With the brief introduction let us explain the humanism of Baba Farid.

Baba Farid's mission was the peace and progress of the humanity at large. To attain this cherished goal he prescribed three paths: (i) the path of knowledge, (ii) the path of self-discipline and (iii) the path of love.

Baba Farid was a great lover of knowledge and scholarship. It was his firm conviction that without knowledge it is very difficult to discipline the self and to traverse the path of love. Knowledge, says Baba Farid, is a divine gift for the individual. Men should make an endeavour to attain it. Mere desire to attain it does not make a man learned. Had it been so, no one in the world would have been illiterate. Therefore, one should make an earnest effort for the attainment of knowledge. He should not mind humiliation and disgrace in the way of attaining knowledge. The religion, in the opinion of Baba Farid, can be protected through knowledge. The Prophet used to say that blessed is the man whose knowledge of his own faults and defects prevents him from disclosing the faults of other.

Baba Farid assigned a respectable position to a learned man in society. He said "The 'ulama (learned men) are nobler than the common people and the faqirs (dervishes) are the noblest of all."

While appointing Shaikh Nizam-u'd-din as his successor, he remarked, God has bestowed on you knowledge, reason and love and one who possesses these three qualities can discharge the duties of the Khilafat of the Shaikh well.

Baba Farid vehemently condemned ignorance. He goes to the

extreme extent and declares, "Do not regard the ignorant as alive." He further says,"Give a wide berth to the ignorant man who poses as a learned one"

After knowledge we come to the discipline of the soul.

Baba Farid attached special importance to purification of the soul, because for the good of humanity it is but indispensable that every member of society should possess a noble and exemplary character. Baba Farid spent most of his long life of ninety years in ennobling the character of the corrupted humanity. He gave the highest position in society to a faqir and he defines a faqir as one who purifies everything, and whom "nothing can make dirty". Thus self-purification is the first and foremost ideal which he wants to inculcate in his followers. For self-purification he prescribes a number of disciplines.

Baba Farid restrains his followers from excessive indulgence in the gross and material world. A man, in his opinion, who busies himself exclusively with feeding an clothing himself, is the meanest of all people. He further says that misery is the by-product of mundane aspirations. Therefore, one should not pay undue attention to the demands of the physical self; the more one satisfies it, the more it demands.

He warns his disciples against pride and arrogance. Pride, according to him, turns the whole into an enemy. Hence, a man should beware of pride. Particularly one should not take pride in committing sin because it makes the heart of a man, which is the sheet of love and truth, a plaything of the devil.

Baba Farid always tried by precept and example to impress upon the minds of his followers the importance of consolation and comfort of the human heart, good work, nobility of character, sense of justice, self-dignity, generosity, gratitude and contentment. These are the positive qualities which the Shaikh wanted to implant inhumanity at large.

The virtue of charity was ingrained in the nature of Baba Farid. What ever unasked gifts (*futuh*) came to his monastery he at once distributed among his visitors. The same spirit of charity he wanted to inculcate in his disciples. His discussion of Zakat (alms) throws interesting light on this matter.

Zakat, according to him, is of thee kinds : (1) Zakat-i-Shari'at, (2) Zakat-i-Tariqat and (3) Zakat-i-Haqiqat.

Zakat-i-Shari'at consits in giving 5 dirhams out of 20; Zakat-i-Tariqat means that one keeps 5 dirhams and gives 15 dirhams, and zakat-i-Haqiqat demands that all should be given and nothing is retained.

He prescribed Zakat-i-Shari'at for those who became his disciples for spiritual betterment yet carried on their worldly pursuits. But for his Khalifas he prescribed Zakat-i-Haqiqat. Thus the Baba Farid's idea was that one should not live for oneself only but should always try to comfort others.

After self-discipline, lastly we come to the path of Love. Love is the basic teaching of sufism. This love includes both the love of God and the love of the creatures, the sufis being unanimous that God cannot be loved without loving the creatures of God. Through love a Sufi wants to create harmony in discordant elements of society. True to this ideal Baba Farid struggled hard to create the atmosphere of love and good-will so that a healthy social order free from dissensions, conflicts, discrimination, hatred and jealousy, may emerge. To achieve this goal he organised and himself supervised the Jama'at Khana. The Jamaat Khana of the Shaikh consisted of a large room where his disciples and visitors used to sleep, pray and study sitting on the floor. It was run by the inmates themselves. Everyone of them had to do something for the management of the household. There was no discrimination there on any ground, not even on the ground of piety and penitence. Hindus and Muslims, seniors and juniors, old and new, rich and poor, Sultan and beggar, the pious and the sinner, all of them were treated on an equal basis.

Baba Farid himself used to preside over the Jama'at Khana. He was a tower of strength to the low born, the downtrodden, the humble and the despised people.

In India of the 13the century where the difference between the conqueror and the conquered, rich and poor, high caste and low caste, privileged and downtrodden was at its height, this Jama'at Khana of Baba Farid served as an oasis. This was a spiritual centre for personalities like Shaikh Nizam-u'd-din Auliya, Maulana Badru'd-din Ishaque, Shaikh Jamal-u'd-din Hanswi and others. The higher sufi ideals were actually translated into action by the followers of the Shaikh. The spiritually starved people flocked to it from far and near and men of different temperaments and attitudes rubbed their shoulders and learnt to live together.

This humanism of Baba Farid brought a tremendous change in the Punjab in particular and in the Indian subcontinent in general. Today Muslim, Hindus and Sikhs alike hold Baba Farid in high esteem and pay respect to his monument. After his name, the Hindu chief, Mokal, named a place Faridkot, which is now a flourishing town, at about 100 miles from Ajodhan, and Ajodhan itself came to be known as Pakpattan, as a tribute to his piety.

The celebration of octocentenary of this great son of Punjab is in itself a shining proof of the living influence of Baba Farid.

13

Islamic Influence on Later Saints

[Abstract: 16th & 17th century saints included Birham, Baba Lal, Laldas, Pran Nath, Charandas, etc.]

A Contemporary of Dadu was Birbhan, who founded the famous sect of the *Sadhs* or *Satnamis*. He was born in 1543 A.D. at Bijesar near Narnaul in the South-eastern Punjab. He was affiliated through Udhodas to Raidas. He was a strict monotheist, he called God by the name of *Satnam*—the Truth.

He looked upon his *Guru* as the inspirer of his teachings, and spoke about himself as *Udho Ka das*, the servant of Udho whom he describes as the *Malik Ka Hukm*, i.e., the order of the Lord, the personified word of God. The teachings of the sect are in Hindi *Bhasa*, and their collection is known as the *Pothi* (the book), which is reverenced like the *Granth* of the Sikhs. The book is read in a *Jumlaghar* (house of assembly) or a *Chauki* (station), and the evening service is attended by men, women and children.

The *Sadhs* do not observe distinctions of caste and rank, they eat and drink together, and marry inside their sect. They permit divorce for offences in which they penalty is expulsion from the sect. They adore one God under the name of *Satnam*, do not keep any material representation of Him, and they do not bow before idol or man. Their worship consists of meditation and the practice of virtue and their ultimate aim is absorption in God. They abstain from intoxicants and animal foods, maintain a strict standard of morals and do not allow the oppression of one by the other. They believe in earning one's living by lawful means only, they discourage inequalities of wealth and give their charities in secret.

Their chief seats are at Delhi, Rohtak in the Punjab, Agra, Farrukhabad and Mirzrpur in the Uttar Pradesh and Jaipur in Rajputana. They became very prominent in the reign of Aurangzeb, when they broke out into rebellion. In 1672 A.D. Khanfi Khan in his notice of the rebellion gave them a very good character, but Iswardas Nagar calls them filthy and wicked; the head and front of their offending was that they made no distinction between Hindus and Musalmans.

Their twelve *Hukms* or commandments which are given in the *Adi Updesh* (first precepts) are deserving of full reproduction. They are given as:—

1. Acknowledge but one God who made and can destroy you, to whom there is none superior, and to whom alone therefore is worship due; not to earth, nor stone, nor metal, nor wood, nor trees, nor any created thing. There is but one Lord, and the word of the Lord. He who medicates on falsehoods, practises falsehoods and commits sin, and he who commits sin falls into hell.
2. Be modest and humble, set not your affections on the world, adhere faithfully to your creed, and avoid intercourse with all not of the same faith, eat not of a stranger's bread.
3. Never lie nor speak ill at any time to, or of anything of earth or water, of trees, of animals. Let the tongue be employed in the praise of God. Never steal, nor wealth, nor land, nor beasts, nor pasture. distinguish your own from another's property, and be content with what you possess. Never imagine evil. Let not your eyes rest on improper objects, nor men, nor women, nor dances, nor shows.
4. Listen not to evil discourse, nor to anything but the praise of the Creator, nor to tales, nor gossip, nor calumny, nor music, nor singing except hymns; but then the only musical accompaniment must be in the mind.

5. Never covet anything, either of body or wealth; take not of another. God is the giver of all things, as your trust is in Him so shall your receive.
6. When asked what you are, declare yourself a *Sadh*, speak not of caste, engage not in controversy, hold firm your faith, put not your hope in men.
7. Wear white garments, use no pigments, nor collyrium, nor dentifrice, nor *mehndi* (henna), nor mark you person, nor your forehead, with sectional distinctions, nor wear chaplets, or rosaries or jewels.
8. Never eat nor drink intoxicating substances, nor chew *pan*, nor smell perfumes, nor smoke tobaccu, nor chew nor smellopium: hold not up your hands, bow not down your head in the presence of idols or of men.
9. Take no life away, nor offer personal violence, nor give damnatory evidence, nor seize anything by force.
10. Let a man wed one wife, and a woman one husband, led not a man eat of a woman's leavings, but a woman may of a man's as may be the custom. Let the woman be obedient to the man.
11. Assume not the garb of a mendicant, nor solicit alms, nor accept gifts. Have no dread of necromancy, neither have recourse to it. Know before you confide. The meetings of the pious (*Sadhus*) are the only places of pilgrimage, but understand who are the pious (*Saduhs*) before you so salute them.
12. Let not *Saduhs* be superstitious as to days, or to lunations, or to months, or the cries or appearance of birds or animals; let him seek only the will of the Lord.

Commentary on these commandments is superfluous; their sturdy commonsense is an evident as their puritanism which borrows from Islam and goes beyond it. The voice of Birbhan must have sounded like a clarion blast gathering together all those who were fighting for light and reason against superstition and darkness. It must, indeed, have been a wonderful age which could produce Kabir and Nanak, Dadu and Birbhan together and which could render it possible for them to spread their purifying gospel broadcast. The account of the *Sadhs* may be closed with one of their hymns, which illustrates the deeply devotional aspect of their faith:—

> "My frame aches without thee! I am wailing at thy door!
> Now appear and let me see thee.
> O my Lord! I pray thee make no delay!
> I have become restless through weeping and wailing.
> I cannot live without the sight of thee.
> Flames rise within me and consume my frame. Who can endure my pain?
>
> I am full of faults and sins; do thou have mercy upon me.
> Take not my faults and facings into thy regard!
> O! thou that freest the soul from sin, maintain my honour!
> Forget me not even for a moment, and have mercy upon me.
> Show me thy form and forget my sins of the present!
> Cast thine eyes full upon me, and sever not thy love from me."

Laldas and Baba Lal flourished about the middle of the seventeenth century. The founder of the *Laldasi* sect belonged to Alwar and came from a predatory tribe known as the Meos. His teachings ran on the same lines as those of Kabir. The teachers of the sect are married men, and the singing of hymns accompanied with music plays an important part in their worship.

Baba Lal who was a Kshatriya was born in Malwa about the reign of Jahangir. His preceptor was one Chaitana, whom he followed to Lahore. He settled down at Dehanpur near Sirhind where he built a temple and a monastery. The unfortunate Dara Shikoh, who was one of his pupils, had many interviews with the saint in which he obtained instruction on religious questions. The conversations at these interviews were embodied in a book entitled *Nadir-un-Nukat* written in Persian. The teaching is in the form of a dialogue between Dara Shikoh and Baba Lal.

What was the creed of Baba Lal? He answers the question in these words:

"The creed of the lower differs from other creeds. God is the faith and creed of those who love Him, but to go god is best for the follower of every faith." And he quotes the verse of Hafiz approvingly:—

"The object of all religions is alike,
All men seek their beloved—
What is the difference between prudent and wild?
All the world is love's dwelling,
Why talk of a mosque or a church?"

Baba Lal and Laldas were not by any means the only representatives of the religious synthesis which attempted to reconcile Hinduism with Islam in the seventeenth century. There were-numerous saints and teachers who advocated the same ideas; but unfortunately the names and writings of most of them have disappeared; *Dabistan* has however, recorded the names of some with whom the author came into contact or of whom he learnt by reputation. Writing of Pirana Kohaly he mentions the *Vairagis* and their beliefs: "This sect do no harm to any living being...They do not admit the *Avataras* (incarnations), and say that God is exempt from transmigration and union; and according to those who profess the belief in the unity and solitariness of the Supreme being, He is not susceptible of intimate friendship." And again of the *Narayanis*, a sect founded by Haridas, who died in 1055 A.H. (1644 A.D.), he says: "This sect knows nothing of idols, nor of temples, nor of the *Ka`bah*, nor of any sort of worship; they do nothing towards obtaining the knowledge of, or union with, God; they confine themselves to the veneration of *Narayan* or the Supreme Being, from which they derive the name of *Narayaniam*. They do not occupy themselves with the affairs of the world; abnegation and solitude is their law." He gives the following account of Gosa'in Jani and his disciples:—

"They call their master Jahan, and his followers, composed of Hindus and Musalmans, adopted the creed of *Visnavi*. This is as follows: They hurt no living beings; they avoid fellowship with men of another creed among the Hindus and Musalmans; they pray five times a day, with their face towards the east; they have the names of God, of the divinities, of the Prophet upon their lips, such as Allah, Mika'il, `Izra`il, Jibtra'il, Muhammad, and others; they bury their dead; they confer benefits upon others to the extent of their power, a number of their *durvishes* pretend to be afflicted with maladies and beg alms, and whatever they so collect they distribute to the blind and lame, and to people of that description."

He goes on to speak of many others who were equally independent in their ideas, among them were Sivarina, Shidayi, Hariram Puri,Sathra, Jadu, Partapmal Chadah, Binavali son of Hiraman Kayastha, Azadah Brahman, and Meharchand Sunar.

To the latter half of the seventeenth century belonged Dharnidas and Pran Nath whose lives extended on to the beginning of the eighteenth century. Dharnidas was born in 1656, and lived at the village of Manjhi in the district of Chapra. He was a Srivastava Kayastha by caste, and a disciple of Chandradas. His teachings are contained in his two works *Satya Prakas* and *Prem Prakas*. The followers of his sect are to be found all over India even to-day. The following poems illustrate his thought:—

> "The lamp is within the house (body), it has neither wick, nor
> oil nor flame,
> Dharni one should attach himself to him in thought, word
> and deed;
> There (in the abode of God) one walks without feet
> and cheers without hands,
> Without eyes one sees the sight, and without cars hears
> the voice,
> Dharni climbed up only half the height, when he saw
> the form of light arise,
> And he beheld the fascinating image of exceedingly
> incomparable form,
> Dharni the throne is in the body, and the Lord (*Sultan*)

is seated on it,
There he accepts in audience (*Mujra*) all life and world (*Jahan*) to its uttermost limits."

and

"He created you from water, hear, O! my foolish mind,
Such is the husband who is known as *Khuda*.
You burnt for ten months (within the Mother's womb),
And when you became helpless you moved.
You then promised with your own tongue, and vainly had the letters (of fate) written.
And then you promised, O! my foolish mind, that you would obey Him this time, if you were released from pain."

Pran Nath, founder of the sect of *Dharnis*, was a Kshatriya who lived in the latter part of the seventeenth century in the reign of the Emperor Aurangzeb. He acquired great influence over Chhatrasal Raja of Panna by the discovery of a diamond mine, it is said. He was well acquainted with the sacred books of Islam, and he attempted to propagate a faith which should combine the two religions. In his *Kulzum Sarup*, a work in the Gujrati language, he brings together texts from the *Qoran* and the *Vedas* and shows that they are not incompatible. His creed proclaims the abolition of the worship of idols, of caste restrictions and the supremacy of the Brahmins. As a test of a disciple's assent to the real identity of the Hindu and Musalman creeds, the ceremony of initiation consists in eating in the society of both religions. He wrote fourteen treatises all in verse; some extracts from the *Qiyamat-nama* are given below:-

"Go to the followers (*ummat*) and tell them, rise the faithful ones, for the day of resurrection has come.
I tell you in accordance with what the *Qoran* says, and I relate before you the story.
He who is a special leader of the following should stand careful.
I will only give this warning, that in the eleventh century (of

the *Hejira*) you will become fearless....

All of you, whether Hindus or Muslims, will have a common faith."

He describes the history of the last eleven centuries, how Jesus Christ came first and then Muhammad and after him the *Imams*; and then continues to give the story of Adam's fall, and Satan's (*'Azazi'ls*) determination to destory the race of man; and then goes on to discuss the various prophecies Judaic, Muslim and Hindu which foretell the coming of the last prophet, with this mission:—

"There was strife in the two worlds, and the path of action (*Karma Kanda*) and of law (*Shari'at*) prevailed. He made known to all the path of reality (*haqiqat*) and gnosis (*ma'rifat*). He cleared away the clouds from the sky, illumined the universe with the sun of light, and united the peoples of the world. The whole creation calls; upon *Khuda*, makes its statement to Him and accepts His command. All worship the word (*Surat*) of the Lord, or the *Kalam* (word) of *Allah*."

The active careers of Jagjivan, Bulla Sahib, Kesava, Charandas, his two lady disciples Sahjo and Dayabar, Gharibdas Shivanarayan and Ram Sanehi, lay in the eighteenth century.

Jagjivandas was born at Sardaha in the Barabanki district of the Uttar Pradesh in 1682 A.D. He was a Chandel Thakur and belonged to the school of Kabir. He spent most of his life at Kotwa between Barabanki and Lucknow. His teachings are contained in his three principal works—*Jnan Prakas, Mahapralaya* and *Pratham Granth*. His disciples were drawn from all classes of people—Brahmin, Thakur, Chamar and Muslim. "He succeeded in establishing some community of thought between himself and Islam. Two at least of his disciples were Musalmans."

He either re-organised the older Satnami sect which had suffered defeat from Aurangzeb's armies, or set up a new one with the same name.

He taught the doctrine of the unity of God, whom he regarded as beyond all qualities (*nirguna*). He laid great stress upon self-surrender and indifference towards the world. He held that the goal of human endeavours was absorption in God through the help of a spiritual guide (*guru*). Truth, gentleness, and harmlessness were the main virtues in his moral code.

In the following hymn he purchase the inwardness of religion:—

> "Oh what avail is the wearing of a rosary, or putting on the mark on the forehead;
>
> Of what avail is the abandonment of food and fasting, or feeding on milk alone.
>
> What is the use of mortification before five fires, of wearing skins,
>
> Of standing with face turned upwards or sitting in smoke or giving up the use of salt.
>
> What is the value of sitting and standing or of keeping silence and repeating the names;
>
> Of being a learned man or a lecturer or of acquiring much knowledge.
>
> Why abandon wife and we retire into forest, and practice asceticism;
>
> The world forgets that without love all is fruitless.
>
> Stay at home, do not run away in all directions, meditate on the One who is beyond thought and beyond support; in the expanse of the mind's sky His image is seen. He is different from all.
>
> He whose belief attains to Him, has ensured his destiny;
>
> O Jagjivan, place your head on the feet of the *guru* and then you will escape from the net of errors."

How to meditate on God is told here:—

> "Give up all thinking (*fikr*), and become absorbed in meditation (*zikr*).

> Make the parrot of attention (*srvti*) sit in the sky, and repeat the name of *Hari* and thus teach him.
>
> The Lord (*Sa'in*) is one, know Him as one,
>
> Never allow your mind to have any doubts
>
> Says Jagjivandas, see there the word (*sruti*),
>
> Fold the two hands together and adore the Lord."

And all human beings are recognised as essentially equal:—

> "O *Sadhu*, the one Light shines in all,
> Think it over in your mind, there is no second.
>
> The blood and the body are the same, there is no Brahman or *Sadhu*;
>
> Some are called men and some women, the Invisible (*ghaibi*) *Purus* (male) is in all."

Bulla Sahib, whose real name was Bulaqi Ram, was a Kunbi by caste, he was employed for ploughing the field of Gulal Sahib; but the latter, struck by his piety and devotion, became his disciple. Bulla was a disciple of Yari Sahib, and set up as a teacher in Bhurkhuda, a village in the Ghazipur district of the United Provinces. His utterances are full of references to Yogic exercises, and the seems to have regarded the control of breath as an important part of worship. Apart from this, however, he is a *Bhakta* of the usual type. Here is an illustration of his teachings:-

> "One who is mad (*divana*) after the Beloved (*Mabub*) drinks the cup, in the abode (*khana*) of the unconditioned (*nirgun*).
>
> The unconditioned is the abode, the *Trikuti* is the goal, and the association of the devotees the means of knowledge.
>
> Every moment one should go so the unconditioned abode, and should remain drunk during the eight parts of the day. Speak to the people of the unconditioned form, O Bulla, and you have found the secret of the heavens."

And this is how he expresses his dependence on God from day to day:—

"O Lord, take my roll-call (*haziri*), and inter it into the register (*daftar*). I am a poor neglected soldier, give me something day by day."

Kesavadas was a Bania by caste, and belonged to the order of Yari Sahib, a Muslim saint (1668—1723), who lived and taught at Delhi. His warning (*chetavani*) is given below:—

"He maintains wealth (*daulat*), standards (*nishan*), display, egotism (*khudi*) and pride.

He shows no mercy to any soul in the world.

He knows well that all this magnificence is transitory, and that Death goes about with its net to kill is an instant.

All this encampment of tents and elephants and horses, all these furnishings are illusory.

Except the name of *Hari* none of them will be of any use at the time of departure.

I warn you over and over again, give up pride and the love of *maya* (world), why, O *Kesava*, are you agitated with the delutions of desire."

Charandas was born in 1703 A.D. at Dehra in Mewat, Rajputana. He was a Dhusar Bania by caste, and he founded his order at Delhi about 1730. He lived the life of a house-holder and accepted both men and women disciples. Of the later Sahjo and Dayabai have acquired fame by their utterances (*bani*). His teaching is similar to that of Kabir. It emphasizes the unity of God, the value of reliance upon His name, the need of devotion and the necessity of having a *guru* who is to be regarded as divine. He died in 1780.

Charandas denounced idolatry. He says:—

"Keep your eyes on the Husband, what have you got to do with any other man?

Leave all the gods alone, and repeat the name of *Hari*."

He had unlimited reverence for the preceptor; says he:

"*Guru* is like *Siva* who awakens you.

"*Guru* is *Brahma, guru Visnu*, he fills up your emptiness.

Guru is like the Ganges which washes away all sins.

Guru is like the Sun which draws all darkness."

Here is an illustration of his devotion:—

> "O benefactor of the poor (*gharib nivaz*), protect my honour, who will put my affairs straight, for everything is wrong with me?
>
> O *Hari*, you are called the lover of *Bhaktas*, the saviour of the fallen, fulfil the aspirations of thy people, look at them with eyes which will cool their burning.
>
> You are a ship, I am your crew, I cannot leave you and go elsewhere.
>
> O *Hari*, if you will punish me and throw me overboard,
>
> I shall never find a place of rest.
>
> O Lord, the whole world knows that Charandas has thrown himself on Your protection.
>
> If he is then laughed at, it will bring slight on You, please think of it."

Sahjo and Dayabar were two sisters belonging to the same caste as Charandas who was their *guru*. Their hymns are full of tenderness and love.

Gharibdas lived from 1717 to 1778 A.D. in the village of Chhudani Rohtak district, the Panjab. He was a Jat by caste and a householder in life. He belonged to the school of Kabir, and consequently his verses abound with Persian terms and Sufi allusions, for instance:—

> "O *Sahib* (Lord), hear the sound of my prayer in Your highest heaven (*ʿarsh*).
>
> You are my father (*pidar*) and mother (*madar*) and you are bestower of favour (*karim*), it is becoming the Father to protect the honour of the son.

I pray to you with folded hands, O Creator,
My body and mind and wealth are an offering to You, vouchsafe to me your sight (*didar*)."

And again—

"Good conduct, patience, discrimination, understanding, mercy, and continuous *dharma*, and maintain also, intelligence (*`aql*), certitude (*yaqin*), and faith (*iman*), and you will obtain the object which is their reality."

Ramcharan, the founder of the *Ram Sanchi* order, was born in 1718, at Surasena, in Jaipur territory. He was at first a *Ramawat,* but later became a staunch opponent of idol worship, and was therefore persecuted by Brahmins. The headquarters of his sect are at Shahpur, but they are represented in several other places. The order consists of *Sadhus* only, and there are no lay members. They "do not worship images. Their religious services are to some extent similar to those of the Muhammadan. Five services are held every day in their shrines." The order admits men of any caste, their religious and moral discipline is strict, and they have regular officers to enforce it.

The *Shivanarayani* order was established about the middle of the eighteenth century (1734 A.D.). The founder, Swami Narayana Singh, belonged to the Narauni Rajput tribe and was an inhabitant of Chandravar near Rasra in the Ballia district. The order has three monasteries in the Ballia district and one in Ghazipur. The *Shivanarayanis* adore the Absolute (*Para Brahma*) alone, and hold their *Granth* (book) in reverence. Persons of all denominations are admitted without any distinction of caste or class.When a member of the sect dies his body is disposed of according to his instructions by burial, cremation or throwing in a river. Muhammad Shah the Mughal Emperor was a disciple of the founder, which is borne out by the following couplet:—

"He taught the word to Muhammad Shah,
And obtaining his seal propagated the sect."

The adhesion of the emperor gave a prestige to the order, which obtained popularity for it. The seal is still kept in the headquarters.

In the latter part of the eighteenth century and the beginning of the nineteenth, flourished Sahajanand, Dulandas, Gulal. Bhika, and Paltoodas. They were among the backwashes of the great wave which had arisen with Kabir in the fifteenth century, and which spread with great force and rapidity all over India in the succeeding three centuries, and which as the eighteenth century wore towards its close gradually ebbed away, creating a cultural hollow into which European currents began to pour down. All of them were devotees inspired by the same ideas, they were reiterators and popularisers, they hardly added anything new to the religiousness or anything of great value to the rich treasures of devotional poetry. The social impulse was exhausted, the empire was crumbling to pieces and society was torn by conflict and disorder. In such circumstances men's minds were benumbed and their activities were clogged. India ceased to create.

Sahajananda, the founder of the *Swami Narayani* sect, was born near Ajodhia in 1780 A.D. He taught the worship of one God whom he called *Krisna* or *Narayana*, and whose incarnation he was himself. He prohibited killing and the use of animal food or liquor or drugs, he insisted upon sirict sexual relations,and denounced theft, robbery, false accusations, suicide and other evils. He observed no distinction of caste, and he rejected the worship of images. His priests were celibate. His ideas spread among Kolis, Bhils and Kathis of Western India. He was presecuted by the Maratha Peshwas, but he taught the doctrine of suffering injury without retaliation, and consequently many of his followers were beaten to death.

Dulandas was a disciple of Jagjivandas who reorganised the *Satnami* order. He was a Sombansi Kshatriya, and lived in the district of Rai Bareili. He speak of Mansur, Shamsi Tabriz, Nizamuddin, Hafiz, in his poems. One of which is given below:

> "Now the sorrow of the heart has vanished, the Beloved has come into sight.
>
> Living in the company of saints, I have bowed my head before the true leader (*hadi*)....
>
> Every moment I have His face in my imagination (*tasavvar*),

and His image shines in my heart, Bu 'Ali Qalandar,
Farid and Tabriz have all sung of this same faith.
With sincerity and patience, he has shown me Allah who is beyond space (*la makan*) and beyond sight.
See O peoples, Dulan, whose *guru* (preceptor) is Jagjivan, has taken the Beloved to his heart.
And the unique Husband, the Invisible Presence (*Ghaibi hudhur*) has entered into my heart."

Gulal, who was born in the last quarter of the eighteenth century, hailed from Bashari, Ghazipur district. He belonged to the Kshatriya caste, and was a disciple of Bulla Sahib. The following lines give an idea of his poetic skill and religious beliefs:

"The bee of the mind plays *Vasanta*,
The unstruck music sounds in infinite space.
The lotus opens and the bees make a noise,
The Light expands its illumination.
The heart is filled with joy to see it again and again;
When the mind becomes entangled, then it is enmeshed in the net.
The current of Light flows in wave after wave.
My heart is placed at the lotus feet.
It does not come (take birth), nor does it go, the soul dies not.
Gladly it drinks the immortal nectar again and again.
The Lord is beyond reach, beyond perception, beyond sight,
I have found the Lord by seeing him with my eyes.
Says Gulal my desire is fulfilled,
I have triumphed over *Yama* and obtained an abode in Light."

Bhika was a disciple of Gulal. He taught in the district of Ghazipur, after the death of his *guru*, as his successor. His pantheistic outlook is expressed in the following poem:

> "He himself (*Khud*) is the earth, from which a multitude of vessels are made, by the potter, whose creation has a wonderful variety.
> The name is like gold, it becomes ornament and appears as other,
> But whether it is pure or impure, the basis is gold itself,
> The foam, the bubble, currents and waves are many,
> Know that the water is the same, whether it is sweet or salt.
> The soul has one caste, *Bhika* holds this opinion,
> The robbers belong to His government (*Sarkar*) as well as the travellers."

Paltoo Das was a resident of village Nagpur Jalalpur in the district of Faizabad. He belonged to the *Kandu Bania* community and was of the school of Bhika. The following lines describe his career.

> "He took birth in Nanga Jalalpur, and dwelt in Oudh says Paltooprasad, his birth created a stir in the world.
> He destroyed the four castes and laid the root *Bhakti,* and in the garden of Guru Govinda, Paltoo the flower, blossomed.
> He became a monk in Jalalpur city, and in Oudh broke the belt.
> God Carries on transactions in the heart, Paltoo says, he is the unconditioned trader."

He showed the same familiarity with Sufi ideas as Kabir, and attempted the same kind of reconciliation of the two faiths as his great predecessor had done. He says,

> "I have known *Nasut*, *Malkut*, and *Jabrut*,
> and I have tasted the delights of *Lahut*.
> The mature devotee is one whose heart is illumined,
> And who takes his seat in the spaceless abode (*lamakan*).
> the secret of heaven has been opened,

And the soul cries in the heart, *Haq* (the truth), *Haq*.

Paltoo Das says, he sees every minute and on all sides, Mecca."

And with regard to Hindus and Muslims:

"They say *Rama* in the east, and *Khuda* in the west,
Who then lives in the north and the south?
Where is the Lord, and where is He not?
Why do the Hindus and Muslims raise a storm?
The Hindu and Muslim have engaged in struggle,
And the two faiths run into two opposing camps.
Paltoo the slave says, the Lord is in all.
He is not divided at all, this is the truth."

Here the account of the radical reformers of Hinduism must close. It was noticed before that there were two classes of religious leaders in India; in the first class were Kabir, Nanak and others whose careers have been traced above, and to the second class belonged those whose thought was of a more conservative type. Among the latter were some who adored *Rama* and others who worshipped *Krisna* or *Krisna* and *Radha*. In all human societies there are groups of men of different spiritual needs; for instance, it is impossible for one group of men to conceive of God except in absolute terms, and their intellectual bias excludes from that conception every human quality; then there is another group which supremely feels the want of a God who has something in common with themselves, who is not a mere abstract impersonal entitiy, an abstract and impersonal consciousness, command, or love, but something that is personal, a teacher, a ruler, a father, a lover; still others need an even more concrete personality on whom they can depend, a person who can stand before them as an ideal, or a person in whose history they can take a living interest, in short, an incarnation of God who dwells amidst men and shares with men his sorrows, griefs and burdens.

The Hindus call the first group the worshippers of the absolute (*Nir guna upaska*), whether their path be that of action or knowledge or devotion; and the second group the worshippers of the qualified

Brahman (*Saguna*); among them some believe in incarnations and the others do not. The Absolute may again be transcendent or immanent or both. The radical reformers were, generally speaking, worshippers of the Absolute who was both transcendent and immanent; and as the Muslim Sufis had the same conception of God, the two came together and saw that there was no essential difference in their religions.

The second group among the Hindus was that of worshippers of *Siva* and *Visnu*, the latter in his two manifestations as *Rama* or *Krisna*. They had their counterparts among orthodox Muslims who regarded God as the Lord and the Ruler; but it was impossible for these two to make any approach towards an understanding, because both were entrenched behind fixed systems of revealed books, inspired and irrevocable commands, and divinely sanctioned rites and institutions. To this group mainly belonged the conservatives, the learned on both sides; and the priests whose interests were vested in the maintenance of a particular social and economic order. But the presence of Islam in India could hardly fail to impress even them, and they too showed in certain aspects its influence. In an earlier chapter it has been shown how Hinduism in the south reacted towards Islam, how contact with Islam accentuated its monotheism, tended to remove disqualifications of caste, strengthened the movement of devotion, introduced new elements in its doctrines about the teacher, relaxed the rigours of the cult without entirely abolishing it, and encouraged the use of the popular languages.

In the north the same features appeared. It is hardly necessary to enter into a detailed analysis of the literature of the two schools, the one regarding *Rama* as the supreme deity to be adored, and the other, *Krisna*. Ramananda and Vallabha were the founders of the two schools in the north, but the best exponents of their ideas in the Hindi language were Tulsidas and Surdas. Both have wielded an enormous influence upon the Hindu mind. But as the object of this thesis is not to describe all the sects which were developed in Hinduism, but only those which show the distinct influence of Islam, they fall outside its ambit. It may, however, be remarked that the language of both Tulsidas and Surdas shows evident traces of this influence, for both use quite a number of words which had been made current by the Muslims.

14

Islamic Impact on Sixteenth Century Saints

[Abstract: Kabir, Nanak, Ravidas, Dadu Dayal are leading leaders, among the others.]

Kabir and Nanak were leaders of the radical school of thought. They had many supporters among their contemporaries and numerous followers after them throughout the centuries. Of the twelve disciples of Ramananda four others besides Kabir have left some of their hymns behind—Dhanna, Pipa, Sa'ina and Raidas. The hymns of the first three are preserved in the *Adigrrantha* of the Sikhs, while Raidas's teachings have been collected and published separately.

Dhanna was a Jat by caste and is said to have been born in 1415 A.D. He belonged to Rajputana, whence he went to Varanasi to become Ramananda's disciple. Nabhaji and Priyadasa relate the legends of the supernatural occurrences of his life, which indicate that he was at first an idol-worshipper. Later a change seems to have come over him, for he says:

"When the *Guru* caused the wealth of divine knowledge to enter me, I meditated on God, and accepted in my heart that He was One.

I have embraced the love and service of God and known
comfort;
I am satiated and satisfied, and have obtained salvation.
He in whose heart God's light which filleth creation is contained,
recognize the God, who cannot be deceived."

The *Bhaktmala* and its commentary gave an extended notice of Pipa, the Raja of Gagaraungarh, and relate many stories of the marvellous events which happened in his life, and of the conversions which he effected. Macauliffe translates a hymn which is found in the *Granth,* and which shows the same tendency as is found in other contemporary saints, that is, God is the Primal Essence, the *Guru* is the means of attaining God, and that worship must be internal.

Sai'n was a barber who lived at the court of the Prince of Bandhavgarh, modern Rewa. He is said to have become the spiritual preceptor of this prince. Of him a story is told by Nabhaji which illustrates the saint's dependence on God and His readiness to help him.

Raidas was a worker in leather and thus belonged to a caste very low in social status. He was born at Varanasi, his father's name was Ragghu and that of his mother Ghurbiniya. He was devoted to religious men and saints and used to spend all the money that he could procure from his father in their service. His father became displeasd and turned him out of the house. He then began to live with his wife in a dilapidated hut, engaged in devotion and earning his living by mending shoes. People were attracted to him by his life of simplicity and contentment, and it is said that a Rajput queen accepted him as her *guru.*

His hymns breathe a spirit of humility and self-surrender. He did not indulge in high philosophic speculation about the nature and essence of God and His relation with the world and man. His cardinal doctrines are not different from those of Kabir, and like him he uses *Rekhta*, even the Persian language, and Sufi terms, to show the identity of Hinduism and Islam. He believed in God as the Absolute Lord of all and identical with self.

He says :

> "*Govind* is immovable, formless, unborn, unique, of fearless gait, unlimited, beyond sight and reason, indivisible, unqualified, extreme joy."

And

> "*Hari* is in all and all is in *Hari,*"
> "Thou art I, and the difference between me and thee is like water in a vessel of gold and in the wave."

Thus although He is one He is yet many:

> "One is many and many is one *Hari*, how am I to say that there is a second," and "He is one, and only two by illustion."

But, according to him, God is not identical with any of the incarnations; says he:

> "The Rama in whom the people recognise Him, they are in error about it, O brother."

Raidas looks upon the world as the play of God, and is inclined to the view that it is illusory, or, at any rate, not worth paying attention to:

> "He arranges it like a player (*Bazigar*), no one knows the secret of his play. The play is false, only the player is true, by knowing this the mind is satisfied." Again, "the body is empty, the *maya* (nature) is empty, emptily hast thou wasted life without Hari. The temple and luxurious living are empty and empty is the dependence on other gods." Raidas has complete faith in His grace, for did He not come to the help of *Ajamila*, the elephant, the prostitute, and if He broke their chains, undoubtedly He will do the same for him. Yet there is a pleasing conceit in his attitude; "Thou hast bound me by chains of illusion (*moha*), I have bound Thee with the ropes of love. I am making an effort to emancipate myself but when I attain freedom then who will adore Thee?"

The other attitude, of complete surrender and humility, is usual with him.

> "*O Rama*, Thou alone art wise, thou art eternity without guise, Thou art King (*sultan*) of kings. I am thy ignorant broken (*shikasta*)

> servant (*banda*). I have no manners, no fortune. I am senseless, foolish and given to evil. I am a sinner, an alien (*gharib*), heedless, cowardly and black-hearted. Thou art powerful (*gadir*) and capable of taking me across the ocean. I am greedy and cunning. This body of mine is shattered and broken, and my mind is full of many apprehensins. Raidas the slave, begs his Lord (*Sahib*) vouchsafe to me a sight (*didar*) of Thee,"

and therefore the calls upon Him out of the deepth of his heart:

> "Save me, save me, O holy Lord of three worlds."

It is necessary then to give up all external rites, the pilgrimages, fasts, shaving of head, singing and dancing in temples, offering of leaves to idols, and to betake to the devotion of One only, by losing the self in Him, as the river loses itself in the sea. Although

> "My caste is low, my actions are low, and even my profession is low,
> Says Raidas, yet the Lord has raised me high."

Kabir had many disciples who spread his message throughout Northern India and the Deccan. They founded twelve branches of the *Panth*, each one recognising some immediate disciple as its head. Some of the branches were merely nominal and took no root where they were planted; others produced important sects. Of his immediate disciples Srut Gopal Das succeeded him at Varanasi and was recognised at Maghar, Jagananth and Dwarka; Bhaggu (Bhagwan) Das is known as the compiler of the *Bijak*; Dharamdas was the author of many poems in which Kabir appears as answering his questions; Jivandas was probably the founder of the famous Satnami sect; and Kamal who is remembered in the *Adigrantha* by the disparaging line, "the family of Kabir foundered when Kamal the son was born," apparently had a following in Western India. Others hardly need mention.

Of those in the generation following one of the most important was Dadu Dayal. According to *Dabistan*, Dadu was a cotton cleaner, who came from Naraina, a village in Marwar, and lived in the time of

Akbar. Wilson follows *Dabistan* concerning Dadu's caste, but adds that he was born in Ahmedabad, from where he removed to Naraina in his thirty-seventh year, and where he lived till the end of his life. Farquhar and Traill, however, state that he was born of Brahmin parents at Ahmedabad in 1544 A.D. But Sudhakar Dwivedt differs from them and is of opinion that he was a tanner or currier (*mochi*) and his family profession was that of making leather bags (*moth*) for drawing water from well. His first name was Mahabali, he retired from worldly pursuits after the death of his first wife and became a disciple of Kamal. The last authority produces the following couplet in proof of his opinions:

> "I found the true and mighty *guru*, who taught me the reality,
> Dadu is the leather bag (*moth*), Mahabalt is the
> vessel who churned and ate the butter."

Dadu spent most of his life in Rajputana and he visited Ajmer, Delhi, Amber and other places. He is reported to have had an interview with Akbar. He died at Naraina in 1603. His poetic utternaces consist of 5,000 verses which are divided into chapters, each dealing with a leading religious question. Their language is a mixture of the dialects *Braja Bhasa* and *Rajasthani*, some of the verses are in *Panjabi* and a number in *Rekhtia* and corrupt Persian. Of the last, one or two instances may be reproduced here:

> *Be mihr gumrah ghafil gasht khurdani,*
> *be dil badkar 'alam hayat murdani.*

which may be rendered thus:

Men are merciless, strayed from the path, heedless, meateaters, heartless, evil-doing, and living yet lifeless.

And,

> *Kul 'alam yake didam arwah akhlas*
> *Bad 'aml badkar dui pak yaran pas.*

which means;

He was the whole universe as one, and the pure souls cleaned of evil actions, evil deeds and of the sin of duality in the company of the Friend.

And again, there is an entire poem beginning with the lines,—

> *Maujud khabar ma'bud khabar arwah khabar wajud*
> *Maqam chi chiz ast dalani sujud.*

This may be translated as follows:

> The existent is known, the adored is known, the souls are known, what is the station of the being to whom it is necessary to bow?

The station of being, according to Dadu, is this:

When the lower self (*nafs*) is dominant, and pride is in possession and anger, egotism, duality, falsehood, greed, obstinacy are present, then there is not the name of righteousness.

The station of souls (*arwah*) is this:

When love, worship, obedience, unity, purity, mercy, affection right, and goodness are present then there is the name of righteousness near.

The station of the adored (ma'bud) is this:

There is one, the beautiful sight of the Beauty is amazing. To drink the cup of inebriation is a wonderful thing.

The animal stage is when men are away from the path and heedless; the first step is to be bound by law (shari'at) to obtain from a wise person the knowledge of good and bad, and of lawful and unlawful. Then having completed this, it is necessary to abandon the world, and to engage in remembering every day and every moment the Highest God to love the Lower, and to feel the pain and to complain and cry.

Then the station of gnosis (*ma'rifat*) is to know that water, fire, heavens (*'arsh*), the chair were all forms of the *Subhan* who had taken the quality of fire (sharar). Says he:

"The Truth is found, I have seen the Light, the object is held which is the sight of the Friend, the spirits of Adam are the being of the being.

"I have told plainly what kind of goal I had attained, the *Pirs* (Preceptors) have informed the soul of the *Murids* (disciples) about the path to the Adored."

Dadu's description of the true Musalman shows how he rose above prejudices of creed and emphasized the true inwardness of religion. He says,

"Dadu the tank of His presence is in the heart and there I take my complete ablution; after performing the ablution in front of *Allah* I says the prayers there.

"Dadu makes his body His mosque, he finds the five members of the assembly (*Jamaat*) in the mind as well as the leader of the prayers (*Mulla`imam*); the indescribable God is Himself in front of him and there he makes his bows and greetings.

"Dadu regards the whole body as the rosary on which the name of the Generous one (*Karim*) is repeated; there is one fast and there is no second, and the world (*kalima*) is He himself.

"Thus Dadu rises before Allah with concentrated attention and goes himself above the heavens (*`arsh*) to the place where the *Rahman* (Merciful) lives.

"Dadu the worshipper continues thus every day till his death, and then he stands before the gates of the Master and neither leaves Him nor goes."

Dadu manifests perhaps even greater knowledge of Sufism than his predecessors, perhaps because he was the disciple of Kamal who probably had greater leanings towards Islamic ways of thinking than others, perhaps because the Sufis of Western India—Ahmedabad and Ajmer—weilded greater influence upon the minds of seekers after God, Hindus or Muslims, then those of the East. At any rate, the effect of their teachings was to make him a staunch supporter of Hindu-Muslim unity. He repeats again and again the sentiment that

"In all vessels whether Hindu or Muslim there is one soul,"

and

> "O Allah Rama, my illusion has passed away, there is no difference at all between Hindu and Musalman."

and

> "The one invisible Ilahi art Thus, Thou art *Rama* and *Rahim*, Thou are the beautiful Master *(Malik),* Thy names are *Kesava* and *Karsm,"*

and he ask:

"What is the *Panth* (sect) of *Brahma, Visnu and Mahes* which is the *din* (faith) of Muhammad and what is the way of Gabriel; the one *Allah* is their *Pir* and *Murshid* (preceptor and director). Dadu knows in his heart to whom they were devoted, the Invisible *Ilahi* is the *Guru* of the world and there is no other besides him."

and lastly says Dadu:

> "The two brothers are hand and feet, the two are the two ears, the two brothers are the two eyes—Hindus and Musalmans."

With regard to ritual and form, priests, caste, idol worship, incarnation, pilgrimages, ceremonial ablutions and so forth, he held the same opinion as his master Kabir; to him also God alone is essential and He is sufficient:

"I am not a *Pandit*, I do not know the good of studying and I have not thought over knowledge.

I am not a prophet, I do not know the light, and I do not possess the ornaments of the face.

I am no ascetic, I have no control over my senses, and I have not performed pilgrimages.

I am not a worshipper in temples, and I do not put my trust in meditation,

I am not an adept in *Yoga* and I do not know the methods of worship.

I do not know anything else, and what after all is the need of other things.

Dadu has placed his whole soul under the protection of one Beautiful *Govind*."

His ideas of God, of the world and of man do not differ from those of his predecessors. He insists upon the unity of God and he regards Him in His two-fold aspect of transcendence and immanence.To him He is one, unchangeable, immortal, incomprensible Being; He is brightness, effulgence, light, illumination, perfection; He is within the heart of all beings. "I stay within me. I am the house for me, I am in the heavens (*arsh*), I am my own support, I depend on myself, so says the merciful One, the Creator", and "the whole of nature is His own form, for He is inside all," Withal He is Creator and Lord, who "by one word created all." and who wills it and the creation comes out of nothing or relapses into nothing.

Man, as long as he is separated from Him, is a sinful creature; his salvation consists in rending this veil; the realising that all otherness and duality, the world of sense, pleasure and pain is a sport and illusion, they are like the mirage in the desert after which the thirsty man runs in vain. The one road to salvation is to know and love Him alone, the one discipline is to die to self in order to live in Him. The man who journeys along this path must be prepared to lay down his life, for he will meet with terrible obstacles, he will feel weary and sick and maddened by pain, so that he will cry out, "my soul is sorely afflicted, because I have forgotten thee. O God, I cannot endure the pain, deliver me." But if he perseveres the clouds will roll away and the sun will shine and the Light will illumine his soul, and filled with wonder he will exclaim "*O Rama,* my God, I am amazed, no one can find Thy end, *Brahma*, *Sanaka* and *Narad* all failed to see Thee; I who am insignificant and low and little minded, Thou vouchasafest Thy vision to me."

Dadu held that man passed through the whole cycle of births and deaths in one life-time. He says:

"The nature of the eighty-four lakhs of lives is within you, there are many births in a single day but few understand them," and

"There are as many incarnations (rebirths) as the changes which come over the soul. This is the transmigration which the Almighty Creator removes away."

"The soul does not know of its births, they take place moment after moment, it undergoes the eighty-four lakhs but does not apprehend."

And again,

"The swine, dogs, jackals, tigers and serpents reside in the heart, also the elephants and the insects, but the *Pandit* knows them not."

It is only by destroying this chain of psychic modifications or spiritual birth and deaths that one can become absorbed in God.

Dadu teaches that the *Guru* is the devotees protector (gual) and the whip which keeps the horse of the mind in control. The *Guru* is greater than books—*Vedas* and *Qoran*—for through Him realisation takes pace and the abode of Light is attained. But it is difficult to obtain the right type of *Guru*, in which case Dadu recommends that one should make birds, beasts and the lord of the forest his *Guru*, for God is in all.

Dadu did not believe in complete actionlessness, for he says,

"Effort (*udyam*) does not produce evil effects, for him who knows it; in effort there is joy, but it should be directed towards the Lord only.

The sect which Dadu established, has its chief seat at Naraina where he died. There they hold an annual festival which gives an opportunity to the *Dadupanthis* to assemble together in memory of the great man who tried to sink all differences of creed and caste in one religion of love.

The sect of the *Khakis* arose from among a group of the followers of Dadu. The reputed name of the founder is Kilh who is mentioned by Nabhaji among the disciples of Paihari Srikrisnadasa. But nothing more is known about him.

Maluk Das is made out by Wilson as a disciple of Kilh, but the editor of the *Sant-bani Pustak Mala*, regards him as the disciple of Vitthaldas, the Dravida saint. Who this Vitthaldas was it is difficult to ascertain. Nabhaji mentions one Vitthaldas who belonged to the sect of Raidas and was a member of Ramanuja's *Sri Sampradaya*, and Rice speaks of Vitthaldas as a *Vaisnava* singer among the Kanarese poets of the sixteenth century. Maludas was born in 1574 in the regin of Akbar and after a long life of one hundred and eight years died in 1682 A.D. Kara in the district of Allahabad is his birth-place. He married and had a daughter, and founded a sect which consists wholly of laymen without any ascetics. His order is said to have monasteries at Kara, Jaipur, Isfahabad (Gujarat), Multan, Patna, Katak, Sita Kayal (Deccan), Kolhapur, Nepal and Kabul.

Malukdas taught the same religious doctrines which by his time had become prevalent all over India. He condemns the externalia of religion—pilgrimage, idol worship, good works and others. He teaches that the true religion is an inward faith, the *Maya* is the enemy of man, and God's name is the only protection against it, that the world is transitory and the wordly relations of no avail, that man is born if dust and will return to dust, that those who are not devoted to spiritual life are the dogs of the world, that salvation is obtained by knowing the self, killing pride and egotism, controlling passions, trusting the *Guru*, and loving God. This is his definition of the true ascetic (*darwish*):

"He who lives apart from the five elements, is the beloved of God, who gives water to the thirsty; his worship is considered great by Muhammad.

"He who feeds the hungry, soon finds the Lord. He who abandons passion and dies while alive, to him `Izra'il bows.

"He who considers all men's pain as his own, Malukdas regards him as the true ascentic."

He too taught oneness of religions and the unity of the Hindu and the Muslim; says he,

"Where is the string of beads (*mala*) and the rosary (*tasbih*), now awake and rely not on them.

Who is infidel (*kafir*) and who is barbarian (*malechchha*) look upon *sandhya* (Hindu worship) and the prayer (*namaz*) as one.

Where does *Yama* live and where is Gabriel? He himself is the judge (*Qazi*), who else keeps accounts?

He calculates the good and the evil deeds, and renders account and sends one where he deserves to go.

Malukdas, why art thou in error, *Rama* and *Rahim* are the names of One."

Sundardas was a disciple of Dadu. He was born in 1596 A.D. at Deosa near Jaipur in Rajputana, in the family of a Bania. It is reated that when Sundardas was six years of age Dadu came to Deosa. He saw the child and was struck with his handsome face. Since then the child became known as *Sundar* (handsome), and lived with Dadu his preceptor at Naraina. He soon became known for his precocious genius as a saint and poet. But on the death of Dadu in 1603 A.D., he left Naraina and returned home. After spending sometime at Deosa he went to Varanasi where he remained engaged in his studies till the age of thirty, and then came back to Rajputana and worked with his co-disciples, Pragdas and Rajjab to spread the religion of *Bhakti* as taught by Dadu. He settled down at Fatehpur Shekhavati and became friendly with Nawab Alif Khan and his sons Daulat Khan and Ta'bir Khan. The Nawab was himself a Hindi poet, and he highly appreciated the talents of Sundardas. In later years he took to travelling and visited numerous places in Rajputana and Panjab. He died in 1689.

Sundardas was a Sanskrit scholar; he had studied Persian and the languages of the North-Western Provinces of India also. His work *Sundarvilasa* is divided into twenty-four chapters. Some of the chapters deal with the six philosophic systems of the Hindus, and the paths of action and knowledge, and show their inadequacy for the salvation of man. In the constructive parts he dwells upon the teaching of Dadu, but draws most of his arguments and illustrations from purely Hindu sources. Sundardas was a man of culture and a fine poet unlike many of the other religious leaders, but his outlook was not so broad and his spiritual experience not as rich as theirs. In the following poem he describes the self-forgetfulness of man:

> "As the fish swallows the flesh overpowered by greed, and distinguishes not the iron hook from the worm;
>
> As the monkey puts his hand into the jar and keeps his first firmly closed, and does not open it forced by the temptation of taste;
>
> As the parrot fixed his beak into the coconut and remains hanging on it, and puts himself into trouble on account of his avidity,
>
> So man united with the body, falls into the power of senses, and urged by his desires for pleasure forgets that He is himself."

15

Ibrahim Ibn Adham

RUSSELL JONES

Ibrahim is mentioned in many works on Islam as one of the early *sufi* saints, often with reference to the sailent facts of his biography, namely, that he is said to have been son of a royal house of Balkh (in northern Afghanistan), that he abdicated his high position, became a religious mendicant, and died in about 776 A.D.

He is in some ways a fascinating figure, but at the same time paradoxical; there seems to be little historically established fact on his life in Balkh, but in legend he enjoys a prominence given to few saints; and though he is often referred to, there has been no major study devoted to him so far.

There are writing on Ibn Adham in many languages, the earliest being perhaps those in Arabic, Persian and Turkish. In a work on *sufism* we fine: "There can, however, be no doubt that Ibrahim was a great figure in his day, and his memory still survives in Islam as far as India." I have not in fact so far come across much material on him in an Indian context. There is a 'versified romance' in Hindustani which is mentioned in the article devoted to him in the first edition of *The Encyclopaedia of Islam*. This article, reproduced in part in the *Shorter Encyclopaedia of Islam*, 1953, comprises a succinct account of Ibn Adham and mentions the main sources on him known when it was published. The rather curious account given in English by Husain R. Sayani seems to be developed from the Persian versions of the anecdotes about Ibn Adham; one anecdote given by him, about the slave girl who incurred Sultan Ibrahim's wrath by falling asleep in the royal bed, is also given by Manucci, an Italian who was at the Mughal court towards the end of the seventeenth century, and it may have also therefore come from the Persian. Perhaps we ought to note here also that he occurs as the subject of Indian miniature paintings, which I hope to discuss in a future article.

It would be of great interest to learn of any other references to Ibn Adham in writings from India. The point I wish to pursue here, however, is that "his memory still survives in Islam as far as India" is an understatement, inasmuch as there is a significant amount of material on him in indigenous sources from even further east, namely the Indonesian Archipelago. This will be apparent from the article in the *The Encyclopaedia of Islam* mentioned. In fact, he many have enjoyed there an even greater popularity than anywhere else in the Muslim world. (Is he known even further afield, for instance among the Muslims of China? And are there no local versions of stories of him in other parts of the Muslim world, e.g., Maghrib, or East Africa?)

The Indonesian languages which have works devoted to Ibn Adham include Malay, Javanese, Sundanese, Buginese and Achenese. Of these I am able to discuss only the Malay versions, which, however, seem to comprise the fullest, and probably the earliest, versions in Indonesia. The Malay literature devoted to him that I have been able to find is:

a. In the writings of Nur al-Din al-Raniri, a scholar writing *circa* 1640 A.D. in Acheh, in North Sumatra, descended possibly from a Hadramaut family which had settled in Ranir (i.e., Rander, in Gujarat). Only unimportant fragments of the passages concerning Ibn Adham have been published.
b. A fairly long (about 125 pages of manuscript) text entitled *Hikayat Sultan Ibrahim*, so far unpublished. An outline of this is given below. (It is alternatively known as *Hikayat Sultan Ibrahim ibn Adham,* the title by which I shall refer to this longer version).
c. An abbreviated form of the same text, published first in 1822 A.D. by the Dutch scholar Roorda van Eysinga, and republished in many essentially similar editions in the

succeeding century. This is also entiled *Hikayat Sultan Ibrahim*.

Al-Raniri devotes only abut a dozen pages to Ibrahim ibn Adham, in a long work entitled *Bustan al-salatin fi dhikr al-awwalin wa'l-akhirin*. What he writes consists of a selection of anecdotes about Ibrahim illustrating the virtues of asceticism, forbearance, trust in God, such as are widely known in Arabic, and it seems probable to me that Nur al-Din himself translated these anecdotes into Malay for his work. Of the twenty five anecdotes, incidents or sayings given, about three quarters will be found in one source, al-Yfi'i's *Raud al-rayahin*, from which they were almost certainly taken directly into Malay. What is interesting, however, is that Nur al-Din has concentrated in one passage material on Ibrahim which is scattered through al-Yafi'i's book. The only anecdote which I have not (so far) traced back to an Arabic source is this:

> Muhammad son of Abu Bakr (may Allah's mercy be upon him) said: Once upon a time Ibrahim ibn Adham went out hunting. Becoming hungry he dismouted from his steed to eat; a cloth was spread out and food was brought for him. Suddenly a crow appeared, took a loaf of bread from off the cloth, and flew up into the air with the loaf in its beak. Ibrahim, astonished at this, at once mounted his steed and set off in pursuit of the crow, which disappeared over a hill. Ibrahim ascended the hill himself, and caught sight of the crow some distance away. When he approached it flew away, but then he raw a man lying there, bound with ropes. Amazed at this, Ibrahim inquired how this had come about. The man replied: "Your majesty, I came to this land as a merchant; I was captured by a Bedouin, who seized all may goods and abandoned me in this place. For seven days have I been here. Fatch day a crow brings bread for me: it perches on my chest, breaks the bread into pieces with its break, and so feeds me. During all this time I have not been hungry." When he heard this, Ibrahim released the man from his bonds, hosited him up on to his own horse, and went back to the place where he was about to have his meal. And so Ibrahim ibn Adham repented to

Allah of all his evil acts, and for his carelessness in his doings.

In Arabic or Persian there are at least nine other anecdotes telling, like this one, of Ibrahim's *tauba*, which was a prelude to his abdication to follow an ascetic life. Most of al-Raniri's anecdotes, unlike this one, are well-known in other sources; the one which follows, for instance, occurs in Persian, English, French, German and Arabic versions, and has been published in Malay. A translation of the Malay version reads:

> Once upon a time Ibrahim ibn Adham came across a drunken man asleep in the roadway with vomit flowing from his mouth. Ibrahim came up, washed the man's mouth, and then proceeded on his way. When the drunken man recovered, he was told what Ibrahim ibn Adham had done for him. He blushed with shame, and gave up drink. Some time later Ibrahim ibn Adham had a dream in which he seemed to bear a voice saying, "Ibn Adham, for My sake you cleansed the mouth of that drunken man; for your sake I cleansed his heart."

The *Bustan al-salatin* also contains a rendering of the anecdote which must have been used by the English poet, Leigh Hunt, for his little poem 'Abou ben Adhem'. In this Ibn Adham wakes at night to see an angel writing the names "of those who love the Lord", and finding that his own name is not included, asks:

> *I pray thee, then,*
> *Write me as one that loves his fellow-men.*

The next night the angel comes and Ibn Adham finds that his name is the first of those who love the Lord. This anecdote is found in its most complete form in an eleventh century Arabic work, and in the Persian of Farid al-Din 'Attar the theme is still intact; the Malay version however reads:

> I dreamed that I saw Gabriel (upon him be peace) holding a piece of paper. "What is that paper for?" I asked him. He replied, "I am writing the names of those who love Allah." I

said, "Be so kind so at set my name down below the names of those who love Allah." Suddently the voice of an invisible speaker was heard: "Gabriel write down Ibrahim ibn Adham's name as first of all the names."

Here Ibrahim is being rewarded perhaps for his modesty but not for the fact that he loves his fellows, which may have been historically one of his most conspicuous qualities. It may be remarked that in al-Yafi'i's version, which this Malay rendering otherwise closely follows, Ibrahim says, "Write below them, as one who love the Lord, Ibrahim ibn Adham."

The longer Malay version of the Hikayat Sultan Ibrahim ibn Adham

As will be seen presently, the longer Malay version of the *Hikdyat Sultan Ibrahim ibn Adham*, which is the object of this study, is quite different from the collection of anecdotes just described. But Nur al-Din al-Raniri's work was not mentioned merely for the sake of completeness, but because it may throw light on what is perhaps the most interesting question: Was the *hikayat* composed in its present form in Malay, or did it already exist in this form in some other language? Further investigation of Arabic and other sources may reveal and early version of the Malay *hikayat* essentially in its present form, but so far I have not been able to identify one. On the other hand, the congruence of *motif* in certain of the anecdotes in Nur al-Din's work with certain incidents in the *Hikayat Sultan Ibrahim ibn Adham* does suggest that Nur al-Din's writings provided some of the raw materials for the Malay version, which would in turn point to a provenance for the story in the Malay-speaking world.

There are four known Malay manuscripts of the longer Malay version, bearing dates varying between 1775 A.D. and 1860 A.D., but the *hikayat* itself could date from a much earlier time.

The authorship cannot be established precisely: Each manuscript in its colophon refers to the narrator as 'Shaikh Abu Bakr, a man of Hadramaut'. This name is so common that identification of the author would be difficult, especially as it is not certain that he was ever in

Indonesia. It is well established that for centuries there has been close contact between Hadramaut and the Indonesian Archipelago, and it may prove to be significant that Nur al-Din al-Raniri himself evidently had connexious with Hadramaut. Several Hadrami scholars to whom I have spoken about this subject instantly recognized the name Ibrahim ibn Adham, but none showed acquaintance with the Malay *hikaya* when it was outlined to them.

From the summary below the legendary character of the Malay version becomes apparent at once: whatever may have been the historical truth, Ibrahim appears here as the illustrious ruler of a splendid court reminiscent of the 'Arabian Nights'. Balkh is not mentioned. Instead, 'Sultan Ibrahim' rules in *negri Iraq* ('the city of Iraq') in an evident identification with Baghdad at the height of 'Abbasid power.

But it has a strong didactive content: not only in the lessons to be drawn from the story itself (e.g., in the merit of abandoning the pleasures of this world in favour of the ascetic existence as Ibrahim did), but also in the numerous homilies put into the mouths of the principal characters at every opportunity. At a more thoughtful level the advice is reinforced by citations from the Qur'an, about twelve in number, and about the same number of non-Qur'anic citations, most of which have been identified as *hadith*. The citations are given in Arabic, and followed by a Malay translation or explanation; no *isnad* is given to authenticate the *hadith*.

On the other hand we do not find in the Malay *hikayat* examples of the many, often striking, little anecdotes which cluster round the name of Ibrahim ibn Adham in arabic literature, nor do we find the preceptive observations often attributed to him. It seems to be a regular phenomenon in legend that the more illustrious figures attract to themselves traditions and stories originally centering on lesser-known figures Ibrahim ibn Adham is not exception to this, and some of the *motifs* in the *hikayat* have parallels elsewhere, but in which they are associated with other figures. Readers conversant with Islamic hagiographic literature will recognize familiar *motifs* in the summary below; but since this paper is only intended to convey the substance of the Malay *hikayat* to the wider readership of this Islamic journal, I shall not attempt here to relate any of these *motifs* to parallels in non-Malay sources; it is my hope that this will be possible in a future publication when my study has progressed further. For the same reason I do not give here full references to manuscripts etc.

Summary of the longer Malay Version of Hikayat Sultan Ibrahim ibn Adham

In Iraq there was a ruler named Sultan Aulia Ibrahim ibn Adham, famed for his asceticism, his generosity and his justice. He had the *kota* (city-wall) of his city reconstructed and was well pleased with the apparently flawless piece of work when it had been completed. However, at the suggestion of a cautious minister the sultan assembled all his people to inspect the wall, commanding them to report any flaws they perceived in it. We are told in some detail how the sultan's subjects were assembled in their hundreds of thousands, and of the measures taken to ensure that no one was missing; one by one they were interrogated, given a *dinar* each, and released. No one could find a flaw in the apparent perfection of the new well.

Officers making yet another check of the surrounding country to ensure that no one had been overlooked came across an old man; and he asserted that there *was* a flaw in the city-wall, but that he would not reveal it until he had been taken into the presence of the ruler, and had forty witnesses. Before the ruler he revealed the flaw in the city-wall was its impermanence.

Sultan Ibrahim asked him what place is permanent, and the old man told him: only heaven and hell. The old man, being *faqir*, refused the gifts offered to him for his revelation. This moved the sultan in course of time to reflect on the transitory nature of everything in this life: he likened his existence to that of a dreamer who dreams that he is adorned in finery, but wakes to find that it was in fact all unreal. He also began to ponder about the problem of the Day of Judgement.

This led Sultan Ibrahim to announce to his people his intention of abdicating the throne; he handed over the regalia and treasure to the minister who was to replace him, emphasizing meanwhile that the people most beloved of God are just kings, and those who incur God's anger on the Day of Judgement are unjust kings.

Sultan Ibrahim left the palace secretly very early on the following morning, "before the wild animals had emerged to seek their food, and before the stars had dimmed." He took with him only a walking staff, a knife, the royal (signet-) ring and a bowl. Alone and on foot, he set off through the forests and across the plains. No destination is mentioned.

Meanwhile the minister in Iraq had discovered the sultan's absence, and he and his retinue and the royal elephant set off in pursuit of the sultan; it was only after they had prayed for divine assistance that they were able to find him. At first Sultan Ibrahim refused to return with them, and was only prevailed upon to do so on condition that he would not rule, but would spend his time performing religious devotions. His ministers were overjoyed at his consent to return with them, "like plants which have been exposed to the hot sun until their leaves fall off, then rain falls and they sprout new leaves."

The sultan set out on his return to his city. But their way took them near the sea-coast: In the sea the sultan espied a large blind heron perching on a rotten log; as he watched, the bird held its beak agape, and fishes came and hurled themselves into it, and thus the bird was fed. Contrasting his own lack of faith in God's providence with this evidence to the contrary, Sultan Ibrahim was moved to dismount from his elephant, and to order his people to return to their city without him. Sorrowing, they returned to Iraq; there the minister carried on the government justly.

Sultan Ibrahim continued on his way, on food and alone. In course of time he hungry and thirsty, and then in the distance he caught sight of a tall tree on a fiver-bank; reaching it, he drank from the river, bathed himself, and washed the sand out of his jacket and trousers. While he waited for his clothes to dry, he wrapped himself in a *musalla*. As he gazed at the river, a pomegranate fruit came floating down; Sultan Ibrahim recovered it, split if into two parts, and had eaten one half before it occurred to him that it must be someone's property, and he was guilty of eating *hakk Adam*. So he dressed himself, and set off along the bank of the river with the other half of the pomegranate to find the owner.

The scene changes to Kufa: There was a pious and wise man named Sharif Hasan who had a beautiful and intelligent 14-year-old daughter named Sitti Saliha. Sharif. Hasan possessed an orchard full of all manner of fruits, in the orchard was a lake, and beside the lake a pavilion. A culvert led the water from the lake to the river; and the orchard was surrounded by a stone-wall. The orchard was tended by two ascetics, Shaikh Isma'il and Miftah al-'Arifin. It came to pass that Sharif Hasan was afflicted with a fatal illness. His devoted daughter was greatly troubled by this; but he comforted her, and predicted that she would one day become the wife of Sultan Ibrahim, who had eaten a pomegranate which had floated from their orchard into the river. He gave her a description of Sultan Ibrahim. Before he died, Sharif Hasan committed his daughter to the care of the two ascetics; it is mentioned that his funeral was attended by a large number of people.

Shaikh Miftah al-'Arifin visited Sitti Saliha from time to time. To comfort her he told her a story about Prophet Muhammad and his daughter Fatima; when the Prophet visited his daughter, he knocked on her door and announced that he had a friend ('Abd al-Rahman) along; Fatima was thrown into confusion as she had only one garment, and that not sufficient to preserve her modesty. The Prophet gave her his own sash. When they were inside the house, 'Abd al-Rahman observed that it was very poorly furnished, with just two chairs and a mat. The Prophet comforted Fatima with the observation that her privations now would be rewarded in the hereafter, 'For this world is the market of the hereafter, and nothing in it is permanent."

Meanwhile Sultan Ibrahim, travelling along the river bank, came to the orchard and saw the culvert out of which the pomegranate must have floated. He called for the gate to be opened, and to his astonishment heard Shaikh Isma'il reply from inside: "Is that Sultan Ibrahim asking for the gate to be opened?" Sultan Ibrahim was led to the pavilion, and narrated the story of the pomegranate; he added that his only possessions were his ring, a knife, a staff and a bowl, so if he were to pay for the pomegranate it would have to be by service to the owner until the value had been worked off. He gave the remaining half of the pomegranate to Shaikh Isma'il, who commented: "O Sutlan Ibrahim, it is indeed a pomegranate which has floated away from this orchard. But I am not the owner of the orchard. Although I live in this orchard—I have lived here some thirty years" (*in some versions it is three years*)"—"I have never tasted a single one of these fruits..." He went on to explain that the owner of the orchard was Sitti Saliha.

Sultan Ibrahim next visited Sitti Saliha's guardian, Miftah al-'Arifin, and together they went to find Sitti Saliha. She listened to the story of the pomegranate, but refused to give retrospective sanction (*halal*) to Sultan Ibrahim for his having eaten it. (*In one version* she observes that during her father's lifetime he had refused to sell a pomegranate even for the price of one thousand *dirham* when it was needed for the sick son of a prime minister.) She would give such sanction only on condition that Sultan Ibrahim married her; the Sultan was obliged to consent to this, and was married by Miftah al 'Arifin to Sitti Saliha.

During Sultan Ibrahim's stay in the orchard, Shaikh Miftah al-'Arifin came to him to receive religious instruction, and was impressed with the Sultan's learning. Next Shaikh Isma'il came to visit Sultan Ibrahim, to try to discover why God had not granted a certain prayer. Sultan Ibrahim named the ten obstacles in his way:

i. Dunia (this world) — he must isolate himself from it.
ii. Shaitan (the devil)—whose weapon is sleep, which leads to forgetfulness of Allah.
iii. Hawa—taking people's goods, stealing, malice.
iv. Nafs—eating the drinking to excess—he should fast and practise *dhikr*.

The other six obstacles are idols (their names being spelt variously);

i. *Halat* or *Halalat*
ii. *Manat* or *Manat*
iii. *'Uzza* or *Mudirra* (?)
iv. *Haluba* (?) or *Hawia*
v. *Ghawia*
vi. *Sawia* or *Sawi* ?

Each of these is associated with something which has to be eschewed.

Sultan Ibahim and Sitti Saliha enjoyed only a brief married life together. After forty days (*alternatively* four or five days, *or*, in *one manuscript*, one night) Sultan Ibrahim informed his wife that he was going to leave her. She entreated him to stay with her; but he refused to be deflected from purpose, emphasizing once more the transitory nature of this world: living in it is no more permanent than the stay in a country of visiting merchants, who always return to their own country when the appropriate season comes. And he likened this world to a fine house extravagantly furnished: a wise man enters it and enjoys its amenities and gives thanks to the owner for his hospitality. But a foolish man takes the amenities as his own, and eventually is driven out by the owner. He also compared this world with a woman dressed in fine clothes; the wise man, when she approaches him, sees that she is in reality old and wicked, and he detests her.

Sitti Saliha's wailing at the departure of her husband was so penetrating that it was heard through the four layers of the heavens, and caused the angels to inquire of God what the noise was.

Sultan Ibrahim set off, bound for Mecca. (*One version recounts an incident which befell him on the way*: Between Mecca and Madina he fell in with some Bedouin who asked him to hand over his provision; but he explained that his provision consisted of *sabr* (patience); *shukr* (thanksgiving); *tawakkul* (submission to God's will); and *rida* (contentment). The Bedouin leader was so impressed with this evidence of piety that the threw himself at Sultan Ibrahim's feet and arranged for a camel to be provided to take him for the rest of the journey.) Arriving at Mecca, Sultan Ibrahim proceeded to the Masjid al-Haram, where he spent his days in religious devotion, without disclosing his real identity.

Meanwhile it transpired that Sitti Saliha was pregnant, and in due course she gave birth to a son who was named Muhammad Tahir. (*In one version* from the age of seven to nine Muhammad Tahir was given instruction in the Qur'an by Miftah al-'Arifin.) One day Muhammad

Thair quarrelled with his playmates, and they taunted him with the allegation that he was the illegitimate son of a wandering *faqir*. This prompted him to inquire of his mother who his father really was, and when she told him the story he resolved to go to Mecca to see his father.

In due course Muhammad Tahir arrived at Mecca, and there he inquired after Sultan Ibrahim. At the time he was eighteen years old (*in other versions* twelve years old). His inquiries at first brought no result, but after having invoked divine assistance Muhammad Tahir caught sight of a *faqir* performing the *tawaf* (circumambulation of the *Ka'ba*), and identified himself. He was warmly received by Sultan Ibrahim; but after sometime the latter became aware that his son's visit had caused him to neglect his religious devotions, and his manner instantly changed; he angrily ordered Muhammad Tahir to depart immediately. In reply to his son's entreaties to be allowed to stay, Sultan Ibrahim narrated this story about Nabi Musa (Moses):

> When Musa was near death he committed his son to God's care. God instructed him to strike the earth with his staff; he did so, and (a rift appeared; he struck the rift with his staff and) a sea appeared; he struck the sea with his staff and a black rock floated to the surface; he struck the rock with his staff and the rock split in two; inside the rock was a caterpillar (*ulat* in Malay) and a green blade of grass; the caterpillar praised God. Musa marvelled that God should see even inside, a rock like that, and should provide food for His creature in it.

Sultan Ibrahim gave his ring to Muhammad Tahir, with the injunction that it was on no account to be disposed of until he reached *negri Iraq*. Muhammad Tahir set off for Iraq; after sometime he came to a fork in the road, one road leading to Kufa, where his mother lived, and one to *negri Iraq*, where his father had commanded him to go; after some indecision he resisted the temptation to go back to his mother, and proceeded on the road to Irak.

When he neared *negri Iraq* he learned that the ruler there was called Wazir al-'alam (or *Wazir al-'alim*' Malay script, like Arabic without vowel-points, does not distinguish between the two). Muhammad Tahir entered the flourishing city and offered to sell his ring to a merchant in the market. The merchant, recognizing it as an item of the Iraq regalia, was smitten with fear and urged Muhammad Tahir to flee the country at once. But Muhammad Tahir instead took the ring and showed it to the ruler.

When Muhammad Tahir told his story *Wazir al-'alam* warmly welcomed him as the son of the ex-sultan. Muhammad Tahir was feasted, and was offered the throne, but this he declined. But he took the opportunity of giving the ruler some advice on the art of government.

He elucidated the quality of justice (*'adl*) under four heads:

i. Give warning to offenders, but for the third offence they should be punished.
ii. Make careful inquiry before passing sentence.
iii. Do not covet other people's goods.
iv. Do not treat poor people less favourably than wealthy people.

Furthermore, advised Muhammad Tahir, a ruler should appoint four principal ministers, and military officers, and should provide swift steeds. Mentioning the *madhhab-i Hanafi* (*one version: madhhab-i Shafi'i*), he enlarges upon the religious obligations of rulers. (*In one version* are listed the four classes of society from which chiefs should be drawn: The *raja* class; the *menteri* (minister) class; the *penghulu negeri* (territorial headman) or *penghulu* (headman) class; and finally the merchant class.)

Muhammad Tahir was seated in state on a dais; he was offered a large amount of treasure, but would accept only a little. He set off on his return journey for Kufa, refusing the escort offered by the ruler. (*But one version* gives an account in some detail of the pageantry of his send-off: the regalia was brought out (it included pennants handed down from Iskandar dhu'l-Qarnain); in the procession were forty maidens, forty ministers mounted on camels, forty war captains mounted on horses. Muhammad Tahir's mount was an enormous white elephant.

The royal standard bearer was a captain entitled Johan Pahlawan, mounted on a brown horse; then came forty soldiers dressed in red tunics; behind them forty spearsmen, then forty ministers, a captain bearing the state sword, then Muhammad Tahir on his elephant. To his right was a captain bearing the state shield, to his left a captain bearing the state lance. Next came ten senior ministers, then the camels of the maidens, then ten more ministers, followed by the soldiers and the common people. Muhammad Tahir took up his position, the sunshades were unfurled, the drum of Nabi Ibrahim was struck up, the raja of Irak mounted, and the procession moved off. Somewhere out on the plain, however, they took leave the Muhammad Tahir, who continued for the rest of the journey on foot.)

In Kufa Muhammad Tahir found his mother sorrowing for him. She prayed unceasingly for her husband. Muhammad Tahir gave her the gems he had brought, and told her about his adventures. Every year for the rest of their lives Sitti Saliha and Muhammad Tahir received from *Wazir al-'alam* eight camel-loads of goods and food.

"Thus is was narrated by Shaikh Abu Bakr, a man from Hadramaut."

16

Sarmad:
His Life and Quatrains

B.A. HASHMI

[Abstract: It is not my aim to survey the influence of mysticism on Persian poetry as a whole, nor do I mean to analyse the theory and practice of mysticism itself. My sole object is to make it clear that nearly all the Sufi poets took to the *Ruba'i,* after partially discarding other types of poetry which had become associated with mundane and sometimes sordid themes.

The list of Sufi poets who lived from the eleventh to the eighteenth century is indeed a long one. Most of them have written excellent *ruba'is.* I am here concerned with only one of them, and what I have to say in this essay falls under two heads: firstly, the life and character of Sarmad; secondly, his *Ruba'iyat* as they have come down to us.]

Persian poetry before the introduction of the mystic element was generally non-individualistic and objective. The *Qasida* was indeed developed on a rather elaborate scale, but it was poetry faked for mercenary ends. The *Tashbib* or the lyric prelude, even when it was adroitly tagged on to the rest of the *Qasida* seldom formed part of an organic whole. The *Masnawi* which came next, was but narrative poetry interspersed with descriptive passages. The *Ghazal* was more subjective but, fettered by the conventions of Muslim society, it assumed rather a depraved tone. The lover of the Arab poets was chivalrous, fearless and true, but the lover of Persian poetry sought his love through power or pelf or self-abasement. The beloved in Arab poetry was a beautiful maiden, who admired manly courage and was jealous of her modesty, but the beloved of Persian poetry believed in tormenting the lover to get the most out of him.

Such in brief was the outlook of Persian poetry before the finer sensibilities of mystics transformed almost all the types of Persian poetry. Sufic thought was surcharged with love of Eternal Truth, of Eternal Beauty and of eternal Goodness. The Almighty was the Beloved. No submission to His will could be interpreted as abject humilliation. The desire for His attainment could not be attributed to earthly passion, and between His lovers there existed not jealousy but a community of sentiment. Each one of His lovers wondered at and admired the great secret of His 'manifest yet hidden beauty.' No doubt the influence of philosophic thought tended to make early mystic poetry abstract; but the subjective element was all the time wedded to the expression of such abstract ideas as 'the Being the Soul, the why and wherefore of all existence.'

Along with the advent of mysticism, another type of Poetry came into its own. This was the *Ruba'i* which for several decades was used by Sufic poets as their chief vehicle of expression. Sultan Abu Sa'id Abul-Khair, a contemporary of Sheikh Bu Ali Sina, was the first Sufi who employed the *Ruba'i* to give expression to his mystic thought. He died in the eleventh century A.D. and was followed by such eminent Sufi poets as Hakim Sanai Ohduddin Kirmani and Khwaja Fariduddin Attar. At this time an event of very great importance took place. The Tartars shook the entire structure of the Muslim world. Many a kind was dethroned and killed. Many a kingdom was devastated and ruined. The contemporary human eye saw all this ruthless annihilation and realized that all was transitory. This bloody vision gave an impetus to mystic poetry and mysticism, which have for their basic principles an unshakeable faith in the controlling forces of destiny, in the transitoriness of worldly glory, in the utter submission of the self to the will of the Almighty, and finally in the realization of self in and through the love of God. As a result of this a larger number of mystic poets flourished in this age than in any other. Maulana Rum, Ohdi, Eraqi, Maghrabi and a host of other minor mystics lived in the years that followed the turbulent days of the Tartar invasion. Henceforth, mystic poetry held undisputed sway over the human heart. It purified and embellished not only the Persian language but also the various types of its poetry. The *Qasida* went nearly out of fashion. Maulana Rum, Maghrabi, Eraqi and Sahabi never attempted it. Strictly conventional *Masnawi* also went out of vogue for the simple reason that in its introductory sections after the *Hamd* and the *Na't,* it was customary to praise the king.

It is important that readers who seek information concerning the life and character of Sarmad should realize how little is known definitely about him, notwithstanding the enormous popularity which Sarmad enjoys amongst the martyrs of the early period of the reign of Aurangzeb Alamgir. Much of what has been written about Sarmad is deplorably uncritical, and I do not believe I need to offer any apology for treating the subject in a scientific spirit. during and even after the reign of Aurangzeb, the entire bulk of *Tazkara* literature was produced by men whose interest did not go beyond the mere mention of a poet's name and giving a few samples of his poetry. Sarmad figures in almost all of these *Tazkaras,* but they do not in any way, improve our knowledge of Sarmad; so much so that we cannot even find his name from these sources. Mirza Mohammad Kazim in his *Deh Saloh,* the writing of which was stopped by royal order, says nothing about Sarmad; even Mustaid Khan in his Maasir-i Almgiri, which was written during the reign of Shah Alam (and which incorporated Deh Salah) has not made the slightest mention of Sarmad. Probably this is due to the fact that the Mughal invasion of Bihar and Assam took place in the same year in which Sarmad was beheaded for his so-called atheism (1659 A.D.).

There are only three books which have anything at all to say about him and it is on these that we must base all our knowledge of Sarmad. The first is *Mirat ul-Kheyal* by Sher Khan Lodhi, a contemporary of Aurangzeb who had no connection with the Royal Court. A manuscript copy of *Mirat ul-Kheyal* which was transcribed in 1137 A.H. has been most kindly lent to me by K.B. Maulvi Zafar Hasan of the Archaeological Department. The second is *Riaz ush-Shu'ara* written by Ali Quli Khan Daghistani, a noble of the Court of Mohammad Shah and a poet and critic of no mean accomplishment and integrity. Lastly there is *Dabistan-i Mazahib,* the authorship of which has not yet been authentically established, though the overwhelming internal evidence from the book leads one to believe that it must be the work of a contemporary author who knew important persons and places of his time rather well. To my mind it appears that these three books clear the ground and define the limits within which a solid reconstruction of Sarmad's life can be attempted. These limits, I have to admit, are exceedingly narrow and create no occasion to speak at length and with certainty about many a point in the life of Sarmad and yet there is nothing more beyond the very meagre internal evidence which the *Ruba'iyat-i Sarmad* offer to the reader. For these reasons, in the present state of our knowledge, the personality of Sarmad must be regarded as an almost inscrutable problem.

The author of *Dabistan-i Mazahib,* in his discourse on the religion of Jews says that "the author had not the chances of keeping company with the wise and the learned amongst the Jews and whatever could be found in the books of non-Jewish authors about their (Jewish) faith could not be relied upon because intolerance often paints a false picture. But in the year 1057 A.H. when I reached Hyderabad Sind, I cultivated the acquaintance of Mohamad Sa'id Sarmad who originally came of the learned of the Jews, from a sect who are known as Ribbani and who (Sarmad) after learning the principles of Jewish faith and studying Torait became a Musalman." This quotation establishes definitely that the name of Sarmad after his conversion to Islam was Mohammad Sa'id. What his Jewish name was, no one can tell. In most anthologies, the various compilers have prefaced the sample of the poetry of Sarmad as 'Sa'ida-i Sarmad' which probably is due to the fact that these compilers used a portion of the name of Sarmad, i.e. Sa'id, as the title of a selection from Sarmad's poems.

The author of Mirat ul-Kheyal says that "Sarmad was originally from Faringistan (Europe) and was an Armenian." Valah Daghistani, in *Riaz ush-Shu'ara,* goes a step further and adds that "his native place was Kashan." In the absence of any other evidence we have no reason to doubt any of these statements which are not which are not contradictory, and can accept the fact that the emigrant ancestors of Mohammad Sa'id Sarmad were European Jews and that they had migrated to Armenia : and that Sarmad became a Musalman, and that prior to his coming to India he lived in Kashan.

None of the *Tazkaras* except *Dabistan-i Mazahib* has anything to say about the education which Sarmad received, although there is unanimity on the point that Sarmad was really a learned man, thoroughly conversant with Arabic. *Dabistan-i Mazahib* says that "he studied philosophy under such learned professors of Persia as Mulla Sadra and Abul Qasim Qandraski and a host of others." The above quotation is a positive proof of Sarmad's learning and erudition, which adds strength to my view that a Jew who had descended from the priestly class and who had studied the sacred books of the Jews would not have changed his faith without first making a comparative study of religions, which incidentally shows that Sarmad was a really fearless person who translated his convictions into action. He certainly was born of rich parents and could afford a more expensive education than was within the reach of the average person.

I have just said that he come of rich parents and to the reader this might possibly appear a rather audacious assumption on comparatively little data. It would indeed be so, were I not able to substantiate it from the fact, that he came to India as a merchant. *Dabistan-i Mazahib* says that 'eventually according to the custom of merchants he came to India by the sea-route.' In the palmy days of the Mughal Empire most of the rich rewards for the fine taste they exhibited in the choice of those unique and priceless samples of art and craft which comprised their merchandise. And who but a wealthy merchant could afford to do this type of business? Indeed Sarmad was one of those numerous merchants, poets, painters and learned men for whom the grandeur of the Mughal Court had a great attraction. He reached India by the sea-route and landed at Thatta—a well-known place in those days. And *Dabistan-i Mazahib* says, "when he (Sarmad) reached the town of Thatta, he fell in love with Abhai Chand—a Hindu boy and withdrew his hand from all things (of the world) and went nude like the Hindu ascetics."

The fact "that the father of that Hindu boy on finding out the purity of Sarmad's love took him into his house and the boy also got so much attached to Sarmad that he never could leave him, and studied Torait and Zaboor and other Gospels from Sarmad," is an indication of that mental and spiritual phenomenon when a seemingly insignificant stimulus may bring mysterious forces into action. This incident closed a chapter in Sarmad's life—that of the trader—and opened up a new phase with which I shall concern myself henceforward.

It is one of the most splendid yet sinister fascinations of life that we cannot trace to their ultimate sources all the storms of influence that play upon the frail craft of an individual's existence. Sarmad had come out to India to add to his worldly wealth, and when he did reach India, he threw away all his worldly wealth and all his worldly wisdom. As I have stated above, he took up his abode in a Hindu family, with the parents of Abhai Chand. This boy, about whom hardly anything is known, studied languages and the Scripture under Sarmad and "translated a chapter from Torait into Persian and the author (of *Dabistan-i Mazahib)* after having it reviewed by Sarmad, and after having injunctions thoroughly corrected and marked, incorporated it with this chapter." The chapter referred to the above quotation is quite a long one and as far as I can judge, its language shows that the writer had acquired a thorough grasp of Persian. In the easy and smooth flow of his style, Arabic words and phrases are so deftly blended that they impart terseness to his sentences and grace to his diction. This Hindu boy must have cultivated a great taste for Persian because, apart from this prose specimen of his, we find also a verse of his which the author of *Dabistan-i Mazahib* has given in his book. There is nothing very remarkable about the verse, but it shows the religious outlook of the Hindu boy who lived and studied under Sarmad's affectionate guidance. It is : "I obey the Quran, I am a Kashish and also an ascetic; I am a Rabbi Jew, I am an infidel and I am a Musalman."

Sarmad stayed in Thatta for quite a long time—how long, no one can say definitely. Towards the close of Shah Jaha's reign, he had reached the Gangetic plain. I think his wanderings took the natural course of a tourist of those days and he eventually reached the great metropolis of the Mughals about the year 1654. Dara Shikoh the heir-apparent was according to the usual custom, the governor of the metropolitan province while the other brothers governed distant provinces of Deccan and Bengal. It is a pity that our historians have not yet paid proper attention to the life and work of Dara Shikoh, who from all available testimony was a Prince of very rare gifts. He was one of the most learned men of his age and his chief interest lay in the comparative study of religions. When Dara Shikoh came to know of Sarmad, he lost no time in inviting him to his court. Sher Khan Lodhi in *Mirat-ul-Khiyal* says, "As Sultan Dara Shikoh had a linking for the company of lunatics, he kept his (Sarmad's) company and enjoyed his discourses for a considerable period. Eventually time took a new turn...."

It is evident that Dara Shikoh took immense interest and pleasure in the company of Sarmad who, in turn, appreciated his royal friend greatly. The circumstances which led to the imprisonment of Shah Jahan and the long and bloody struggle which ensued between his sons, do not require any comment from me. I have only to mention that this ended in the capture, imprisonment and finally the death of Dara Shikoh and Aurangzeb's accession to the throne. *Mirat ul-Khiyal* says that, with the accession of Aurangzeb, the new and foolish creeds of Akbar and Jahangir were rooted out, the customs of Murad Bakhsh and Dara Shikoh were set aside and religion once again had the sway which it deserved. In the new regime, Sarmad whose life was not led in accordance with the *Shariat* was not to be tolerated any more. He had many a crime in his charge-sheet for which sooner or later he had to stand a trial.

There is a diversity of opinion about the causes which led to the execution of Sarmad. It is said in *Tazkirat ul Khiyal* that the Moulvis took offence at a certain quatrain of Sarmad which to them appeared to deny the bodily accession of the Prophet Mohammad (peace be on his soul) to the heavens. "Whoever came to know the real secrets of existence, he traversed long distances easily; the Mulla says that Ahmad ascended the heavens and Sarmad says that the heavens descended to Ahmad."

It is also said that Aurangzeb, who know all about the close friendship of Sarmad and Dara Shikoh, did not like any one of Dara Shikoh's admirers to survive. He got rid of most of them on political pretexts; but for Sarmad, the subterfuge of religious disbelief was needed. It was not very hard to find one, and so Mulla Qavi, the Qazi-ul Quzzat, was sent to Sarmad, to ask him the reason of his nudity.

Sarmad in reply recited the following *Ruba'i* incidentally hurting Mulla Qavi's feelings by an insulting pun on his name. "The eyes by giving me two wine-cups have taken me out of my senses; he is by my side and I am in search of Him. This novel thief has stripped me of everything."

Mullah Qavi took the story to Aurangzeb who has Sarmad summoned before a religious court where he was to be tried for his various religious crimes. Valah-i Daghistani writes on the authority of Khalifa Ibrahim Badakhshani who lived his pious life towards the end of the reign of Aurangzeb, that when Sarmad refused the order of the court to put on clothes, Aurangzeb argued that no one could be hanged with any justification for going undressed. At last Sarmad was asked to recite *Kalima-i Taiyaba.* He, according to his habit, recited only *La ilaha* —there is no god—and did not go any further. When he was questioned about his heretic utterance, he said that in his life he had so far met only with the negation of life and love, and as he did not actually know the positive side of it, he would not speak of it. Now the charge of heterodoxy was completely established and Sarmad stood condemned, firstly, for being a partisan of Dara Shikoh, secondly, as one who did not believe in the bodily accession of the Prophet to the heavens *(Miraj-i Jismani);* and thirdly, as one who went about nude and denied the existence of God because he had not had any personal knowledge of Him. Judgment was delivered and Sarmad was sentenced to be executed. When Sarmad was taken to the place of execution and the executioner wanted to bandage his eyes according to the custom, he asked him not to do so and looking at the executioner smiled and said:

"Come in whatever grab you may, I recognise you well." So saying, he bravely placed his head under the sword and gave his life.

Some people believe that the place where Sarmad lies buried is not the spot where he was beheaded, but Valah Daghistani is definite on this point. He says, "At a side of Masjid Jamay they beheaded him and buried him at the same place. The writer of these words has twice had the honour of visiting his sacred tomb and in all the four seasons there is plenty of verdure on his grave. In reality it is a source of great peace to be able to visit this sacred shrine."

There are only two tombs on the sides of the Jami 'Masjid; one is on the north which is in a very uncared-for condition and is said to be the grave of an unknown saint while the other which lies on the eastern side to the right is rather well kept, and the popular belief is that this is the tomb of Sarmad. It is generally known as the grave of Haray Bharay, and is held in great reverence by the citizens of Delhi. Valah Daghistani mentions on the authority of Khalifa Ibrahim Badakhshani that although Sarmad never recited the whole of *Kalima-i Taiyaba* in his life time, yet after his execution, people heard his chopped head reciting the whole of the *Kalima.* It is strange that this story is current in Delhi even now when about three centuries have passed, and I do not doubt that it had its origin in the popular belief of Sarmad's contemporaries and the successive generations that Sarmad was a great saint to whom the shackles of convention and the rituals of religion were irksome, and that he had the courage of his convictions when he broke those fetters and paid the penalty by giving his life. Nothing is known of Abhai Chand's fate. It cannot even be said whether he was with Sarmad at the time of the execution.